Sources and Analogues of
Old English Poetry II

The Major Germanic and Celtic Texts in Translation

SOURCES AND ANALOGUES
OF
OLD ENGLISH POETRY II

The Major Germanic and Celtic Texts in Translation

Translated by

Daniel G. Calder and Robert E. Bjork
(Germanic Texts)

Patrick K. Ford
(Welsh Texts)

Daniel F. Melia
(Irish Texts)

D. S. Brewer　　　　　•　　　　　Barnes and Noble

© D. G. Calder, R. E. Bjork, P. K. Ford, D. F. Melia 1983

First published 1983
by D. S. Brewer Ltd
240 Hills Road, Cambridge
an imprint of Boydell & Brewer Ltd
PO Box 9, Woodbridge, Suffolk, IP12 3DF
and Barnes and Noble
81 Adams Drive, Totowa, NJ 07512, U.S.A.

ISBN 0 85991 135 7

British Library Cataloguing in Publication Data

Sources and analogues of Old English poetry.
2: The major Germanic and Celtic texts in
translation.
1. Latin poetry, Medieval and modern—Translations
into English   2. English poetry—Translations
from Latin   3. Anglo-Saxon poetry—Sources
4. Anglo-Saxon poetry—Translations into English
5. English poetry—Translations from Anglo-Saxon
I. Calder, Daniel G.
871′.02′08   PA8122

ISBN 0-85991-135-7

Library of Congress Cataloging in Publication Data

Sources and analogues of old English poetry II.

  Bibliography: p. 000
  1. Anglo-Saxon poetry—History and criticism—
Sources.   2. Germanic literature—Translations into
English.   3. Celtic literature—Translations into
English.   4. English literature—Translations from
other languages.   5. Literature, Comparative—Themes,
motives.   I. Calder, Daniel Gillmore.
PR182.S66   1983   829′.1′09   83-12288
ISBN 0-389-20434-X (Barnes & Noble Books)

Printed in Great Britain
by St Edmundsbury Press, Bury St Edmunds, Suffolk

CONTENTS

Preface

I

This book supplies the vernacular backgrounds of Old English poetry and thus becomes both companion and foil to *Sources and Analogues of Old English Poetry: The Major Latin Texts in Translation* (Allen/Calder). The similarities between the two volumes are entirely predictable: both follow the order and titles of *The Anglo-Saxon Poetic Records*, and both fix Old English poetry within certain circumscribed traditions. But the differences between the two books are more significant and perhaps more instructive. The Latin volume provides direct sources for Old English poems. Those sources most often occur in prose form, generally appear as theological treatises or tracts, and uniformly derive from a tradition that can be considered external to the native Germanic ethos. The Germanic and Celtic volume, on the other hand, contains mostly analogues rather than sources. With one exception, these analogues are in poetic form. All the Germanic analogues come from a native tradition, one that informs and controls each work in the whole spectrum of the literature *Germania* produced. The strong correlation between the Latin and the Old English reminds us just how thoroughly Christianity pervades the surviving Old English literature. By contrast, the Germanic and Celtic texts gathered here etch out distinctly the basic conceptions and genres of early medieval poetry, often before the touch of Latin Christianity had forever changed its art and spirit.

Like the first volume, this book may resemble an anthology because of the chapter headings and generic divisions of poems—modern conventions imposed on the material for the reader's convenience—but the book should be read as a whole. Although categories are necessary to delineate individual relationships, most of the analogues cast as much light on Old English poetry generally as they do on any specific poem or genre. Battle poems turn elegiac, elegies describe battles, wisdom poetry runs throughout the selections. *The Lay of Vafðrúðnir*, printed under *Solomon and Saturn* to illustrate "dialogue poetry," contains as much Norse lore as *The Lay of Grímnir*, entered under "Wisdom Poetry." This book will have most value for those who approach it from this broad perspective: as a basic collection of the more-or-less contemporary poems produced by those exerting strong pressures on Anglo-Saxon culture, either by speaking closely related languages or by living in close geographical proximity.

The Germanic texts represent only a selection from many possible inclusions. Although an early stylistic branching in the development of Germanic literature produced both the stichic, rhetorical verse paragraphs from England and Germany and the cryptic strophes from Scandinavia,[1] the Germanic aesthetic reveals itself in every ancient lay.[2] One could argue that the Germanic analogues for Old English poetry encompass all poems composed in other Germanic tongues through the Middle Ages. Some Old Norse and German pieces resemble their Old English counterparts more closely than others, but scholars have reached little agreement about the kinds of correspondences that exist for the greater part of the canon.

A secondary level of interaction that took place among the various old Germanic literatures makes the problem of selecting analogues still more complex. The continental Germans (and perhaps the Icelanders) learned to read and write from the Anglo-Saxons; in Germany the missionary efforts of the Englishman Boniface (Winfrith) and the founding of the monastery at Fulda had profound effects—some immediate, some delayed—on the development of Old Saxon and Old High German poetry and prose.[3] The colonial literature in turn affected the poetry of the fatherland: *Genesis B* is an Old English translation from Old Saxon, even though the original was itself an imitation of Old English biblical narratives. However, the literary interrelations of Old English and Old Norse are not so clear, and scholars still debate what the contacts between the two cultures produced.

Chronology also presents a thorny problem: the dating of both the Old English texts and their Germanic relatives is rough and speculative at best.[4] For Old English poetry, the end of the eleventh century would be an obvious cut-off date if we were sure of the chronology; but to insist on that historical boundary would mean omitting pertinent analogues for the elegies, the Norwegian *Rune Poem*, and others. We have, therefore, gone at times well beyond

[1] Lehmann.
[2] Smith.
[3] Bostock and Duckett.
[4] Lindblad.

the eleventh century when analogues corresponded to whole genres or categories. When they represented only incidental topics or themes, we chose not to include them. One example is the poem at the end of *Sagan af Starkaði Stórvirkssyni*. Margaret Schlauch has noted that Starkaðr's recounting of his unnaturally long life produces a catalogue of names and experiences akin to that in *Widsith*.[5] But the work is very late and the similarity, though interesting, quite remote. We have omitted other twelfth- or thirteenth-century Eddic poems for similar reasons.

Limits of space have dictated policy too. We would have liked to include complete translations of the Old Saxon *Heliand* and Otfrid's *Evangelienbuch* in Old High German as analogues of the Old English biblical verse narratives. But those two works alone would comprise a book larger than the whole volume as it now stands.[6] We thus decided to eliminate any text that was simply another version of a common Latin model or tradition. The exceptions to this rule were made for obvious reasons: the Old Saxon *Genesis* must be kept because it is a direct source; the Old Irish *Exodus* offers one brief example from Celtic literature; and the analogues under "Saints' Lives" give us a glimpse of other attempts at poetic hagiography. Their crudeness highlights the much earlier and more sophisticated development of hagiographical verse in England.

The relative importance of the Old English poems likewise governed some decisions. The elegies struck us as requiring ample illustration, for they comprise such a disparate group: some have female speakers lamenting lost loves, others have male speakers bemoaning exile or loss of favor, a few contain portions of Christian moralism, and other, longer narratives also contain elegiac passages. To cover all situations and attitudes meant abundant documentation, especially since the related literatures offer a large selection of possible texts. On the other hand, wisdom poetry, while extensive in the records of Anglo-Saxon verse, seemed to require less attention. The available Germanic and Celtic analogues do not resemble their Old English counterparts closely enough to warrant more than a sampling. As in the Latin volume, we include no analogues for *Beowulf*; a complete survey of those works in a good translation is readily available.[7]

The works we translate here include only one prose text, the description of the battle at Vínheiðr from *Egils saga*. While no

[5] Schlauch 1931.
[6] A translation of *The Heliand* is available; see Mariana Scott, trans., *The Heliand* (Chapel Hill, N.C., 1966).
[7] Garmonsway.

certain identification of this battle with that celebrated in *The Battle of Brunanburh* is possible, the likelihood that the two refer to the same conflict is strong.[8] The Old Norse piece sheds light on a historical event commemorated in an Old English poem.

Apart from this single prose example, however, we translate only poetry and have chosen to do so in prose. Prose renderings can give the plain sense of a poem more directly than verse, and we see little point in trying to imitate verse forms for their own sake. So we have excluded Egill Skallagrímsson's *Hǫfuðlausn*, which has been cited as an analogue to the Old English *Rhyming Poem*, but only because of its bizarre experiments in rhyme.[9] Furthermore, we find that attempts to recreate the poetic forms and meters of Scandinavian verse founder: either they are metrically so true to the Norse that they are almost incomprehensible in English, or they are comprehensible but only roughly suggestive of the original style. Four major variations on North Germanic meter are represented by the poems translated here: the three distinct types of Eddic meter—*fornyrðislag*, *ljóðaháttr*, and *málaháttr*—and skaldic poetry, primarily the favorite meter known as *dróttkvætt*.[10] This last kind of poem, brilliant but curious, was written by named poets and is an anomaly in the Germanic tradition. A later development, skaldic poetry preserves many of the features, both metrical and imagistic, of the earlier pan-Germanic heritage, but in many respects it departs sharply from this common legacy for reasons not yet fully explained. Our selection of skaldic poems is thus small and limited to a few well-known items.

In translating these works, we have tried in all instances to be as faithful to the original as possible, hoping that our renderings, usually on the side of the literal, would encourage those who have only an elementary knowledge of a language to tackle the texts, using this book as a guide. Where published translations exist, we have consulted them; where the original was obscure or conjec-

---

[8] Campbell and Einarrson, B.

[9] *ASPR* III, xlviii–xlix.

[10] For detailed explanations of the Eddic meters, see Gordon, Hallberg and Hollander; for explanations of *dróttkvæt*, see *ONCP* and *ScP*. Briefly, *fornyrðislag* ("Old Lore Meter") is a stanza of eight half-lines. Each independent rhythmic unit closely resembles the half-line of OE poetry. *Málaháttr* ("Speech Meter") is related to *fornyrðislag*, but each half-line contains more syllables (from five to seven, compared to four or five). *Ljóðaháttr* ("Song Meter") is a symmetrical stanza made up of two *fornyrðislag* lines (1 and 3), combined with two shorter lines (2 and 4). The complexities of the skaldic *dróttkvæt* cannot be explained briefly; we note only that it is an eight-line stanza.

tural, we have emended—sometimes silently—to produce a reasonable version in English; where a text was so opaque that we and all editors are merely guessing at its meaning, we have so indicated by a question mark in parentheses. Before beginning, the reader should also note the bibliography with its abbreviations for the works cited and the glossarial index which explains the many names occurring in the texts. Foreign words or symbols appear in italics, indicating either a Latin original or, in the rune poems, a runic character.

D.G.C./R.E.B.

II

Early Welsh poetry is quite unlike that of the Germanic tradition. It is characterized by a sparseness, an economy of expression that frequently deletes the verb as well as the definite article. Tenses are often dispensed with in favor of the unmarked verbal noun. What emerges is a canvas where images sometimes blend with one another, where there is a spiralling of thought instead of linear progression.[11] Adjectives frequently take the place of nouns, and archaic and obscure words abound. The Welsh poets and their patrons coexisted in a geographically contiguous plain with the Anglo-Saxons, and no doubt shared many of their experiences, emotional, physical, and intellectual. But the reactions to these experiences, expressed officially by the formally schooled bards in the courts of their patrons, were profoundly different.

Welsh poetry traditionally has its roots in the sixth century. 'Nennius' writes in the *Historia Brittonum* (ca. 800) that during the reign of Ida, king of Northumbria (547–59), five poets were famous among the native Celtic tribes of Britain.[12] Two of them, Aneirin and Taliesin, are represented here; there is no extant poetry attributed to the others. But no literature survives directly from the sixth century, nor do we have any substantial secular texts until the period of the great vernacular codices of the high Middle Ages. The work of Aneirin is found in a manuscript known as The Book of Aneirin, written around 1250; the poems of Taliesin are extant in a manuscript also bearing his name and written around 1275. Two other manuscripts which contain allegedly early poetical works are

[11] *WP*, p. 11.
[12] *PLlH*, p. 18; *BWP*, pp. 42–5.

the Black Book of Carmarthen (end of the twelfth century), and the Red Book of Hergest (ca. 1400). Linguistic evidence permits us to date many of these poems to about the ninth or tenth century, and since scribes tended to modernize the texts in their exemplars, the original works could date from a much earlier period.[13] We are on unsteady footing in attempts to date these poems precisely, but given the conservatism of Welsh tradition, we may comfortably assume that the poems translated here belong to the period of Anglo-Saxon England.

The Welsh and the Anglo-Saxons shared the isle of Britain for some six centuries; sometimes their coexistence was harmonious, often it was not. Although some of the strife that generated the Welsh poetic output was intertribal and internecine, most of it was between the native Celtic tribes and the expanding Anglo-Saxon kingdoms. As the Anglo-Saxons pushed relentlessly on, the British tribes continued to oppose them, with occasional success. But from those conflicts arose great leaders and able warriors, and it is these who are celebrated in the early verse of Taliesin and Aneirin.[14] While we speak of this poetry as "Welsh," suggesting the country situated to the west of present-day England, the language of these poems was in fact a form of late-British that was common to the Northern British kingdoms, extending right on down to Lancashire, and to those of the West from Chester to the mouth of the Severn. It seems safe to say that the traditions of the Northern heroes came to their western kin in Wales after the eventual collapse of the North.[15] In any case, the poetry is preserved in the Welsh language and in manuscripts written in Wales.

The native British kingdoms thus had a close relationship with the growing Anglo-Saxons, and we might be justified in looking for closer analogues to Anglo-Saxon poetry in the Welsh examples than in the Irish or Germanic. Some scholars have made serious attempts to demonstrate just that,[16] but without great success. As with the Germanic selections, the Welsh poems presented here are in no sense sources of Old English poetry. They are, however, analogues in a special way. Celtic society, like Germanic society, had its special class of literati that functioned in a more or less strictly prescribed manner; that class was, no doubt, of Indo-European origins.[17] One of the chief functions of this class in Celtic society was

[13] *BWP*, pp. 41–9; see also Green.
[14] Bromwich 1954; Dillon; Lloyd; Parry; Jarman 1976.
[15] *GO*, pp. 63–7.
[16] Henry; Pilch.
[17] Jarman 1976; Williams 1971.

the singing of praise to its rulers. Praise entailed the attribution to the patron of those virtues held dear by the warrior aristocracy—the dominant class. A chieftain was expected to be strong enough to gain the respect of his peers, to assemble and command hosts, lead them into successful combat, and divide the spoils freely among his court, his retinue and, of course, his poets. He was expected to have a valid claim to his throne, and so genealogies were of primary importance.[18] He was expected to be gentle and kind to the weak, the old, and the needy, and to be rough, unsparing, and unyielding toward the mighty—especially those from the other side of the border.

The bards of Wales, descended from the class of Celtic learned men, took this charge as their primary one. The uppermost rank among them, the *pencerdd*, "chief of song," or *prydydd*, "shaper," had praise poems as his principal obligation.[19] To praise his chief properly, he had to know his lord's pedigrees, the histories of places and events associated with him, as well as conventional diction and themes. All this was passed on orally for generations before any of it was committed to velum. But the training of the poet doubtless included other kinds of traditional knowledge, too: the meanings of place and personal names, names of heroes, where they fought and where they died and were buried, the histories of great battles, proverbial wisdom, and gnomic utterances relating to both man and nature. The accumulated wisdom of the entire society, mnemonically codified, is likely to have been the poet's fodder. Certainly no one grade of poet was responsible for all of it; indeed, the evidence suggests that the poets were ranked according to how much or what kinds of knowledge they had committed to memory. For the Welsh bard, as for his Irish and Anglo-Saxon counterparts, poetry was not idiosyncratic, personal, lyrical, or subjective: it carried a social message and it was functional.

And that raises the problem of genre. Because the point of departure in this book is Old English poetry, the sections have been divided according to the extant texts in that corpus: Elegies, Wisdom Poetry, Riddles, Battle Poems, and the like. The problem of genre crops up everywhere in early Welsh poetry; scholars have been content to use the analytic categories of earlier generations and too often of other cultures, fitting the corpus into this or that genre. Accepting the fact that nature poetry is one thing and gnomic poetry another, they reject the validity of a native genre that combines the two, speaking of "irrelevant" lines and "filler" lines in

[18] Bartrum.
[19] Parry.

some of the poems.[20] A good example is the poem that begins "Snow on the mountains . . .". It appears to comprise a set of linked stanzas of nature description, and yet the third line of each verse contains some sententious saying. To what "genre" do we assign such mixed texts? What do these two "discrete" (in some cultures) types of poetry have to do with each other? Are the gnomes dependent upon the descriptions or the other way around?[21] Again, early Welsh poetry has no battle poems *in sensu stricto*, that is, no poems that narrate the particulars of a certain battle (*The Battle of Argoed Llwyfain* is as close as we come). And yet, in a broad sense, most of the early poems *are* battle poems, for they speak of carnage, of valour, of flashing blades, of gore-glutted battle-ravens, and of disaster as well as victory.[22] Their tone is more elegiac than journalistic and they should, perhaps, be classed as elegies. The problem of genre, then, is a real one, and the reader should beware of making hasty comparisons of the works gathered together here without further study.

A considerable party within the scholarly community accepts the theory advanced by Sir Ifor Williams that the poems of the so-called Llywarch Hen and Heledd cycles are fugitives from lost sagas.[23] The textual tradition of these poems offers no support for that theory, even though it may be true. But clearly these poems, and others like them in the Red Book of Hergest, were preserved and presumably valued only as poems, and it is as such that we must try to understand them. From a modernist perspective they appear to be highly subjective and personal. Still, we must reserve judgment on that issue, realizing that our present knowledge of them and the tradition from which they spring is very limited. We still know far too little about the nature of professional bardic performances, including dramatic dialogue or assumption of personae.[24] But whether subjective and personal or not, many of these stanzas will sound familiar to readers of such Old English elegies as *The Wanderer* and *The Seafarer*. There is in them a lamentation of the transitoriness of things, a drumming on the *ubi sunt* theme, a protest over encroaching age and desolation.

Of the present translations, the two poems, *Taliesin's Travels* and *The Battle of the Trees*, are virtually unchanged from their published form in *The Mabinogi and Other Medieval Welsh Tales (M)*. The

---

[20] *EWGP*, p. 1ff; *CLlH*, xliii–xliv.

[21] *PLlH*, pp. 37–8.

[22] Jarman 1967; Parry.

[23] *BWP*, chap. viii; Dillon; Parry; Williams.

[24] *PLlH*, pp. 48ff.

stanzas from the Llywarch Hen cycle have also been translated before in *The Poetry of Llywarch Hen (PLlH)*, but a comparison with the earlier work will show that the present translations differ to a greater or lesser degree. At times, the meaning of a line has been altered considerably; elsewhere, only occasional words or syntax have been changed to provide a more felicitous reading. The underlying reason for revising the earlier translations was to emphasize the fact that *no* translation is ever final or perfect. Perhaps that point will make it unnecessary to defend the fresh translations of the remainder, for any translation of such difficult material without copious accompanying notes begs the reader's indulgence.

P.K.F.

III

Ireland, geographically isolated from Britain and the rest of Europe, still remained in political and social contact with both the Welsh and others throughout the early Middle Ages. Raids and tribal migrations from the fifth century on brought settlers from Ireland to Wales, western Scotland and the west coast of England.[25] Of these settlements, only Gaelic Scotland survived as an area dominated by Irish culture. But from centers in northern Britain Irish missionaries evangelized the Anglo-Saxons during the sixth and early seventh centuries, particularly from such monasteries as Lindisfarne and Iona. The Irish church educated many English clerics, including Aldhelm (ca. 640–709), abbot of Malmesbury and the "first Anglo-Saxon man of letters."[26] They sent missionaries to the continent during the "golden age" of the Irish church in the seventh and eighth centuries: St. Columbanus is the foremost example. But official Irish influence in the Anglo-Saxon church came to an end at the Synod of Whitby (664) with the rejection of the "Celtic" position on the calculation of Easter.[27] Informal relations continued, yet the conflict over the Easter question reinforced the cultural separation of the Irish from their nearest Germanic neighbors.

[25] Dillon, pp. 38ff.
[26] Kenney, pp. 226ff.
[27] Kenney, p. 224.

Some of the works translated here from Old Irish reflect this relative isolation of medieval Irish culture. Although the Irish poetic tradition grew from the same roots as the Welsh and shared both an Indo-European past and the influence of Christianity with the Anglo-Saxons as well, the native strain in Irish poetry remained especially strong. Poetic matters in Ireland, as in the rest of the pagan Celtic world, had been in the hands of a hereditary caste of poet/seers (*filid*). Their very name, cognate with Welsh *gwel-* ("to see"), suggests the ancient Indo-European connection between poetry and prophecy, and historically their functions indicate their cultural descent from the pre-Christian druid caste. Caesar says of the druids of Gaul:

> They are said to learn thoroughly here [at the druidic schools] a great number of verses. Therefore a good many stay in training for twenty years. And they do not think it right to put these things in writing. . . . There seem to me to be two reasons for adopting this attitude: because they do not want their special knowledge to become common, nor to have those who study it, by depending on writing, to develop the memory less.[28]

Even in Christianized Ireland, the *filid* continued this same tradition: "He was a learned man, not an entertainer. Counsellor of Kings, conservator of the social order, guardian and interpreter of tradition, his protracted training was designed to set him apart from lesser men and to equip him adequately to discharge these responsibilities."[29] In a warrior aristocracy, the *filid* functioned as upholders and praisers of their princes well into the later Middle Ages, but because their craft continued to be oral, we have few direct examples of what they said. Nevertheless, their influence strongly colors the written vernacular works produced and preserved by Christian monks.

Christianity came to Ireland in the fifth century and was firmly established by the seventh. As in the Anglo-Saxon world, the remnants of pre-Christian Irish literary tradition have been preserved and passed on by men who were, by their own lights, convinced Christians, and usually members of religious communities. Some of these men were sharply aware of the contrast between their own views and those which preceded them. The incorporation of new Christian ideas into the older poetry was sometimes comfortable, sometimes not. The author of *The Fall of Tara* gloats over the growing strength of the centers of monastic Christianity and compares them to the desolated old centers of

[28] Caesar, VI, 14, p. 339.
[29] MacCana, p. 18.

pre-Christian worship such as the Hill of Tara. He may also use the vocabulary of the older heroic poetry ironically, calling the monks of Armagh "warriors" and "heroes". But in contrast, the author of "Lorica II" seems to have little trouble integrating pagan elements into a Christian framework.

Most of the poems included here were written after the shock of the ninth-century Viking invasions. The lack of early written poetic records of panegyric and of battle poetry probably reflects a long-standing division between monastic and secular vernacular poetry in medieval Ireland. Thus the destruction of many great Irish monasteries disrupted a flourishing Christian Latin literature, and this allowed both the establishment of new native literary genres and the recording of older poetry, formerly confined exclusively to the oral tradition. Our selections, then, may well reflect important aspects of the native, pre-Christian strain. The prominent families of many monastic scribes and abbots were descended from the old poetic caste; their interest in tribal history and genealogy undoubtedly accounts for the preservation of the large extant corpus of early Irish material.[30] This earlier poetry appears in the ritual *Advice to a Prince* from the *Audacht Morainn*, in Amargein's claims of supernatural knowledge of nature, and in the invocation in the "loricas" of natural and supernatural phenomena—Christian and pagan—to protect the poet. "Let us adore the Lord" and *Adam and Eve*, however, present obviously foreign Christian material in the dress of native form. *Adam and Eve* is a good example of a poem which earlier would have existed only in Latin, while the *Audacht Morainn* represents a written slice of druidic tradition.

Two important aspects of the Irish poetic tradition deserve mention. First, these poems were composed with a "competent audience" in mind; the poets expected their audiences to understand oblique references to an entire body of knowledge about legendary persons and events. *The Hag of Beare*, like *Wulf and Eadwacer* or *Widsith*, indicates how much of this information we have lost. Second, we note the poets' deep interest in onomastics, which a translation cannot make clear. Two simple illustrations of this interest are the Hag of Beare's discussion of places as if they were people, and the transparency of the name "Armagh"—*Árd Macha* in Irish means "the high place of Macha" (*The Fall of Tara*). Translation can neither render the appropriateness of certain meters to certain poems, nor the striking distinction between the so-called "new meters" (*núa crutha*) and the cadenced

[30] Kelleher.

meters of the oldest Irish poetry. The "new meters" employ
isosyllabic lines, stanzaic structure, obligatory end-rhyme, and
other features familiar to us from later western European poetic
tradition. The "loricas," *Audacht Morainn*, and *Amargein's Song*,
however, are all composed in the archaic cadenced meters of pre-
Christian Irish poetry, characterized by varied stress and line-
length, stichic structure, largely ornamental (though frequent)
alliteration and rhyme, and fixed line-ending cadences. One critic
has argued persuasively that these verse forms descend directly
from primitive Indo-European metrics.[31] Whether the "new
meters" are a development of traditional native forms or a trans-
mogrified import from late Latin hymn meters, they provided a
medium for a new amalgam of traditional and Christian poetic
culture in Ireland.[32]

The translations are as literal as possible without violating
English grammar, but they cannot hope to capture more than a hint
of the original style. In these traditional and formal genres, the
abruptness of the phrasing, often conditioned by metrical con-
straints, produces an almost telegraphic effect on a modern reader.
The interplay of metrical requirements and aesthetic demands is an
interesting aspect of many of these poems. For every *cheville* that
seems to be a pure line filler ("I will not conceal it," *Adam and Eve*,
l. 841), there is one which gives an unexpected or beautiful turn to a
poem ("great disaster," *The Fall of Tara*, l. 169, can only be
interpreted as ironic.)

Given the archaic nature of these poems, the versions here are
sometimes heavily indebted to previous translators. Readers may
wish to compare translations to appreciate more fully such difficult
works. The spellings of personal and place names generally follow
the orthographic conventions of ninth-century Irish, with the
exception of such well-known names as Armagh and St. Patrick.
The word *ráth* has been left untranslated. It designates a ring-fort of
the kind whose ruins litter Ireland even today, and which is
characterized by one or more stone or earthen walls surrounding a
central compound. These structures were both multiple dwellings
and defensive retreats in the Middle Ages, and it seems misleading
to translate the word as "fort" and equally misleading to leave it as
"dwelling" or "farmstead."

If medieval Irish poetry resembles the Anglo-Saxon, this results
in large part from similar historical developments; in the Middle
Ages few direct literary connections occur. Because of the distance

---

[31] Watkins.
[32] *EIL*, pp. xiv–xvii and Melia.

between the two worlds and their independent cultures, comparisons can cast only a reflective, though interesting, light.

D.F.M.

A note on the maps: The maps contain a mixture of medieval and modern spellings. In general, medieval names were used where identifications were certain, and modern names where identifications were only probable.

ACKNOWLEDGMENTS

Several people have generously given us aid on this book. We would like to thank Michael J. B. Allen for reading the first draft and Henry A. Kelly both for reading that draft and for pointing out the connection between the *improperia* and the OIr *Exodus*; Matthew Miller for his assistance in compiling the Index and for completing the maps; Karen Borst-Rothe for bibliographical assistance on the OIr materials; Carol P. Hartzog for her comments on the Introduction; Stephen P. Hartzog for his help on the maps; Terence H. Wilbur for answering questions on some cruces in OHG; and Roberta Frank and G. Darryl Wieland for their help with the poems from the *Eddica Minora*. To Theodore M. Andersson and T. Craig Christy we owe a special debt. Andersson's painstaking review of the ON texts and Christy's equally careful examination of the OHG and OS works were acts of generosity which cannot be properly acknowledged. We would like to express our gratitude for their work and to accept any and all remaining errors as our own. The Research Committees of the Academic Senates at UCLA and UC Berkeley provided funds for this project.

ABBREVIATIONS

CSc	Common Scandinavian
OE	Old English
OIr	Old (and Middle) Irish
OHG	Old High German
ON	Old Norse
OS	Old Saxon
MW	Middle Welsh

I

GENESIS

A. Germanic Source and Analogue

The Caedmonian "revolution" in OE poetry, which produced
what may have been a near flood of biblical verse narratives, even
though only a few survive, has its roots both in the exegetical
tradition of hexameral commentary (see Allen/Calder) and in the
Latin custom of poetic biblical paraphrase (see Kartschoke). The
Anglo-Saxons took this new kind of poetry back to their continental
homeland through the missionary efforts of Boniface and others.
The Saxons copied the English model, and at least once the Saxon
imitation was returned to the English through translation. In 1875
Sievers speculated that the OE *Genesis B* must derive from an OS
exemplar; in 1894 the OS *Genesis* fragments were discovered and
his guess proved true. Only a few lines of *Genesis* survive in both
languages (OS 1–26; OE 790–817a). But the other portions illustrate
what may have been additional sections of the OE poem, and they
also offer analogues germane to parts of *Genesis A*. The OS *Genesis*
is a mid ninth-century poem, which was translated into English
sometime during, or shortly after, the reign of Alfred (see Timmer).

1. The Old Saxon *Genesis*

(Text: *HG*, pp. 233–48.)

I.

"Alas, Eve," said Adam, "you have now sealed both our fates with evil. Now you can see dark hell greedily gaping; now you can hear it roaring from here. The kingdom of heaven is not like such hell-fire. This was the most beautiful of all lands, which we two were to possess through our Lord's grace, if you had not listened to him who caused us this grief—that we violated the command of the Ruler, the King of heaven. Now afflicted we may grieve over that fate, since He Himself commanded us to be on guard against such wrong, the greatest of harms. Now hunger and thirst oppress me already, the bitter evil deed—we were free of both before. How shall we live now? How shall we exist in this world, now that the wind comes at times from west or east, from south or north? Darkness gathers, a hail-cloud comes clinging to the sky: it presses forward. That is very cold. At other times the bright sun shines hotly, blazes from heaven. We stand here thus naked, unprotected by clothes. There is nothing here before us, neither for shade nor for shelter, nor cattle provided us for food. We have made almighty God, the Ruler, angry with us. What shall become of us now? Now I may lament that I ever prayed to heavenly God, the Ruler, for this . . ."

II.

Then he went to his house; he had committed a sin, bitter against his brother. He left him lying on his back (?) in a deep dale, spent from loss of blood, empty of life, to occupy a death-bed, the man on the ground. Then God Himself spoke to him, the Ruler with His words (He was angry in His mind, enraged at the slayer). He asked where he had [left] his brother, his young kinsman. Then Cain spoke to Him again in return—he had committed a great crime with his own hands through evil deeds: by this the world was so very stained in sins—: "I will neither grieve about this," he said, "nor care where he may go; God did not command me that I had to watch over him anywhere here, to guard him in this world."

He hoped strongly that he could hide [it] from his Lord, conceal the deed. Then our Lord spoke to him again: "You have brought it all about," He said, "that your spirit will be afflicted throughout your life; for you did this with your own hands, so that you became your brother's slayer: now he lies bloody, weary from wounds. Although he had not committed any evil deeds, sins, against you, nevertheless you now have slain him, done him to death. His blood now sinks into the earth, the blood lies scattered; the soul departs, the sad spirit according to God's will. His blood cries out to God Himself, and says who did that deed, that crime on this middle-earth. No man among men may sin more greatly in the worldly kingdom by bitter slaughter deeds, than you have done against your brother [by this] crime."

Then Cain was afraid after the Lord's words; he said he knew certainly that none of his deeds on earth could ever be hidden from the Ruler. "So now," he said, "I must bear in my heart the grievous thought that I slew my brother through my hand-might. Now I know that I must live in your hate, henceforth in your enmity, since I myself performed these wicked deeds, so now my sins seem heavier to me, my misdeeds greater than your merciful spirit. Therefore I am not worthy, O good Ruler, that you might absolve me of these evil things, might acquit me of these transgressions. Since I did not want to keep my faith, my spirit against your pure mind, therefore I know that I cannot live here any longer, because he will murder me, whoever finds me along the way. He will slay me on account of these sins."

Then the Ruler of heaven Himself spoke to him again in return: "Nevertheless," He said, "you shall now live here for a long time. Though you may be thus despised, encircled with sins, still I will give you protection, mark [you with] such a sign, that you may be in peace in this world, though you may not be worthy of it. But now as a fugitive and as an exile you shall henceforth live in this land, as long as you dwell on earth. Pure people shall curse you. You shall never again come to speak with your Lord, converse there with your words. Revenge for your brother stands boiling, bitter in hell."

Then he went thence with a grim spirit, God Himself had entirely forsaken him. Sorrow was then made known, the great evil deed to Adam and Eve, the murder of their child, that he was no longer alive. For this reason Adam's spirit within his breast was very distressed, when he knew his son was dead. So was his mother also, who had nourished that son, the child at her breasts. When she washed the bloody shroud, then was her spirit grieved. Sorrowful to them was both their son's death, the hero's departure, and that Cain had committed a sin with his hands in such a murder. They did not then have any more children living in the world, except that one, who was then despised by the Ruler for his evil deeds. There they did not eagerly take any joy, since he had raised such hatred, that he became his brother's slayer. About this they were both, the married couple, troubled in heart. Often they stood mourning that on the ground, the married couple together. They said they knew that their [own] sins had done that to them, that afterwards no heirs, thanes, would succeed them. They both suffered a great death-misery, until mighty God, the high Guardian of heaven, again healed their spirits, so that heirs were bestowed on them, thanes and maidens, [who] afterwards prospered well, grew splendidly, acquired wisdom, wise speech. The holy Lord, He who could, fostered His handi-work, so that a son was born to them; they created Seth as a name for him with true words: to him the Ruler of heaven granted growth and good spirits, prosperity—he was worthy to God—He was generous to him in His heart.

So it goes well for the man who always can serve the Lord with such devotion. Most of all he praised God's grace to the sons of the people, to men. From him came good men, thanes, wise in words [who] acquired wisdom, faith, and afterwards prospered well. Then again from Cain came powerful peoples, hard-hearted warriors. They had a strong mind, a rebellious will; they did not want to follow the Ruler's teachings, but they raised hostile strife. They grew into giants: that was the worst race, [which] came from Cain. Then the men began to buy women among themselves. For this reason, Seth's family was at once ruined. The race of men became mixed with sin and the sons of men became hateful peoples to Him who created light, except that one of them had a noble understanding, virtuous thought. He was an admirable man, sage and wise of words; he had great wisdom: he was called Enoch. Here on earth he became famous among men over this middle-earth, because the best King [took] him hence while he was still alive, living in his body, so that he never died in this world. But thus the Ruler of the heavens fetched him here and set him where he always could be in joy, until the high Guardian of heaven sends him into this world again to the sons of men, as a teacher to the people. Then the devil will also come here, so that Anti-Christ will destroy all nations, [all] mankind when, through his hand-might, he becomes Enoch's slayer with weapons, with sharp swords. His soul will turn, the spirit on the way of salvation, and God's angel will come, punish him, the devil, with a weapon's edges. Anti-Christ will be deprived of life, the fiend overthrown. The people will again be converted to God's kingdom, the family of men for a long while, and the land will stand inviolate thereafter.

III.

Then the people of Sodom, the men, had so greatly sinned again, that our Ruler, the mighty Lord, was hostile towards them, because they committed evil, performed sinful deeds; the sons of wicked men had shown so much crime. Then the Lord, ruling God, did not want to suffer that [any longer], but He commanded three of His angels to fare from the east on His errand, to journey to Sodom, and He Himself was there with them. As the mighty ones crossed over Mamre, then they found Abraham standing by a temple. He was guarding a holy place and he was to make an offering to our Lord; the best of men was to serve God there at midday. Then he felt God's power, when he saw them coming. He went toward them and bowed to God; he bent and prayed and asked urgently that henceforth he might have His grace: "Where do You want to go now, Ruler, my Lord, almighty Father? I am Your own servant, loyal and obedient. You are so good to me, Lord, so generous of treasures. Do You want to have something of mine, Lord? Lo, it all stands at Your disposal, I live on Your estate, and I believe in You, my good Lord: may I ask You now, Victory-Lord, where You want to go?"

Then God's answer came to him in reply, mighty it came to pass: "I do not want to keep it from you now," He said, "conceal from the loyal man how my mind inclines. We must travel southward hence: there are such depraved men around Sodom. The priests call out to me now day and night, those who report their deeds, tell their sins. Now I myself want to know, if the men under them commit such wickedness, the men [do such] evil deeds. Then welling fire shall fall [on them]; their heavy, evil sins shall destroy them: fiery brimstone will fall from heaven, deceitful ones will die, the sinful men, as soon as morning comes."

Abraham then spoke (he had a good spirit, wise word-speeches), and replied to his Ruler: "Lo, You do so much good," he said, "Lord God of the heavenly kingdom; all this world stands in Your power, according to Your will. You have power over this middle-earth, the races of men, so that it could never happen, Lord, my Ruler, that You would make evil and good, love and hate, equal, because they are not alike. You strive so for the right, powerful Lord, because You do not want men of goodwill to suffer there for the deeds of evil-doers, although You have the power to bring that about. May I ask You now, God of the heavenly kingdom, as long as You will not thereby be the angrier at me: if You find fifty wise men there, faithful people, may that land stand safe and protected, Ruler, according to Your will?"

Then God's answer came to him in reply: "If I find fifty there," He said, "wise men, good men, who have held fast to God, then I will grant them their lives, because I want to preserve the righteous men."

Then Abraham spoke another time; he questioned his Lord further: "What will You do about it then," he said, "my Lord and Leader, if You can find thirty thanes there, sinless men? Will You still let them live, that they might occupy that land?"

Then the good God of the heavenly kingdom said to him at once that that was what he wanted to do in the land: "If I can find there," He said, "thirty faithful thanes, God-fearing men, among that people, then I will forgive them all the evil and the wrong-doing, and let that race of men dwell in Sodom and be safe."

Abraham then spoke eagerly—he followed his Lord—uttered many words: "Now I shall ask of You," he said, "that You do not become angry with me, my good Lord, because I may speak so much, may exchange my words with You: I know that I am not worthy of that, nor could it be unless You wanted to allow it through Your goodness, God of the heavenly kingdom, Prince. I have a great need to know Your will: whether that people may live safe, [or whether] they must perish, fall in death. What will You do about it then, my Lord, if You can find ten loyal ones there among that people, will You then grant them their lives so they may abide in Sodom, dwell in the cities, if You are not angry with them?" Then God's answer came to him in reply: "If I can find even ten," He said, "loyal men there in the land, then, because of those devoted men, I will let them all enjoy their lives."

Then Abraham did not dare question his Lord longer, but he fell before Him in prayer, the strong one, on his knees: he said [that] he would gladly make ready his sacrifice and would serve God, work according to His will. He left thence to go again to his hall. God's angels journeyed on to Sodom, as the Ruler Himself ordered them with His command, when He bade them to set forth on the way. They were supposed to determine which of the men in the city of Sodom were devout, free of sins, those who had not done much of evil, of sinful works. Then they heard the cry of the doomed in every house, the sinful people doing their evil deeds. There was a throng of fiends, of hostile demons; they had led the people into crime. The reward was then at hand, a great one for murder, since they often practised evil.

There within dwelt a noble-born man, Lot, among the people, who often wrought the praise of God in this world. He had acquired there enough possessions, property; he was worthy to God. He was of Abraham's noble lineage, his brother's son. There was not a better man in manly virtues, endowed with understanding, about the banks of the Jordan: our Ruler was gracious to him. As the shining sun, the brightest of all beacons, sank to its seat, he stood before the city gate. Toward evening he saw two angels going into the dwellings, as they came from God, endowed with understanding. Then he spoke to them at once with his words. He went towards them and thanked God, the King of the heavens, because He granted him this joy, that he could look on them with his eyes. And he kissed them on the knees and asked them politely to visit his house. He said that he would give them according to their own liking such goods as God had bestowed on him in that land. They were not hesitant in any way, but went into his house, and he devoutly gave them service. They said many true words to him. There he sat on guard; he protected his Lord's holy messengers, God's angels. They told him much of good and truth. Darkness glided further, the narrow night in a cloud-cover; morning approached in every house. The dawn-bird sang a morning call.

Then our Lord's messengers confirmed the sins, those which the men had committed there in Sodom. Then they said to Lot, that there should be a great slaughter of the sons of men, of that people, and also of that land as well. Then they commanded him to get ready, and commanded him then to go hence, to distance himself from the enemies, and take his wife with him, the noble-born lady. He did not have there more of his noble kin besides his two daughters. They commanded him to be up on a mountain with them before daybreak, so that the burning fire would not touch him.

Then quickly he was ready for the journey. The angels departed, they had him by the hand, the messengers of the heavenly King. They led him and instructed him a long time, until they brought him outside the city. They commanded them that should they ever hear a great noise roar in the cities, not to look back, if they wanted to live in that land. Then the holy guardians turned back again, God's angels went quickly, travelled to Sodom. Thence southward Lot fared according to their instructions; he fled the throng of people, of wicked men. When day came, there was a great din rising heavenwards; it burst and roared. Each of the cities was filled with smoke; there was so much fire falling from the heavens. There was a cry of doomed ones, of evil people. Flames completely surrounded the broad plains where the cities sat. All burned together, stone and earth, and so many war-like men died and sank. Burning brimstone welled over the dwellings. The criminals suffered recompense for evil. That land sank in, the earth into the abyss. Everything in the kingdom of Sodom was destroyed, so that not a man of it was spared; and just as it was put to death in the Dead Sea, so it still stands today filled with water. All the people of Sodom had greatly atoned for their evil deeds, except for one of them, [whom] the Ruler in His mercy led out, and his wife with him, [and] three thanes with them. When they heard the death-cry of the people, the cities burning, then the noble-born woman looked back there—she would not follow the angels' orders. That was Lot's wife, as long as she could live in that land. When she stood on the mountain and looked back, she turned to stone. There she must stand as a sign to men throughout middle-earth, for ever and ever, as long as this earth remains.

B. Celtic Analogue

1. *Adam and Eve*

(*Saltair na Rann*; text: *AE*, I, 11–111.)

This poem is only a small part of a tenth-century collection of biblical and assorted religious material which runs in its entirety to over 7,000 lines. The title of the larger work, *Saltair na Rann* ("Psalter of the Quatrains"), refers to its overall plan, apparently based on sets of 150 quatrains. Perhaps the need to conform to such a scheme accounts for the collection's repetitive nature, even in the Adam and Eve segment. While this poem, like *Genesis B*, pays considerable attention to the fall of Lucifer and the self-justification of Satan, the Irish version of the Genesis story is in many respects more traditional than the OE version. The Irish poet seems to draw much of his material from the apocryphal "Adambooks" (see Murdoch 1976, Dumville, and MacNamara), and Satan appears himself as a serpent, approaching Eve first. A large amount of descriptive matter fleshes out the Irish version, augmenting its difference from the OE version still more. The stanza numbers used here come from *SnR*.

833. My regal King over every champion said to Lucifer: "In response to your shining petition there will be many hosts of archangels under you.

837. Give, as is proper, honor from you to Adam, to the one who is in my likeness. The nine generous, fine, pure orders [of angels] will be prepared to receive you."

841. "Honor to Adam—I will not conceal it—I will not give, because I am the elder. For it would be ensnaring—with every host as witness—if I were to put myself under my junior."

845. His just and pure Lord, the King of the constellations, said to him: "Real honor will not be yours, since you do not submit your will to Adam."

849. Zealous Lucifer spoke this proud, ill-intentioned reply: "I will be manifest king over every plea; the angel multitude will serve me.

853. The angels will be under my sway. I will raise my muster myself. I will be overlord of my own troop; there will not be another king over me."

857. Those opposing him overthrew Lucifer, with numbers of his ilk. They subdued his sick pride; they forced him into hell.

[Extended description of hell omitted.]

953. There the hosts were all punished, in the greedy maw of bright-red hell. If I were to have a hundred good tongues, I could not tell it in my lifetime.

957. The house of hell: with abundant pains there will be continued sorrow under everlasting earthquake; a narrow valley of sobbing, its color horrible. My mighty King made it.

961. A King who made beautiful paradise, a perfect steadfast circle of protection, a fair fruitful land, an unassailable resting-place for mankind before they sinned.

[Extended description of paradise omitted.]

1029. The King who formed paradise in its splendor, He is our ingenious armed protector. He put a golden wall completely around it with many strong barriers.

1033. The King of the stag-rich, green-covered world, the King of the full-fruited paradise, created then a pair of all the animals,

1037. the King who made splendid Adam in a noble form, without fear, with charity, without harm—it has been heard—in paradise, before sinning.

1041. Adam was three days without warmth, dead to love, purely inert, on solid earth without movement, without soul, without coming to life.

1045. The body of Adam was—according to sure prophecy— three days without a soul, waiting to begin, without sadness—clear tidings—expecting Christ to arise.

1053. And after that he was named from the four stars: Archon, Dissis—God created you—Anatole, Missimbria.

1057. Nine full months—precious saying—from when Adam received a soul to the time his woman was created, according to the stream of tradition, sound historians,

1061. whose name was splendid Eve, perfect, royal, modest, precious, shapely, choicest of her kind, excellent source of true children.

1065. After that, Adam rose up out of his sleep, without fear, and he saw the woman, with her soft complexion, favored, illustrious, well-formed.

1069. As he saw her face he chose her beyond every true treasure. He promised her—clear wisdom—that she would be the special love of the multitude.

1073. "It is for you—without concealment—that everyone will leave his mother and his father. From today until the end of this age—timely triumph—each one of us will exist for your satisfaction" [said Adam].

[Obscure stanza omitted.]

1081. The King spoke a clear message to Eve and Adam: that it was the fruits of paradise that they should eat—a statement without limitation—following the command of God.

1085. "So you may eat—for [your] special compensation—the fruits of sweet-smelling paradise; some, all, a bit for refreshment—it is your lawful possession, save for a single tree.

1089. [This is] so that you know you are under command—without misery, without vexation, without care or compulsory toil, without age, evil, or defect,

1093. without aging, without harsh sickness, in permanent life with permanent goodness, going to heaven—bright celebration—in the pre-ordained state of thirty years of age."

1097. A thousand years—a triumphant moment—and six hours, without falsehood or fear, it has been heard, that Adam was in paradise.

[Obscure stanza omitted.]

1105. Because of this, the devil envied Adam and his children: that they should be borne, faultless—bright notion—to heaven in their whole bodies.

1109. All the animals alive, my holy King created them. It is Adam who ruled them—without fighting—outside of paradise.

1113. When the hosts of the seven heavens used to go from every border around the High-King, all the fair-bodied animals came to Adam.

[Description of the gathering of the animals omitted.]

1133. Lucifer, with a number of clear evil intentions, went into the midst of the animals and into the host just outside paradise, and it is there he found the serpent.

1137. "It is not for nothing that you are outside [paradise]," the devil said to the serpent, "but because of your quick cleverness—

well-known—because of your cunning and wit.

1142. It was great harm and wrong, the ranking of Adam, the youngest of created beings—feeble fame—above you; destroying him would not be a crime for us.

1145. Because you are the more famous in battle, because you were created first, you are smarter in every way, my dear one; do not put yourself under your junior.

1149. Take my counsel without unhappiness: let us make an agreement and alliance. Listen yourself to my clear argument and do not go to Adam.

1153. Give me a place in your body according to my regulation and my plan, that we may go eagerly across the plain, the two of us, to Eve.

1157. Let us urge on her together the fruit of the forbidden tree, so that she may, purely, then urge the food upon Adam.

1161. Thus the two of them together may go against the order of their Lord. They will not be loved anymore by God; they will come without profit out of paradise."

1165. "What recompense am I to have—before every host," the serpent said to the devil, "for welcoming you into my fair body, to cohabit with me without [sexual] sin?"

[The serpent repeats his query in various forms.]

1173. "What is the greatest recompense I will give you by the measure of our great evil? We will usually be spoken of in anger as a single being," [answered the devil].

1177. When the devil had obtained a dwelling in the shape of the serpent for the treachery he contemplated, quietly he came straight to the gate of paradise.

1181. "I ought not to talk to anyone," Eve said to the serpent. "I am going outside to feed the wild animals."

1189. "If you are that Eve who has been heard of famously for excellence in paradise, the wife of Adam, a beauty who is not miserly, I look to her for my full redress."

1193. "When Adam is not here, I am the one who cares for paradise, without difficulty; though a soft, womanly being, I give satisfaction to the animals."

[Eve describes her stewardship further.]

1201. "He leaves to me—a pure entertainment—feeding the animals, when according to pure renown he himself goes, without fail, to worship the Lord."

1205. "I want to ask you something," said the hard, thin serpent, "because your fine mind is pure and precious, O Eve, Adam's wife."

1209. "Whatever it is you are planning to say will not offend me, O animal of little status. It is certain that there will be no lack of clarity either. I will tell you in simplicity.''

1213. "Tell me, noble Eve, since we are conversing, is it good living in paradise with the nobleman who brought you?"

1217. "Until we go, as ordained, without sin, in our bodies to heaven, we are not seeking here a sovereignty greater than the good we have in paradise.

1221. Every food—as has been heard—which God made in paradise, except for a single tree, all, without exception, is under our control.

1229. 'Leave the tree alone completely,' He commanded me and Adam. 'The fruit of this rough tree will be death if you eat it.' "

1233. "Although you and Adam may be equal in renown, O Eve, you are not smarter, fair and pure one, than any of the animals," [said the serpent].

1237. "Though there may be a great host subject to you outside, it is a shame that you don't have intelligence. You are on the same level as the brute animals.

1241. You cannot have full sovereignty because He did not show you anything of evil, only things obviously good; it is the worse for your judgment.

1245. Great is your defect in understanding. God is tricking you, for it is of the one tree of good and evil that He does not let you eat.

1249. For this was the sharp tree created and for this is it not allowed you: so that you will not have enough sense to distinguish between good and evil.

1253. Don't be slow. Go to the tree and try just a single apple. The difference between good and evil will be yours [to know], exactly, as from the high Prince."

1257. "Although your understanding may be good—a clear reckoning—although your advice may be full of virtue, I don't dare go to the tree at all, so that I may not die," [said Eve].

1261. "Come to the tree yourself, serpent, and take an apple from it. Should that apple but reach me, I will share it between me and Adam.

1265. We shall know—in the sight of every multitude—if we but eat the apple, whether your story (without ire—a clear reckoning) is true as you say."

1269. "O shining Eve, open the door of paradise for me without conditions. Quickly, if I but enter there, will I get the apple from the tree."

1273. "If I open up for you, you must go [back out] there. If you take an apple from the tree, there won't be dawdling on your part, [or] staying any length of time in paradise.''

1277. "So long as I give you the apple for distinguishing good and evil, I will go out without any [problem], unless some hindrance comes to me.''

1281. Secretly, Eve opened the door to the serpent. Without any resistance he went—and it wasn't slowly—running to one certain tree.

1285. He gave the entire apple from the apple tree to Eve—a sad story it was. She ate half of it; it was not pure. She left the other half for Adam.

1293. From the point when Eve, by herself, ate half the malignant apple, her body changed for the worse—heavy punishment—her beautiful covering fell from her.

1297. To Eve, beginning without sin, it was a marvel being naked. Trembling took hold of the woman without pure form and she let out a cry to Adam.

1301. At Eve's cry—as was right—sinless, unblemished Adam came straightaway and saw his wife naked.

1305. "You cannot endure as you are," said Adam to his good wife. "How did you come to be in slavery? Who stripped you of your holy covering?''

1309. "I won't tell you that, Adam, my lord, until you have taken this apple from me, fearlessly and swiftly.''

1313. After Adam had openly taken the malignant apple, his covering left him, without beauty, so that he was himself naked.

1317. "Who betrayed you, silly woman? Who was aware that you did not have true wisdom? He who has brought us to misfortune—may he be in trouble—has betrayed you; you have betrayed me.''

1321. "Truly, the serpent" (as has been heard) "begged of me that it come into paradise. After coming here, it took an apple from the forbidden tree.''

[Eve recapitulates for Adam the events just narrated.]

1341. "The serpent has overcome us—his fang is sharp—he has brought us to tribulation by his tempting. He plotted his splendid deed a long time ago. His treachery has destroyed us, Adam.''

1345. "O, Eve, of many transgressions, it is not good that we saw your apple. It is manifest from the way we are naked that we have suffered great evil because of it," [said Adam].

1349. "There is worse from it as well: separating body and soul; the corrupted body into the hard earth, the soul to hell.''

1357. The complexion of their bodies was manifest to each of them because they had been left completely naked. To cover their shame—tradition is clear—they took the leaves of the fig tree.

[Gabriel assembles the hosts of heaven.]

1377. The mighty King came to paradise with His great host firmly before Him, without sin; a choir of angels singing in unison.

[Description of the hosts of heaven.]

1393. "Have you heard clearly the deed which Adam has done: going—without pure integrity—against my orders, against my teaching?" [said the Lord to His creatures].

1397. Each of them [Adam and Eve] went, individually, in flight into the shadow of the tree and the voice of God said from heaven, "You have not been good, Adam."

1401. Adam spoke his pathetic reply—with clear sense—to God: "If it be that I violated your ordinance, it was my wife who tempted me."

1405. God said clearly to Adam: "Because you did not confess your sin, after this your children will always dispute their sinfulness."

1409. If Adam—with all his faults—had done penance, his sins would have been forgiven him clearly.

1413. The keen-sighted Prince Himself clearly ordered His angels: "Send Adam, [a man] without pure deed, out of paradise to earth."

1429. "Do you hear me, dear God? For your angels, for your archangels, will you allow me, through grace, some of the fruit of the tree of life?" [asked Adam].

1433. "You will not taste the fruit of the tree—as is the desire (?) of a great multitude—while your body and your soul are together in living warmth."

[The Lord berates Adam.]

1445. "Go into a foolish, shrivelled, twisted, ever-laborious life; sadly weary, without cause for rest; this will be repayment for your sins.

1449. Your children, your sons, your wives rendering service for you every single day; they do not have any possessions, until sweat—hard work—comes upon their brow.

1453. The many hurts that are upon you: separation of body and soul, fated to trouble and toil, age, and withering of trembling hands.

1457. Be prepared for the temptations of the devil every day, every single year, so that he may not bring you with him to his house: to horrible hell.

1461. If your deeds are pure, following my commandments, my instructions, heaven will be given—wonderful appearance—to everyone according to his real merit."

1469. The King bestowed the earth's surface upon Adam after his transgression. He would not have been unsatisfied with good God if his lifetime were not to run out.

1473. Adam was a week here after his expulsion from paradise, complaining, without fire, without shelter, without drink, without food, without clothes.

[Adam complains of their fallen state and remembers paradise.]

1525. Eve responded, for she was bound and in sorrow after transgression: "Adam, famous over every land, why do you not kill me for my sins?

1529. It is I who went against the commandment, it is I who made the transgression. It is proper for you to kill me for that, my lord Adam."

[Eve continues her offer of death.]

1537. "We have offended the King enough, woman," said Adam without contempt. "I will not commit kin-slaying upon you, even though I may be hungry and naked."

1553. "Our circumstances are not good," said Eve. "Adam, without clothes for us, without a warm house, without food, we will die of hunger.

1557. We had food, we had covering while we were without transgression; after our transgression and falling away we do not have covering or good food."

1565. Adam zealously went on an expedition, near and far. In the end he did not find food that was pure except the plants of the earth.

1569. "The plants of the earth, their color green, food of the senseless animals, they are not soft for us as a feast after the smooth foods of paradise.

1573. Eve, let us, purely, do enduring penance and repentance, so that we might wash away, before the King of Laws, something of our sins, of our transgression.

1585. Let us worship the Lord together in silence, without speaking together. You go into the strong pure river Tigris and I will go into the river Jordan.

1589. Thirty-three days—a precious measure—for you to be in the river Tigris; I, under penalty, in the Jordan forty-seven full days."

[Further description of the immersion.]

1625. Angels of God came from heaven every day to care for Adam, to instruct him—as had been ordered—until nineteen days were over.

1629. Adam prayed then a powerful prayer upon the river

Jordan, that it should fast with him against dear God with all its numerous animals.

1633. The stream stopped in its tracks, from its course, from its wandering. The royal stream ceased its running in aid of God absolving Adam.

1637. After that the stream brought together every living animal that was in its womb: the full complement of the host it ruled, until they all were around Adam.

1641. Both of them prayed: Adam and the stream—and all the animals. Sadly they poured out their noble cries to the pure host of the nine holy orders.

[Further description of prayers.]

1653. For the sake of his orders [of angels] God gave full absolution for the sin of Adam, with permanent possession of the earth, and with worthy, pure, high, holy heaven.

1657. And he then forgave his children, his descendants; but he who does not bear the right, let him go into unrighteousness against the command of God.

1661. When the black devil heard that forgiveness had been given to Adam: "I will go splendidly in fair state to Eve again,

1665. to bring her from the river, owing to her weakness, to bring her on a specious course so that I might remove something of her effort and devotion."

[Eve comes out of the river.]

1689. Eve did not clearly recognize Lucifer on account of his many [different] appearances. It was hard for the excellent woman, her mind was doubtful.

1693. "Eve, what is the matter with you? You are doing a lot of thinking. I came all the way from heaven at the behest of dearest God.

1697. Let us go to Adam, woman; do not be so tardy. We have all prayed to dear God about forgiving your sins."

[They go to Adam.]

1713. [Adam speaks:] "O miserable Eve, without fair form, what has brought you from the river Tigris without permission of the King of Right, without a holy guardian angel?

1721. Lucifer, devil, why are you pursuing us? You tricked us— as has been heard—you betrayed us in paradise.

1725. Since our contracts have been sundered, do not pursue us, Lucifer. We are in captivity on account of your plan. We do not want your company.

1729. It is not we who took your possessions or put you from your proper sovereignty. It is not we who asked secretly for your expulsion from the heights of heaven.

1749. Truly, it was your rebelling against the King of Laws that brought you to helplessness. You have found much trouble through your pride and through your lack of submission.

1753. Why are you assaulting us here, after we have been put out of paradise? You have struck our pure lives from us; you have given us into sin."

1757. "Do you remember, Adam, the evil that I have encountered because of you: putting me from the plain of noble heaven, my living in sorrow, without status?"

[Lucifer repeats a litany of the evil he has suffered and recapitulates the story of his fall and the fall of Adam and Eve.]

1873. "I offer you this hard saying: whatever harm and hurt I am able to do, in heaven and afterwards on earth, I will do to you, Adam.

1877. I will destroy everything in the world around your children, around your descendants, openly in rough battle, in sickness, in plagues."

1881. When the two of them had poured out their pure passion in their strife, Adam rose up out of the river. He sent Lucifer away from them.

1885. Clearly, after that Adam was for a year on the land of this world, in a wandering state, without anyone else save himself and his wife,

1889. without strengthening produce—tradition is clear—but grass, the portion [created] for the animals, without food, or fire, or a house, without customs or singing, or clothing;

1893. [nothing but] a drink of water from his fine palm to wash down the green herbs under the shelter of clean trees in the dry caves of the earth.

1897. Eve gave birth to a child—a fine exploit; right away he started walking. His careful help to the household was good: reaping the grass for his father.

1905. "God has been good to us, O fair, faithful Eve," [said Adam]. "It was great sense on my part here that I did not foolishly kill you."

1909. Adam named his son Cain—rough, fierce, powerful. Shame and deceit filled him, a headstrong, destructive man.

1913. When God, at last, felt sorry for Adam eating the grass, He decided wisely, "It is time to help Adam."

1917. God sent Michael—a pure means—from heaven to earth with the essence of every fine fruit and with various seeds.

1918. And he gave every individual seed in [their proper] order to Adam. And thus he taught him plainly the methods of husbandry.

[Adam is given knowledge of plants and animals.]

1933. It was fully seven years after that until Eve bore another child to Adam—fair was the hostage—a son who was named Abel.

1937. Selected by God—a clear course—a just man, truly perfect, who was, after the victory of dear God, serving his parents.

1941. "A dream-vision has appeared to me," said she, said Eve to Adam, "Cain's drinking Abel's blood with swift power."

1949. "Woman, certainly there is help for that if God thinks it proper. They will not spend the night in the same house; each of them will be in his [own] dwelling."

1953. Adam built two houses: a house for each of the two of them, individually. A house for Cain—admirable the effort—and another house for Abel.

1957. God sent pure Gabriel to Adam with the real truth of the tale: "Rude, dark Cain, without sense, is intending to kill Abel.

1961. But do not let Eve discover from him the story in [its] extraordinary, true sorrow: Cain will take a drink of his blood, for he [Cain] is the beloved son of the devil.

1965. And do not let your wits be disturbed if Cain kills Abel; you will have (?) a son of his fair form whose name will be Seth, particularly dear."

1969. There were born to Adam—as has been heard—without fear, without transgression, seventy sons, and two of them notable, and the like number of daughters.

1973. The King exalted two sons of Adam over the vast tribes: Abel, and famous Cain, with their powerful children.

1977. The King granted the earth with its good possessions to man. He was satisfied with Abel for a long time, and unsatisfied with Cain.

1985. Two hundred years—pleasant dignity—is what was completed by Abel (it is not a lie—it has been said for a long time) until he was killed by Cain.

1989. The King then declared to every one of the children of Adam that they should obey His will and that they should not kill Cain.

1993. "Whoever under heaven should kill Cain for that crime will not be accepted for his furious deed; sevenfold retribution will be put upon him."

1997. After that, my shining King put the sign of sin upon Cain. So that the sin would not be hidden, he put a bump on his forehead.

2001. Unfortunate Cain died afterwards, one evening, in the valley of Jehosaphat, when a crooked tree struck with painful force on the bump which was on his forehead.

2005. Since Cain fell there, in the narrow valley of Jehosaphat, it is under a sentence of blame, without fruits or profitability.

2009. After a space of time, the King gave noble Seth to Adam in place of Abel, so that from him, after that, sprang the noble families of the seed of Adam.

2013. Forty years—not silently is it related—without rough battles, in tranquility, without sickness or fighting, until Seth began propagating.

2021. So that you may know, without error, Adam's lifetime (it was not short): he had 930 years, in excellence, it was precise.

2025. After that a true illness came—as it comes to everyone— to Adam. Eve was, in dignity in every way, at his deathbed.

2029. Adam knew his fate. He said to fair, modest Eve, "I have parted from you and our children. It is of this sickness that I will die."

2033. "Would to God, truly stated," she said, said Eve to Adam, "that you were not leaving here, that I were the one to go first."

[Eve mourns Adam.]

2049. "Tell me correctly, husband, what am I to do with your beloved body, as you are sure of your dying from that [illness], my lord Adam?"

2053. "Foot or hand should not touch me, nor men come to disturb me until God send from heaven to arrange my beloved body."

[Adam repeats that his body should be left alone.]

2089. Sorrowful Eve bends her knees on the ground, speaking with difficulty. "My tear is for you, O King of heaven, until the warrior, Michael, comes to me,

2093. to cleanse the soul of Adam, to separate him from his sins, to lead him, after going to death, to the hosts of archangels."

2097. [The Archangel Michael replies:] "Rise from the ground, Eve. Abundantly (?) your words have been heard. Your tale has reached the height of heaven; the warrior Michael has come to you.

2101. His soul has gone from Adam's body, O well-formed Eve. Put his fair body in order, without terror, with your own two hands—fine the treasure."

2105. After that Eve came quickly to Adam. She found Adam— great dignity—without the inhalation of breath.

[Eve watches Adam's soul rise to heaven.]

2169. The pure host of holy, noble angels all bent to the ground. They prayed to dear God to forgive Adam's guilt.

[The angel host continues its prayers.]

2189. The soul of Adam, of noble status, threw itself down on the ground; it was lying in front of the Overking for three whole days.

2193. Until the King, after that, put His hand under Adam's soul and commended it—a fine tale—without any struggle, to Michael.

2205. "*In the third heaven*," said God, "the name of which is Ficconicia, may it be there, without display of punishment, until the time of the resurrection."

[The orders of angels praise God.]

2217. There the oil of mercy and the herb *odoramentum* were put about the body of Adam by them to cleanse it of its sins.

2221. Three full winding-sheets—a mark of nobility—were wound about the body of Adam, and it was buried with care next to the grave of Abel.

2225. So the body of our ancestor, Adam, was buried, long ago (according to the numerous arts of the learned) in Hebron under the harsh captivity of sad death.

2233. The flooding of the deluge over every plain dug up much of the earth. It took Adam's head from him and brought it to Jerusalem.

2237. The head remained after that at the gate of Jerusalem. Later, without sorrow, the cross of Christ was set in the body of Adam.

II

EXODUS

Celtic Analogue

1. *Exodus*

(From *The Poems of Blathmac*; text: *PoBl*, pp. 26–33.)

This account of the Exodus is contained in an eighth-century poem addressed to the Virgin. Like the *Saltair na Rann*, it is arranged in groups of 150 quatrains to imitate the psalms. Embedded in an account of the Crucifixion, the Exodus section presents a complaint about the Jews' ingratitude. This may indicate that the poem had liturgical origins. The section parallels the *improperia* ("reproaches") of the Good Friday liturgy, in which the voice of the crucified Christ asks, "O, my people, what have I done unto thee?" (*Popule meus, quid feci tibi?*). The voice goes on to remind the faithful, "I smote the Kings of the Canaanites," and mentions bringing fresh water from the rock for Moses. The parallel is highly suggestive even though we do not know exactly what Good Friday liturgy Blathmac may have known (see Schmidt, pp. 793–96 and 929–46, and Andrieu, pp. 245–60).

77. It was hard, it was a shameful deed for the Jews—as we have mentioned—the Crucifixion of the Son of God, the Father; he smote the strong for their forefathers in Egypt.

78. For he heard their cry from captivity, under heavy enslavement, because of the ancient covenant which he had with Abraham.

79. It was for these men, then, that he brought the ten chief

21

plagues [to Egypt]; one of those [was] weeping in every household: each cried for his firstborn.

80. When they came in their march, Egypt was under total mourning. When they were released on the road, it was not voluntarily, it was by necessity.

81. In the day a dark cloud was brought from heaven for their protection so that with it enemies might not judge where they were and would not recognize them.

82. At night a fiery cloud—unique in kind—was brought for their protection, so that no one might set up their gravestones [kill them], so that their setting forth might be fortunate.

83. It was to their leader—a kingly gift—that the mighty rod was given with which he struck the Red Sea so that it split into two high walls.

84. After that, it was they who went across that sea with dry feet; Pharaoh was drowned with his splendid host, with chariots and many horses.

85. It was to them—splendid gathering—that God gave a fine gift: the Manna—more than fine treasures—with its four chief flavors.

86. For them limpid water was brought from the rock of the stream that they might not be harmed by drinking from poisoned waters.

87. He taught them at the same time how to make bronze serpents. Terror seized the serpents fleeing before them.

88. To them was sent a certain flock of birds when meat was their true desire. It was to them the law was given that used to expound every wrong.

89. Before them—two worthies—the river Ernon and the river Jordan divided; and it was before them as well that the seven walls of Jericho cracked.

90. It was to them the king granted the fruitful Land of Promise; before them he cut down—in splendid battle—the seven great tribes of the Canaanites.

III

THE ELEGIES

A. General

1. Germanic Analogues

While the OE Elegies are among the most read and most admired of early Germanic lyrics, scholars have yet to establish that the "Elegy" existed as a specific genre in the various branches of Germanic poetry. The problem of definition stems from the difficulty of uniting such widely varying poems and the numerous "elegiac" passages in other texts under a single generic heading. Some scholars are very restrictive in drawing their boundaries; Malone believes that only *Wulf and Eadwacer* and *The Wife's Lament* belong together, since both are *Frauenlieder* (Malone 1962). Others, however, maintain that all the OE examples share a common heritage with certain ON lyrics and, presumably, unrecorded German Elegies (see Sieper, Heusler, and Harris). They posit that the "Elegy" derived from funeral verse or ritual lament known to all the Germanic tribes. Recent work stresses the integrity of the genre. Greenfield suggests that a first-person narrator and a pattern of loss and consolation are the salient features of the Elegy; later he defines the genre in terms of our modern response (see Greenfield 1966, 1972). Harris goes further and outlines an inclusive pattern of development within the genre, from heroic autobiography, through the addition of gnomic and homiletic material, to allegory. Given the disparate nature of the OE Elegies, the analogues selected for this collection will relate to the individual poems in different ways.

a. *The First Lay of Guðrún*

(*Guðrúnarqviða* [*in fyrsta*]; text: *Edda*, pp. 202–6.)

Although *The First Lay of Guðrún* comes first in the *Guðrún* poems, it is not the oldest of the group, and may even be as late as the twelfth century. In this lay, written in *fornyrðislag* meter, Guðrún sits by Sigurðr's dead body; he has been slain through the plotting of Guðrún's brothers, Gunnarr and Hǫgni. In some versions of the legend Brynhildr has egged them on to this deed. Jealousy and a thirst for the Rhine gold are the principal motives (see Bellows, Hollander, Hallberg, and Andersson).

1. There was a time when Guðrún was ready to die, when she sat sorrowful by Sigurðr; she did not wail, nor wring her hands, nor cry like other women.

2. The all-wise jarls went towards her, those who would relieve her heavy heart. Yet Guðrún could not weep, she was so sad she would burst.

3. The noble wives of the jarls sat, gold-adorned, before Guðrún; each of them told of her great grief, the bitterest she had suffered.

4. Then spoke Giaflaug, Giúki's sister: "I consider myself the most miserable on earth: I have suffered the terrible loss of five husbands, three daughters, three sisters, eight brothers—though I still live."

5. Yet Guðrún could not weep, she was so sad at her husband's death and stony-hearted by the prince's corpse.

6. Then spoke Herborg, the queen of the Huns: "I have a heavier sorrow to tell: my seven sons in the southern land, and my husband, the eighth, fell in battle;

7. the wind played with [my] father and [my] mother, four brothers, on the waves; the billows beat against the bulwarks.

8. I myself had to adorn [them], I myself had to bury [them], I myself had to make [them] ready for their hell-journeys. I suffered all that in one half-year, without any one offering me comfort.

9. Then I was bound and taken captive; that happened in the same half-year. Every morning I had to dress the chieftain's wife and bind [her] shoes.

10. She threatened me out of jealousy and goaded me with hard blows; nowhere did I find a better master, nor anywhere a worse mistress."

11. Yet Guðrún could not weep, she was so sad at her hus-

band's death and stony-hearted by the prince's corpse.

12. Then Gullrǫnd spoke, Giúki's daughter: "Though you may be wise, fostermother, you can bring few words of consolation to the young wife!" She persuaded them not to cover the prince's corpse.

13. She swept the shroud from Sigurðr and turned the pillow towards the wife's knees. "Look on your loved one; lay your mouth to his lips, as you embraced the prince when he was alive!"

14. Guðrún looked a single time: she saw the hero's hair run with blood, the prince's gleaming eyes now dimmed, the warrior's breast pierced by a sword.

15. Then Guðrún sank down, slumped against the bolster; her hair came loose, her cheeks turned red, a drop of rain ran down toward her knees.

16. Then Guðrún wept, Giúki's daughter, so that the tears flowed through her tresses; in the courtyard the geese cried out, the glorious birds, which the young wife owned.

17. Then Gullrǫnd spoke, Giúki's daughter: "I do not know of a greater married love than yours among all men over the earth; you were content neither outside nor in, my sister, except near Sigurðr!"

18. "So was my Sigurðr above the sons of Giúki, as the garlic grows above the grass, or the bright stone set on a band, a jewel among chieftains.

19. And to the prince's warriors I seemed higher than any of Heriann's maids; now I am as little as the leaf on the meadow laurel (?), since the prince's death.

20. In the seat and in the bed I miss my closest friend; the sons of Giúki caused [that]. The sons of Giúki caused my misfortune and their sister's bitter tears.

21. Thus you strip the land of people, just as you broke your sworn oaths. The gold will bring no joy to you, Gunnarr, the rings will be your slayer, since you swore oaths to Sigurðr.

22. There was often greater joy in the courtyard when my Sigurðr saddled Grani, and they travelled to woo Brynhildr, contemptible bitch, in an evil hour."

23. Then Brynhildr spoke, Buðli's daughter: "May that bitch be without husband and children, who brought you to tears, Guðrún, and who gave you speech-runes this morning."

24. Then spoke Gullrǫnd, Giúki's daughter: "You hateful woman, do not speak those words! You have always been the deadly fate of chieftains, every wave of evil fate tosses you, cruel sorrow for seven kings, and the most evil husband-killer among women."

25. Then spoke Brynhildr, Buðli's daughter: "Atli, born of Buðli, my brother, alone caused all this misfortune;

26. when in the Hunnish hall we saw the fire of the serpent's lair [gold] around the prince, I later paid the price of that ride. I always see that sight before me."

27. She stood under the pillar, she gathered her strength; a fire burned from Brynhildr's eyes, Buðli's daughter; she snorted out poison, when she saw the wounds on Sigurðr.

Guðrún went away from there to the woods in the wilderness and travelled all the way to Denmark and was there with Þóra, Hákon's daughter, seven half-years.

Brynhildr did not wish to live after Sigurðr. She had eight of her thralls and five bondmaids killed. Then she killed herself with a sword, as is told in the Short Lay of Sigurðr.

b. *The Second Lay of Guðrún*

(*Guðrúnarqviða* [*ǫnnor*]; text: *Edda*, pp. 224–31.)

This disconnected poem is usually called the *"Old Lay"* of *Guðrún*. As Hollander notes, here "we may recognize the prototype of the various other laments of the [*Edda*]. It is unquestionably older than most—or all—of them" (p. 269), and may go back as far as the tenth century. Brynhildr is absent and Sigurðr's death is blamed on the jealousy of Guðrún's brothers. The meter is *fornyrðislag* (see Bellows, Hollander, Hallberg, and Andersson).

1. I was the maid of maids, my mother bore me, bright in the bower, I loved my brothers well—until Giúki gladdened me with gold, gladdened me with gold, gave me to Sigurðr.

2. So was Sigurðr above the sons of Giúki as the green leek grows above the grass, or the long-legged stag [towers over] the fawn-colored (?) beasts, or ember-red gold [is valued] above gray silver.

3. But then my brothers begrudged me a husband better than all; they could not sleep nor judge cases before they had had Sigurðr killed.

4. Grani ran from the Þing, there was a din to hear, but Sigurðr himself did not come hence; the saddle-beasts were all drenched in sweat and used to toil under the killers.

5. I went weeping to speak with Grani; with tear-stained cheeks I asked the horse for the tale; then Grani hung his head, he let it

droop to the grass; the horse knew that his owner no longer lived.

6. Long I wavered, long my mind was divided, before I asked the warlord about the prince.

7. Gunnarr bowed his head, [but] Hǫgni told me about Sigurðr's sorrowful death: "He lies hacked to pieces beyond the flood [Rhine], Gothormr's slayer, given to the wolves.

8. Go look for Sigurðr on the southern road! There you will hear the ravens scream, the eagles scream, glad in carrion, the wolves howl about your husband."

9. "Why, Hǫgni, do you want to tell me, bereft of joys, such woes? May ravens tear your heart wherever you roam (?) over the wide lands."

10. Hǫgni answered one time only, heavy at heart from the great grief: "You would have more to cry about, Guðrún, if the ravens should tear my heart."

11. Alone I turned away from those words to the forest, to gather up the leavings of wolves: I did not wail, nor wring my hands, nor cry like other women, when I sat close to death by Sigurðr.

12. The night seemed to be pitch dark to me, when I sat in sorrow over Sigurðr; the wolves seemed better than all: if they would [only] let me forfeit my life or [if I could just] burn up like birch wood.

13. I travelled from the fell five days all told, until I noticed Hálfr's high hall.

14. I sat with Þóra, Hákon's daughter, seven half-years, in Denmark. To give me joy, she embroidered in gold the southern halls and Danish swans.

15. In the tapestry we had what warriors play, and in our handiwork the ruler's thanes, red shields, Hunnish warriors, sword-company, helmet-company, the ruler's followers.

16. Sigmundr's ships sailed from the land with gilded figure-heads and carved prows; in the web we wove what they fought, Sigarr and Siggeirr, south in Fión.

17. Then Grímildr, the Gothic woman, learned what I intended (?); she cast aside the tapestry and summoned her sons to ask sternly who would compensate their sister for her son or make amends for the slain husband.

18. Gunnarr said he was ready to offer gold, to settle the claim and Hǫgni as well. She asked who would go to saddle the horse, to harness the wagon, to ride the horse, to let the hawk fly, to shoot arrows from the yew-bow.

19. Valdarr the Dane with Iarizleifr, Eymóðr the third with Iarizkárr went in then like princes, the Langobard (?) men; they

had red cloaks of coarse wool, ornamented byrnies, high helmets, and were girded with short swords; they had dark brown hair.

20. Each wanted to choose treasures for me, choose treasures and comfort me with words, [to see] if they might win a truce from me in my great sorrow, but I did not trust them.

21. Grímildr brought me a horn to drink, cold and bitter, so I would not remember my grief: that was mixed with power of destructive fate, the ice-cold sea, and the blood of a sacrificial boar.

22. On the horn was every kind of rune stave, carved and reddened—I could not interpret them—a long serpent from the land of the Haddingiar, an uncut ear of grain, and the entrails of beasts.

23. Many evil things were mixed in that beer, all the herbs of the forest and burned acorns, the hearth's dew [soot], entrails of sacrifices, boiled swine's liver, because it would deaden my grief.

24. When I had taken the drink, then I forgot the slaying of the prince by sword (?) in the hall: three kings came to my knees, before she herself [Grímildr] began to speak with me.

25. "Guðrún, I give you gold to own, all the great treasures that were your dead father's, red rings and Hlǫðvér's halls, and all the hangings that the prince had;

26. Hunnish maidens, those who can weave linen and make gold fair to please you; you alone shall control Buðli's wealth, honored with gold, and given to Atli."

27. "I will not take a husband, nor have Brynhildr's brother! It is not fitting for me to raise a family with the son of Buðli, nor to live content."

28. "Do not dwell on revenging your feuds with the warriors, although we were the first to start trouble; so you will act as though both were alive, Sigurðr and Sigmundr, if you bear sons."

29. "Grímildr, I may not presume to have joy, nor have hope in the warrior, since the wolf and Huginn sorely drank Sigurðr's heart's blood together."

30. "Now I have found a prince from the noblest of all races and the best of any man; you shall have him until your life comes to an end. You will be without a husband unless you choose him."

31. "Do not keep offering me that sinister race so stubbornly! He will do harm to Gunnarr and tear out Hǫgni's heart. I will never quit until I have taken the life from that restless starter of battle."

32. Weeping, Grímildr heard the words, which boded ill for her sons and great calamity for her offspring:

33. "Lands I give you and a band of retainers, Vínbjǫrg,

Valbiǫrg, if you will accept them; you will have and enjoy them for life, daughter."

34. "I will choose him from among the kings, and have him for my kinsmen, although unwillingly. A husband will be no delight for me, nor will my brothers' suffering be a shelter for my sons."

35. Soon each warrior was seen on a horse, and the Frankish women lifted into wagons: seven days we rode through cold lands, and another seven we struck against the waves, and a third seven we crossed barren lands.

36. There the guardians of a high fortress opened up the gates before we rode into the courtyard.

37. Atli woke me, but I seemed to be full of bad thoughts from my kinsmen's deaths.

38. "Just now the Norns woke me." He wanted me to interpret the vision of evil. "I thought that you, Guðrún, Giúki's daughter, pierced me through with a poisoned sword."

39. "That means fire when one dreams of iron; pride and willfulness, a woman's wrath: I will burn you to ward off evil, comfort and heal you, though I loathe you."

40. "I dreamed that here in the courtyard saplings fell, those I wanted to let grow, ripped up by the roots, reddened in blood, brought to the bench, you bade me chew them.

41. I dreamed hawks flew from my hands, hungry for meat, to a house of woe; I dreamed I chewed their hearts mixed with honey, sorrowful in spirit, soaked in blood.

42. I dreamed I loosed whelps from my hand, lacking all joy, they both howled. I thought their flesh turned to carrion; unwilling, I had to eat the corpses."

43. "There will men speak about sacrifice and take the heads of victims (?); they are doomed to die in a few nights, before daybreak, for the troop to consume."

44. "I lay down then—I did not want to sleep—defiant on my sick bed; I remember that clearly."

c. *The Third Lay of Guðrún*

(*Guðrúnarqviða* [*in þriðia*]; text: *Edda*, pp. 231–3.)

An oddity among the other laments, this lay is essentially a Scandinavian re-telling of German material treating a wife's infidelity. The ordeal by boiling water, introduced into Norway from Germany at the beginning of the eleventh century, means that the poem must be relatively late, perhaps twelfth-century.

Guðrún's review of her sorrows forms the poem's elegiac core. The meter is *fornyrðislag* (see Bellows, Holland, Hallberg, and Andersson).

Herkia was the name of one of Atli's bondwomen; she had been his mistress. She told Atli that she had seen Þióðrekr and Guðrún together. Atli was very grieved. Then Guðrún said:

1. "What is wrong with you, Atli? Buðli's son, you are always sad at heart; why do you never laugh? It would seem better to the jarls, if you spoke with men and looked on me."

2. "That grieves me, Guðrún, Giúki's daughter, what Herkia told me in the hall, that you and Þióðrekr slept under a roof and were lovers under the bed linen."

3. "I will swear to you all oaths about this, at the white, holy stone, that I did nothing with Þióðmarr's son, which woman and man should not do.

4. Rather I embraced the prince of hosts, the noble warrior, just one time; quite different were our talks, when full of sorrow we two sat down to speak in confidence.

5. Þióðrekr came here with thirty, not one of the thirty men still lives; they have deprived (?) me of my brothers, of the byrnied men, they have deprived me of all my closest kin.

6. Send for Saxi, the prince of the southern men! He can bless the boiling kettle."

7. Seven hundred men went into the hall, before the king's wife thrust [her hand] into the kettle.

8. "Gunnarr will not come now, I will not call Hǫgni, I will not see my sweet brothers any more; Hǫgni would avenge such affliction with his sword, now I myself must clear me of this taint."

9. She plunged her bright hand to the bottom, and she picked up the precious gems: "See now warriors—I am proved guiltless by the holy trial—, although the kettle boils."

10. Then Atli's heart laughed in his breast, when he saw Guðrún's hands unscathed: "Now shall Herkia go to the kettle, she who expected harm for Guðrún."

11. No man ever saw a wretched sight who did not see how there Herkia's hands were singed; they led the maiden to the foul moor; in that way then Guðrún paid back (?) her injuries.

d. *Brynhildr's Ride to Hel*
(*Helreið Brynhildar*; text: *Edda*, pp. 219–22.)

This lay, written in *fornyrðislag* and recounting Brynhildr's meeting with and devotion to Sigurðr, is manifestly late, probably twelfth-century; commentators frequently mention the traces of Christian influence that appear here. Of all the lays, this is the only one that portrays Brynhildr sympathetically (see Bellows, Hollander, Hallberg, and Andersson).

After the death of Brynhildr, two pyres were built; one for Sigurðr, and that burned first, and Brynhildr was burned on the other and she was on a wagon, which was adorned with costly fabric. It is said that Brynhildr rode in the wagon on the road to Hel and travelled to a homestead where a certain giantess lived. The giantess said:

1. "You shall not go through the courtyard, which stands on stones; it would be better for you to weave than to seek another's [Guðrún's] husband.
2. What do you, foreigner, seek at my house, you with the fickle heart? Goddess of gold [woman], you have washed the blood of men from your hands, O 'gracious one,' if you want to know."
3. Then Brynhildr said: "Do not reproach me, woman, from the rock, although I may have been in battle [as a valkyrie]. I will seem the better of us two where men know both our lineages."
4. The giantess said: "Brynhildr, Buðli's daughter, you were born most ill-fated into the world; you have ruined the sons of Giúki and destroyed their noble dwelling."
5. Brynhildr said: "I, wise from my wagon, will tell you, great witless one, if you want to know it, how the heirs of Giúki made me loveless and forsworn.
6. The bold king had our skins [the feather coats of the eight sisters] borne under an oak; I was twelve winters old, if you want to know, when I pledged my troth to the young prince.
7. Everyone in Hlymdalir who knew me called me Hildr-under-helmet.
8. Then I made old Hiálm-Gunnarr of the Goths go to Hel next; I gave victory to Auða's young brother; Óðinn was very angry with me about that.
9. He surrounded me with shields in Skatalundr, red and white; the rims touched. He bade him break my sleep, who knew no fear anywhere in the land.

10. He had the ravager of all the forest [fire] burn southward, high around my hall; there he bade one thane only to ride over, he who would bring me the gold that lay under Fáfnir.

11. The good one, the gold-giver, rode on Grani, where my fosterfather ruled his hall; there the Danish viking seemed better than all the retinue.

12. We slept and were content in one bed, as if he had been born my brother; neither of us laid a hand over the other for eight nights.

13. But Guðrún, Giúki's daughter, reproached me, [saying] that I had slept in Sigurðr's arms; then I became aware of that which I did not want to, that they had deceived me in the taking of [Gunnarr as] a husband.

14. Women and men are born into the world for deep sorrow all too long; we will forfeit our lives together, Sigurðr and I—sink down, giantess!"

e. *The Lament of Oddrún*

(*Oddrúnargrátr*; text: *Edda*, pp. 234–9.)

The character of Oddrún, Atli's sister, is a northern addition to the Sigurðr-Atli cycle. No parallel explains Gunnarr's and Hǫgni's deaths through Atli's discovery of a love affair between Gunnarr and Oddrún, as occurs in this poem. While *The Lament of Oddrún* has been characterized as "the most elegiac of the whole collection" (Hollander, p. 279), it has a very late date (the end of the twelfth century?). The meter is *fornyrðislag* (see Bellows, Hollander, Hallberg, Turville-Petre 1964, and Andersson).

About Borgný and Oddrún

There was a king called Heiðrekr; his daughter was called Borgný. Vilmundr was the name of the man who was her lover. She could not give birth to children before Oddrún, Atli's sister, came to her; she had been the beloved of Gunnarr, Giúki's son. About this story is here told:

1. I have heard it told in ancient tales, how a maiden came to Mornaland; no one over the earth could give help to Heiðrekr's daughter.

2. Oddrún, Atli's sister, heard that this maiden had a great sickness; she brought from the stall the bitted-steed, and laid a saddle on the black [horse].

3. She made the horse go over the even ground, until she came to the high, towering hall, and she went in the whole length of the room; she jerked the saddle from the tired horse, and these were the first words she spoke:

4. "What is going on in the world, or what has happened (?) in the land of the Huns?" "Here lies Borgný, overcome by labor, your friend, Oddrún; see if you can help her!"

5. "Who was the ruler who committed this outrage? Why is Borgný suddenly sick?"

6. "He is called Vilmundr, friend of warriors; he enveloped the maiden in warm bed linens, five winters in all, but she kept it secret from her father."

7. Then, I think, they spoke little more. Helpful she went to sit at the maiden's knees; Oddrún sang mightily, Oddrún sang strongly, powerful charms for Borgný.

8. A girl and a boy set their feet on the earth, those happy children [born] to Hǫgni's slayer; then the deathly-sick maiden began to speak, she had said nothing before these words:

9. "May the holy powers help you, Frigg and Freyia and many [another] god, as you delivered me from danger."

10. "I did not kneel to help you for this, because you were ever worthy of it; I promised and I fulfilled what I spoke earlier, that I would help all, when chieftains get offspring (?).

13. Then the sorrowful woman sat herself down, to tell her misfortune from heavy griefs:

14. "I was brought up in a prince's hall—most were good to me—according to the decree of men. I lived happily and [had] my father's riches, for five winters only, while my father lived;

15. then the weary king spoke these last words, before he died: he bade that I be dowered with red gold and given to Grímildr's son in the south;

16. he said, 'a better maiden would not be born on the earth, unless fate destroyed her.'"

11. "You are crazy, Oddrún, and out of your wits, since you have spoken most of these words to me in spiteful fury; but I followed you on earth, as if we had been born of two brothers."

12. I remember what you spoke one evening, when I mixed the drink for Gunnarr; you said such a bad example would never be [given] again by a maiden, except by me alone.

16. But he bade Brynhildr get the helmet, he said she would be a valkyrie.

17. In her bower Brynhildr wove, she had people and lands under her; earth and heaven resounded, when Fáfnir's slayer saw that fortress.

18. Then war was waged with a foreign sword, and the fortress broken that Brynhildr owned; it was not long after this, but unfortunately soon, when she knew all their wiles.

19. For this she made her vengeance hard, as we have all learned from experience enough; that [tale] will travel to men of every land, how she killed herself at Sigurðr's side.

20. I was told to love Gunnarr, the giver of rings, as Brynhildr should have.

21. They offered Atli red rings and no small payment to my brother; and he offered fifteen farms for me, and Grani's burden [the Niflung gold], if he would have it.

22. But Atli said he would never accept a dowry from Giúki's kinsman; we could not struggle against the desire, and I laid my head against the ring-breaker.

23. Many of my kinsmen spoke, they said the two of us had been together; but Atli said I would not take a false step nor do wrong.

24. But of such matters a man should never speak for someone else, where love is concerned.

25. Atli sent his agents through Myrkviðr to test me; and they came where they should not have come, where we two shared a bed.

26. We offered the thanes red rings, so they would tell Atli nothing; but they hastily told Atli and eagerly hurried home.

27. But they completely hid it from Guðrún, although she most of all should have known.

28. A clatter of plated hoofs was heard, when Giúki's sons rode into the courtyard; they cut out Hǫgni's heart and placed the other [Gunnarr] in the snake pit.

29. I was still away on a journey to Geirmundr to mix his drink; the wise king struck the harp, because he thought, the high-born king, that I would come to help him.

30. From Hlésey I heard how the strings there spoke of sorrow; I bade the serving-maids be prepared, I wanted to save the prince's life.

31. We made the ship sail over the sound, until we saw all of Atli's court.

32. Then came the wretched one crawling out, Atli's mother, may she rot! And she bit to Gunnarr's heart, so that I could not save the noble one.

33. I have often wondered, gold-bedecked woman, how I could afterwards stay alive, for I loved the valiant giver of swords as myself.

34. You sat and listened while I told you the many evil fates—

mine and theirs; every man lives by his passions—now Oddrún's lament is ended."

f. *Guðrún's Chain of Woes*

(*Guðrúnarhvǫt*; text: *Edda*, pp. 264–8.)

Guðrún's Lament, as the title of this poem is also translated, treats the final episode in Guðrún's life. A work of uncertain date, the lay depicts Guðrún with her third husband, Iónakr. She tries to incite Hamðir and Sǫrli, her sons by that marriage, to avenge the death of their half-sister, Svanhildr, child of Guðrún and Sigurðr, who had been trampled to death by horses on orders from Svanhildr's husband, Iǫrmunrekkr. The poem is composed in *fornyrðislag*. Many affinities exist between *Guðrúnarhvǫt* and an older version, *The Lay of Hamðir* (q.v.; see Bellows, Hollander, Hallberg, and Dronke).

1. Then I heard the most evil-bringing dispute, reluctant words spoken from great sorrow, when Guðrún, hard in heart, goaded her sons with grim words to battle.

2. "Why are you sitting, why are you sleeping out your lives? Why does it not grieve you to speak words of good cheer, since Iǫrmunrekkr trampled your sister, young in years, with steeds, white and black, on the battle-way, the gray, pace-trained horses of the Goths?

3. You have not grown up like Gunnarr, nor in hearts are you as Hǫgni was; you would have sought to avenge her, if you had the courage of my brothers or the hard hearts of the Hunnish kings."

4. Then Hamðir, the great-hearted one, spoke: "Little would you have praised Hǫgni's deed, when they wakened Sigurðr from sleep; your blue-white bed covers were reddened in your husband's gore, drenched in the blood of slaughter.

5. You had wicked and sore revenge on your brothers, when you murdered your sons; we could have all, one in spirit, avenged our sister on Iǫrmenrekkr.

6. Bring out the treasures of the Hunnish kings! You have incited us to sword-play."

7. Laughing, Guðrún turned to her storehouse; she chose helmets of kings from the chests, broad byrnies, and bore them to her sons; the brave ones leaped onto the backs of their steeds.

8. Then Hamðir, the great-hearted one, spoke: "So will the spear-god [warrior], come to visit you again, mother—killed

among the Gothic people—so that you will [have to] drink to us all at the funeral feast, to Svanhildr and your sons."

9. Weeping, Guðrún, Giúki's daughter, went sorrowfully to sit in the forecourt and, with tears on her cheeks, to tell her painful tales, in many a way:

10. "I have known three fires, I have known three hearths, I have been taken home by three husbands; Sigurðr alone was better than all for me, he whom my brothers slew.

11. I did not see nor feel a harder sorrow; [but] there seemed more pain prepared for me when the chieftains gave me to Atli.

12. I called my keen boys to secret speech; I could not win recompense for the evil until I chopped off the heads of the Hniflungar.

13. I went to the sea, angry with the Norns; I wanted to escape their truce of woes [commit suicide?]; [but] the high waves bore me up, they did not drown me, so that I climbed up on land and had to live.

14. I went to bed—I'd hoped for better—for the third time with a king of the people; I bore children, rightful heirs, in the sons of Iónakr.

15. And bondwomen sat around Svanhildr, whom I loved best of my children; in my hall Svanhildr was as beautiful to look at as a ray of sunlight.

16. I dowered her with gold and costly fabrics before I gave her to the Gothic people; that to me was the hardest of my griefs when Svanhildr's fair hair was trampled in the mud under horses' hoofs.

17. But it was the saddest when they killed my Sigurðr in his bed, robbed of victory; and the grimmest when the flashing snakes gliding took Gunnarr's life; and the sharpest when they cut to the heart of the brave, living king [Hǫgni].

18. I remember many evils . . . Sigurðr, bridle the black steed, the fleet-footed horse, let it run here! Neither son's wife nor daughter sits here who might give treasures to Guðrún.

19. Remember, Sigurðr, what we said when we both sat on the bed, that you, courageous man, would seek me from Hel and I you from the earth.

20. Jarls, heap up an oak-wood pyre, let it be the highest under the warrior! May the fire burn my grief-stricken breast . . . may it melt the sorrows around my heart!"

21. May it lighten the lot of all jarls, lessen the sorrow of all women, that this tale of woe has been told.

g. *Víkarr's Piece*

(*Víkarsbálkr*, from *Gautrekssaga*; text: *EM*, pp. 38–43.)

The author of *Gautrekssaga*, written probably in the early fourteenth century, used *Víkarsbálkr*, attributed to Starkaðr, as a source. The poem itself has been dated between the eleventh and twelfth centuries (see *EM* and Pálsson/Edwards). *Gautrekssaga* is one of the *Legendary Sagas*, tales dealing with events which supposedly took place before the settlement of Iceland in the ninth century (see Schlauch). Their value as history is slight, although Starkaðr is identified in the *Landnámabók* as having lived around 750 (see Pálsson/Edwards). Óðinn grants Starkaðr a life three times that of an ordinary man, but Þórr decrees that he must commit a terrible deed in each life. In return for his gift of longevity, Óðinn demands that Starkaðr sacrifice King Víkarr, his lord and friend (see Turville-Petre 1964). This tragic conflict stands at the heart of Starkaðr's account of his life. The poem, like the others that follow from the *Eddica Minora*, has been characterized as a *Rückblicksgedicht* (a "retrospective poem"; see *EM* and de Vries). For the most part, the poem imitates the *fornyrðislag* meter of the Eddic lays.

1. I was young when a great number of seamen burned to death along with my father in his house; [there he lies] near the sea inside Þruma, the great warrior and retainer of Haraldr of Agðir. The brothers-in-law betrayed the necklace-breaker, Fiǫri and Fýri, heirs of Freki, brothers of Unnr, my mother.

2. When Herþiófr betrayed Haraldr, he deceived in his truce his superior; he robbed the life of Agðir's lord and contrived fetters for his sons.

3. Hrosshársgrani carried me, three winters old, from there to Hǫrðaland; I grew up on Askr; I did not see kinsmen for nine summers.

4. I got quite strong, limbs grew, long legs, and an ugly head; I sat like a laggard in the ashes down in the hall, curious about little;

5. but then Víkarr came from the signal beacon, Herþiófr's hostage; he walked into the hall. He recognized me, he told me to stand up and answer.

6. He measured me with hands and fingers, the whole length of my arms. . . . Hair grew down from the chin.

7. Then he gathered a troop, Sǫrkvir and Grettir, heirs of Haraldr, Hildigrímr, Erpr and Úlfr, Án and Skúma, Hrói and Hrotti, sons of Herbrandr;

8. Styrr and Steinþórr from Staðr in the north; there was old

Gunnólfr blesi; then we were thirteen altogether. It would have been difficult to find a finer band of warriors.

9. When we came to the king's enclosure, we shook the gates, hewed the door-posts; we broke the locks, drew our swords, there where seventy choice men stood before the king. In addition there were all the thralls, laborers, and water-carriers.

10. Víkarr was hard to follow, because he stood first and foremost in the host. We hewed helmets along with nose-bands, split their byrnies and broke their shields.

11. Honor was granted to Víkarr and to Herþiófr hostilities were repaid; we wounded warriors and we killed some. I was not standing far away when the king fell.

12. You were not with Víkarr east at Vænir early one day long ago, when we attacked Sísarr on the field; that was a hard task, greater than it seemed.

13. He wounded me with a blow from his sharp-edged sword, through the shield and the helmet on my head; he cut my skull and cleaved my chin-bone to the teeth. He smashed my left collar bone.

14. And the powerful one struck with his sword into my side above the hip; into my other side he thrust the cold spike of his halberd, so that the point stuck deep in my body; you can see the healed wounds on me.

15. I sliced his side with my sharp sword right across his belly. I let my sword swing in rage, and put forth all my strength.

[Interpolated stanzas omitted.]

16. Víkarr gave me foreign gold, the red ring which I wear on my arm, three marks in weight; and I gave him Þruma. I followed the prince for fifteen summers.

17. I followed the prince whom I knew to be the greatest; then was I best contented with my life, before we went—but that the witches caused—for the last time to Hǫrðaland.

18. It was on that mission, that Þórr created for me the name of traitor, [and] misfortunes of many kinds; inglorious, I was destined to commit bad deeds.

19. I had to sacrifice Víkarr to the gods, Geirþiófr's slayer, in the high tree; I pierced the prince to the heart with a spear: that is to me the most grievous of my hand-works.

20. From there I wandered aimlessly, hated by the Hǫrðar, in bad spirits, without rings and songs of praise, kingless, sad in all thoughts.

21. Now I sought Sweden, the home of the Ynglingar at Uppsalir; here the sons of the king treated me like a dumb jester, as I will long remember.

22. Here they set me in the midst of warriors, mocked and white-browed; the men ridiculed and made a laughing-stock of me, [they were] all too cruel (?) toward the prince's retainer.

23. They imagine they see on me, Hergrímr's slayer, the marks of my giant origin left by the eight arms which Hlórriði tore off with his hands, north of the cliffs.

24. Men laugh when they see me, the ugly jaw, the long snout, the wolf-gray hair, the dangling arms, the rough neck, the wrinkled hide.

h. *The Song of Hrókr*

(*Hrókslied*, from *Hálfssaga*, text: *EM*, pp. 44–8.)

Hrókslied, a late poem, probably did not originate before the second half of the twelfth century (*EM*, p. xxxvii), though dating of all these poems is problematic. In this *Song*, Hrókr enn svarti ("the black") reviews his life and laments the fall of King Hálfr. Hrókr has lived in Skáney unrecognized by King Haki, whose daughter, Brynhildr, is engaged to Vifill, son of Jarl Heðinn. King Sveinn had courted Brynhildr unsuccessfully and has vowed to kill her future husband and her father. Hrókr recites this lay after following Brynhildr into a forest.

1. Now the son of Hámundr will tell what was the origin of my brother and me: my father—a true hawk at heart—was greater by far than yours, Haki.

2. No one would compare himself with Vifill, even though he tended the flocks of Hámundr; I saw no swineherd there more cowardly than the heir of Heðinn.

3. My life was better by far when we followed the wise Hálfr; we all took counsel together and we harried across every land.

4. We all had the tempers of hawk-men [warriors], wherever the wise-minded one strove to advance; full-grown men, with gray helmets, we went through nine homelands.

5. I saw Hálfr hack with both hands, the ruler had no protecting shield before him; no man could find, though he travel wide, a stronger or more noble heart.

6. Men say, those who do not know, that Hálfr's courage amounted to foolishness; he does not understand the king of Hálogaland who attributed to him the strength of a fool.

7. He asked his warriors to feel no apprehension of death, nor to speak any words of fear; no one should follow the prince, unless he held to his orders.

8. They should not groan, even though they may have received great wounds in battles, friends of the king, nor have their wounds bound before the same time the next day had come.

9. He asked that [his men] not distress a woman captive nor harm a man's wife; he asked every maiden to be bought with a wedding payment of fine gold, according to her father's wish.

10. There were not so many men on the warships that we would take to flight, even though we had a smaller troop by far: the odds were eleven to one.

11. We all had the upper hand wherever the tree of Hildr [the warrior] beat against shields; I knew one prince equally bold: King Sigurðr in Giúki's halls.

12. There were many men on the warships, good and bold, with the prince himself: Bǫrkr and Bryniólfr, Bǫlverkr and Haki, Egill and Erlingr, the sons of Áslákr.

13. The best cherished men to me were, Hrókr, my brother, and King Hálfr, Styrr the strong, both Steinar, resolute men, the sons of Gunnlǫð.

14. Hringr and Hálfdanr, both hawks [warriors], the judges of the Danes, Dagr the noble, Stari and Steingrímr, Stúfr and Gauti; you will never find a finer band of warriors.

15. Valr and Haukr, both bold in battle, friends of the king; few from Haki's kingdom would seem more able than those prince's warriors.

16. In no way did I ever consider myself the black sheep of my race on that ship; they called me the most vigorous man, because each sought praise from the others.

17. Vémundr, who dared attack, bore the banner, Biǫrn and Bersi, before the king: the prince drew up his troops in the foremost rank while he still lived.

18. The bold ruler did not enjoy his life as he should have by his bold deeds; at the age of twelve the prince began to harry, and the lord was thirty when he died.

19. Many a night I feel like sleeping little and I stay wide awake, since my brother had to be burned alive in the fire with the king's warriors.

20. That day has become for me the dreariest thing in the world by far that men experience; we never thought ourselves happy afterwards, when we were able to band together with dear kinsmen.

21. All of my sorrow would be lighter if I could have avenged King Hálfr, so that I could have pierced the breast of Ásmundr, the ring-breaker's slayer, with a sharp, shining sword.

22. Hálfr the bold will be avenged, because they betrayed the

noble prince in the truce; King Ásmundr caused murder and manslaughter in an evil hour.

23. Then I will test and give trial, if we meet Sveinn in battle,
which of the two will be the better in the fight, the son of Hámundr
or the thanes of Haki.

24. I say as it was reported by the wise woman, that I would
woo Brynhildr, if I might know, whether she would love Hrókr,
Hámundr's son.

25. I could hope for wise men, sharp warriors, if we could
marry; I found no maiden more gifted in any land than Haki's
daughter.

a. I have never found, although I have travelled widely, a more
charming maiden than Haki's daughter; she is everything that I
could wish.

26. Here in Haki's kingdom I now seem to be the outcast of
every nation; they have all gone to sit farther in, the men of the
hall and Hálfr's warriors.

i. *Hiálmarr's Death Song*

(*Hiálmars Sterbelied*, from *Qrvar-Oddssaga*; text: *EM*, pp. 49–51.)

Hiálmarr's Death Song exists in several versions, as well as
appearing in two different sagas in quite dissimilar contexts. As
Lönnroth states, "In *Hervarar saga* . . . the battle is fought as a
hólmganga, or duel, to decide whether Hjálmar or Angantýr shall
marry the Swedish princess, but in *Qrvar Odds saga* . . . the
combatants come upon each other by chance, not by arrangement,
and they fight primarily to prove their viking valor, not to win any
woman's hand" (1971, p. 19). The verses attributed to Sóti in the
EM text are usually assigned to Oddr and can be dated near the
end of the twelfth century, at the latest (see *EM*).

1. Sóti: "What is wrong with you, Hiálmarr? You have changed
color; many wounds, I say, make you weary; your helmet is hewn
and the byrnie on your side. I think your life is now departing."

2. Hiálmarr: "I have sixteen wounds, a slit byrnie, darkness is
before my eyes; I do not see my way; Angantýr's sword pierced my
heart, the sharp sword-point, hardened with poison.

3. Women on the earth will not learn that I shielded myself
before the blows; she will not mock me for giving ground in the
battle, the wise, quick-witted woman in Sigtúnir.

4. I turned from the beautiful singing of the women, willingly

from my pleasure, away with Sóti; I sped my journey and went into the host, for the last time from my loyal friends.

5. The ruler's fair daughter led me out to Agnafit; the tale she told me will prove true: that I would not come back.

6. I parted from the young Ingibiorg—that was quickly done— on the appointed day; hard-gripping grief will the woman have— that we two will never meet again.

7. I owned five homesteads all together in that land, but I never took pleasure in my lot there; now I must lie, deprived of life, wounded by sword on Sámsey.

8. Bear to her sight—such is my wish—my helmet and byrnie into the king's hall; the heart of the ruler's daughter will pine away when she sees the shield hacked to pieces at my breast.

9. Take the red ring from my arm, bear it to young Ingibiorg; heart-fast grief will she have—that we two will never meet again.

10. I see where the women sit in Sigtúnir, those who tried to keep me from leaving there; neither ale nor warriors will ever gladden Hiálmarr again in the king's hall.

11. The company of jarls cheerfully drinks ale with the prince at Uppsalir; drink makes many a warrior weary, but the tracks of the sword-edges constrain me on the island.

12. Out of a high tree the raven flies from the south, the eagle flies after him in comradeship; I shall give food to that eagle for the last time; he will sup on my blood."

j. *Hildibrandr's Death Song*

(*Hildibrands Sterbelied*, from *Ásmundarsaga kappabana*; text: *EM*, pp. 53–4.)

Written perhaps in imitation of *Hiálmarr's Death Song*, this retrospective lament portrays a situation obviously related to the Sohrab and Rustem confrontation as it was found in Germanic tradition (see Schlauch 1934). The name Hildibrandr, of course, recalls the father-son duel of the OHG *Lay of Hildebrand* (q.v.). Here the two combatants are half-brothers, unknown to each other, each equipped with a magic sword.

1. "It is very difficult to foresee which brother is destined to become the death of the other; Drótt bore you in Denmark and me in Sweden.

2. There were two swords made, heirlooms of Buðli, now is one of them broken; the dead dwarves forged them, as no one has before or since.

3. The broken shield stands at my head . . . there are counted between seventy and eighty of those men, whom I killed.

4. My own dear son lies at my head, an heir, whom I begot . . . and, without wishing to, bereft of life.

5. I beg of you, brother, one request, one request, do not refuse it! You shall wrap me in your clothes, as few will do for the slayer of another.

6. Now I must lie, deprived of life, wounded by the sword, that puts a spell on wounds."

k. Skaldic Poetry

1. *The Loss of Sons*

(Egill Skallagrímsson, ca. 900–83, *Sonatorrek*;
text: *ScP*, pp. 28–41.)

This lament for the deaths of his sons, Gunnarr and Bǫðvarr, by fever and drowning, is Egill Skallagrímsson's masterpiece and one of the great achievements of medieval poetry. *Egils saga* relates how his daughter tricked him out of death by starvation and into writing the poem, which became a consolation for his loss. The poem falls into the class of *erfikvæði* ("memorial poems") and is written in *kviðuháttr* ("speech meter," a version of *fornyrðislag*, with three syllables in the odd lines and four in the even). Egill wrote the poem around 960. At times the text remains enigmatic and obscure and we have relied heavily on Turville-Petre's edition and translation (see also Kershaw, Hallberg, and Bouman).

1. It is very difficult for me to move my tongue or the air-weight of the steelyard of song; now there is no hope to expect Óðinn's stolen goods [poetry], nor is it easily drawn from the secret cavern of thought [heart].

2. The glad find of the kinsmen of Frigg [mead of poetry], borne of yore from Iǫtunheimr, is not easily forced to spout from the place of thought—because of a heavy grief.

3. Faultless when it [the mead of poetry?] came to life on the dwarf's ship [poetry]; the wounds of the giant's neck [the sea] roar down under the boat-house door of Náinn [cliffs?].

4. For my race stands at its end, like the dead trunk of the forest maple; a man has no spirit, who bears the joints of a kinsman's corpse down from the hall.

5. Yet first I will tell of my mother's corpse and my father's fall;

I bear these timbers of praise [poetry], covered with the leaf of speech, out from the word-temple.

6. Bitter for me was the space which the wave ripped in the circle of my father's family; I see unfilled and standing open the breach [left by] my son, which the sea made for me.

7. Rán has shaken me very roughly, I am stripped of beloved friends; the sea has snapped the bonds of my race, a hard-twisted strand [son] from my own being.

8. You [daughter] know that if I could avenge the crime with a sword, the ale-smith [the sea god] would have lived out all his time; if I could fight, I would take on the brother of the turmoil of the waves [the sea?] and the wife of Ægir [Rán].

9. But I thought I could not get the strength to fight against the slayer of the ship [the sea], because the lack of a following for the old thane appears before everyone's eyes.

10. The sea has stolen much from me; it is bitter to tell of the fall of kinsmen, since the shield of my race turned from his life on to the happy roads.

11. I know myself that the substance of a bad thane had not taken root in my son, if that shield-tree [warrior] had been allowed to ripen until the hands of Óðinn could take him.

12. He always heeded most what his father spoke, although all the people said something else . . . and he supported my strength most.

13. Often the lack of a brother comes into my favorable wind of the moon's bear [mind]; I think about it as the battle mounts, I look around for him and think about this,

14. what other thane would stand brave by my side in the furious battle; I often need this against clashing men; I become unable to fly as my friends diminish.

15. It is very hard to find one whom I can trust among all the people of Óðinn's gallows [Yggdrasill?], for he is an evil deceiver of kinsmen who sells his brother's corpse for rings.

16. I often find when he asks for money . . .

17. It is also said that no one may get compensation for a son, unless he himself should beget yet another son who may be for others (?) a man born in his brother's stead.

18. The fellowship of men is not agreeable to me, although each by himself keeps the peace; the son (?) has come into the realm of the bee-ships [Valhǫll?], the son of my wife, to seek his kin.

19. And, as it seemed to me (?), the ruler of the brew [Ægir] was standing against me, firm in his thought; I cannot prop up the land of the face, or hold straight the chariot of the runes [the head],

20. since the vengeful fire of sickness took my son from the world, he whom I knew to be careful, on guard against faults, to avoid evil talk.

21. That I still remember, when the friend of the Gautar [Óðinn] raised up into the realm of the gods the ash of my race, he who grew from me and from my wife's family tree.

22. I was on good terms with the lord of the spear [Óðinn]; I became trusting, believing in him, until the friend of the chariots (?), the judge of victory, broke off with me.

23. I do not sacrifice to the brother of Vílir [Óðinn], the god-guardian, because I am eager to; yet the friend of Mímr has given me booty in compensation for my misfortunes, if I count better.

24. The foe of the wolf [Óðinn], used to battle, gave me the skill, devoid of flaws, and those wits with which I made for myself certain enemies out of plotters.

25. Now it is difficult for me: the giant sister of Tveggi's enemy [Fenrisúlfr] stands on the promontory; yet glad I shall await Hel, with good will and without grief.

2. Egill Skallagrímsson

(from *Egils saga*, chap. 78; text *ONCP*, p. 76.)

Egill's patron has died and he mourns the "diminishment" of his income (see *ONCP*).

Now diminish the heralds of Ingvi, those who diminished the brightness of the meadhorn [gold]; where shall I seek generous men, those who beyond the isle-studded girdle of the earth [the sea] hailed upon my hawk's high mountains [forearms] crucible-snow [silver] in exchange for words.

3. Egill Skallagrímsson

(from *Egils saga*, chap. 55; text: *ONCP*, p. 78.)

Egill's brother, Þórólfr, has died in a battle, which the saga identifies as the battle at Vínheiðr (see *The Battle of Brunanburh* and *ONCP*).

The jarl's slayer, he who feared nothing, went swiftly into the great din of Óðinn [battle]; strong-minded Þórólfr fell; the earth grows over my noble brother near the Dvína; that is a death-sorrow, but we must bury grief.

4. Egill Skallagrímsson

(from *Egils saga*, chap. 57; text: *ScP*, p. 23.)

Egill's description of a storm he encountered sailing out from Norway (see *ScP*).

With raging breath the enemy of the mast [the storm] mightily beats out a file before the beak on the calm path of the prow-bull [ship] with the chisel of storms; while the cold-clad enemy of the willow [the troll-wind] mercilessly files with it the swan of Gestill [the ship] with gusts over the beak before the prow.

5. Sighvatr Þórðarson, ca. 995–1045

(from *Heimskringla, Magnúss saga ins góða*, chap. 8; text: *ONCP*, p. 131.)

Sighvatr laments the death of Saint Óláfr, remarking on his own fall from favor as a court poet and the tyranny of Óláfr's successor (see *ONCP* and Turville-Petre 1953). Óláfr, King of Norway (ca. 995–1030), was largely responsible for the conversion of Norway to Christianity.

It seemed to me the high, sloping cliffs were laughing all over Norway while Óláfr lived; I was recognized on the ships before. Ever since the slopes seem much less happy to me; such is my woe; I have lost all the prince's favor.

6. Sighvatr Þórðarson

(from *Heimskringla, Óláfs saga*, chap. 71; text: *ScP*, p. 79.)

From his experiences on a diplomatic mission for Saint Óláfr, Sighvatr composed twenty-one strophes called the *Austrfaravísur* (*Verses on a Journey to the East*). This stanza describes a sea journey.

Merry was I often when the stormy weather out in the fjords shredded the wind-blown sail of the chief of the Strindir [Óláfr] in the storm; the horse of the deep [ship] waded [through the water], prancing nobly; the keels carved the sea of Listi when we made the warships rush out over the ocean.

7. Holmgǫngu-Bersi Véleifsson, ca. 950–1000

(from *Kormaks saga*, chap. 16; text: *ONCP*, p. 146.)

Spoken by Bersi in his old age just before he kills a man (see *ONCP*).

Ullr of the gold of the forearms [the warrior] has lost his footing with old age; many things must now be endured from the wielding-gods of the shield [warriors]. Although the shield-trees [warriors] may create cold life in the grave for the poet, sooner will I bloody the stormwand of the helmet [sword] on the island than I should fear that.

8. Bjǫrn Ásbrandsson Breiðvíkingakappi, fl. ca. 1000

(from *Eyrbyggja saga*, chap. 29; text: *ONCP*, p. 171.)

Bjǫrn's mistress, Þuríðr, has informed him that her husband intends to ambush him that evening (see *ONCP* and *ScP*).

We two would wish this day longest between the golden woods and the dark blue—sometimes I receive harm by the support of a ribbon [woman]—since, young pine-tree of the arm-serpent* [woman], at dusk I myself will begin to hold a wake for my joy which has often vanished.

*arm-serpent: ring

9. Bjǫrn Ásbrandsson Breiðvíkingakappi

(from *Eyrbyggja saga*, chap. 40; text: *ScP*, p. 65.)

Bjǫrn explains how his love for Þuríðr made him return to Iceland after a long absence. (see *ScP*).

I cut the ice-stiff land of the swans [sea] with nailed planks [ship], for with love the heedful woman led us hard from the east with a laden ship; far and wide I got weary from the cold; now for a time the courageous tree of battle [warrior] dwells here in a cave instead of a woman's bed.

10. Óláfr Haraldsson (Saint Óláfr), King of Norway, ca. 995–1030

(from *Saga Óláfs konungs hins helga*, chap. 203; text: *ONCP*, p. 174.)

Saint Óláfr sees his former fiancée ride off on a journey and this provokes an elegiac response (see *ONCP*).

Formerly the precious oak of the jarldom [woman?] stood all green with blossoms, as the men of Hǫrðaland knew each season; now has the tree of the bench [bride] suddenly become pale with the tears of Freyia [gold]: the ruler in Garðar has bound the linden of the linen headdress [woman] with gold leaf.

1. *Memento Mori*

(Text: *AHDL*, pp. 142–4.)

A late OHG poem, the *Memento Mori* has been associated with Hirsau Abbey because of its strong ascetic perspective. Hirsau Abbey was the first German monastery to adopt the spirit of the Cluniac Reform movement, and this poem was probably composed there around 1070 (see Garland, Barber, and Schützeichel 1962).

1. Now consider, woman and man, where you shall end up. You love this transitory life and hope you will always be here. No matter how dear it seems to you, you shall have it [only] for a short time. Even if you desire so eagerly to live a long time, you must exchange this life.

2. Over there is a great crowd. They believed they would be here forever, they loved this misery; today they are very sorrowful. No matter how dear it seemed to them, still they have left it forever. I do not know where they have gone: may God preserve them all.

3. They expected to live here; they thought to fare away to eternal joy, where they should always be. How little they thought about that, where they at last should go! Now they have found out; they would gladly be freed.

4. Paradise is far away from here. There very seldom has any man come who might return here, and who might bring us news or

might have told you what kind of life they lived there. You shall always have bliss there, [but] you must be the messengers yourselves.

5. This world is made thus: whoever tries to seize it, for him the world makes everything so wonderfully pleasant [that] he cannot get away from it. When he has grasped enough of it, [still] he would gladly have more of it. That he does up to his end; thus he has nothing here nor there.

6. You hope to live here always: you must at last give an account of it. You will all perish; you cannot escape it. Man passes away in a moment, as quickly as the brows blink together [in the twinkling of an eye]. This will I boldly say: just as quickly will he be forgotten.

7. God created you all. You came from one man. Then He commanded you to live, to exist here with love, so that you would be as one man. You have transgressed against that. If you had done nothing else, you would for that reason always suffer punishment.

8. Though you all come from one man, you are nevertheless separated by manifold deceits, by great evils. The one is wise and prudent . . .

9. . . . for this he will be damned. The poor man has need of justice (?): unfortunately, he may have none of it, even if he buy it very dearly: for this they all go to hell.

10. If [only] they would think how it goes at the end. As he goes away irrevocably, so he is dead forever. Because he sold away the right, so he fares to hell. He must always remain therein. He has given up God Himself.

11. If you all live according to one law, so you would all be summoned into eternal joy, where you would always be. The one you keep for yourselves; therefore you may not go in. The other you give to the poor, you must always stand by that.

12. Blessed is he who contemplates the long journey, who prepared himself for it, as God Himself commanded, so that he would be ready whenever he might see His heavenly messenger! In truth I say that: he always comes unexpectedly.

13. There is no man so wise, that he may know [the time of] his departure. Death, which resembles a thief, will leave nothing of you behind here. He is a leveller: no one is so noble that he would not have to die: wealth will be of no use to him for this reason.

14. He has used his riches so that he departs without toil: at beautiful inns he finds his sweet reward. The time he has not lived in the world, how little does it trouble him there: one day there seems better to him than a thousand here, that is true.

15. Whatever he leaves behind here, that will be held against him [there]. If he has given something away, for that he may henceforth always live. Even if he should do it as long as he can, nevertheless the day will yet come. If he has done nothing of the kind, then he can never atone for it.

16. This man is not at all wise: he is on a journey, he finds a beautiful tree; thereunder he goes to rest. There sleep oppresses him, so he forgets where he was supposed to go. When he leaps up, how sorely he rues it then!

17. You all resemble this man: you must irrevocably depart from here. The tree signifies this world: you are somewhat delayed here. [You thought you would live here; you did not think that you would have to depart.] The journey seemed troublesome to you, you come from there above: there must you return. That you will discover well. [You should hasten there well-prepared in every-thing, [yet] you should not trouble yourselves about the reward. Good to him who here does good: he will be well rewarded for it.]

18. Yes, you very evil *world*, how you deceive us so! You have taken control of us, so that we are all cheated. If we do not leave you for a little while, we will lose soul and body. As long as we live here, God has given us free will.

19. Lord, noble King, *have mercy upon us*! You must give us understanding for the short time we are here, so that we may protect the soul; because we must irrevocably fare hence. So must you always be joyful: Noker made all this.

2. Celtic Analogues

a. *The Sick Man of Aber Cuawg*

(*Claf Aber Cuawg*; text: *PLlH* [=*CLlH*, VI. 1–32].)

The Sick Man of Aber Cuawg may belong to the so-called Llywarch Hen cycle of poems (see Jarman 1976). Llywarch appears in early Welsh genealogies as a first cousin to Urien, prince of Rheged, and he must have lived therefore in the latter half of the sixth century (see Bartrum). Most agree that Llywarch did not write the poems, which were instead the work of a professional poet assuming his persona sometime in the ninth or tenth century. Presumably Llywarch speaks the lines below, although the tone is typical of the elegiac mode of much of early Welsh poetry (*EWP*, p. 202). The form here (and in b. through g.) is the *englyn*, pl. *englynion*, a self-contained stanza of three or four lines, depending upon the type of *englyn*, with end-rhyme and frequent ornamentation by alliteration and internal rhyme (see *BWP*, Henry, Jarman 1967 and 1976, Parry, Pilch, *PLlH*, Williams 1944).

1. My mind seeks to be sitting on a hill, and still it does not move me; short is my journey, my dwelling desolate.

2. Keen the wind, cowherds bare; today, when trees wear the fair colors of summer, I am extremely ill.

3. I am not nimble, I keep no host, I am not able to walk about; while it pleases the cuckoo, let him sing.

4. The clamorous cuckoo sings at dawn—lofty song in the dales of Cuawg; better generous than miserly.

5. In Aber Cuawg cuckoos sing on blooming branches; clamorous cuckoo, let him sing long.

6. In Aber Cuawg cuckoos sing upon blooming branches; sad for the sick one who hears them ceaselessly.

7. In Aber Cuawg do cuckoos sing; 'tis bitter thinking that he who heard them hears them no more.

8. I listened to a cuckoo on an ivy branch. My garments grow slack; grief for what I loved is greater.

9. From the top of the mighty oak I listened to the sound of birds; lofty cuckoo, each remembers what he loves.

10. Singer of ceaseless song, longing in its voice, journey of purpose, hawk's pace, eloquent cuckoo in Aber Cuawg.

11. Loud are birds, streams wet; the moon shines, midnight cold; raw my spirit from the burden of disease.

12. White the hilltops, streams wet, midnight long; every wise one is honored: I deserve this reward in old age.

13. Loud are birds, gravel wet; leaves fall, the homeless is dispirited; I do not deny that I am ill tonight.

14. Loud are birds, the shore wet; sky is bright, the wave full; heart withered from longing.

15. Loud are birds, the shore wet; wave is bright, its motion full; the passion of youth—I would love to have it again.

16. Loud the birds on Edrywy hill; the howl of dogs is desolate; loud are birds again.

17. May, and every growth is lovely; when warriors rush to battle, I will not go; a wound prevents me.

18. May, and it is beautiful at the border; when warriors rush to the battlefield, I will not go; a wound torments me.

19. Pale the mountain top, tender the tips of ash; from estuaries flows a shimmering wave; laughter is far from my heart.

20. Today is the end of the month for me in the lodging that he left; raw my spirit, fever has seized me.

21. Clear the sentry's eye; pride causes indolence; raw my spirit, sickness enfeebles me.

22. Cattle in sheds, mead in bowl; the content desire no war; patience is the bond of acquaintance.

23. Cattle in sheds, beer in bowl; slippery the road, the shower fierce, and deep is the ford; the mind brews teachery.

24. Treason brews wicked work; there will be grief when it is cleansed; selling a little in exchange for much.

25. A cauldron of wicked will be readied when the Lord judges on that long day; sad will the false be, the true shining.

26. Cups raised, the warrior ragged, men merry over beer; reeds withered, cattle in sheds.

27. I have heard the heavy thudding surf, loud betwixt sand and gravel; raw is my spirit, depressed tonight.

28. Antlered are the oak-tops, bitter the taste of ash; pleasant the cow-parsnip, a wave laughs; the cheek does not conceal a heart's hurts.

29. Many a sigh escapes me, as is my custom; God allows no good to the wretched.

30. Good fortune comes not to the wretched—only sadness and anxiety; God does not undo what He has done.

31. The wasted one was noble once, a bold warrior in a king's court; may God be gentle to the outcast.

32. Whatever is done in an oratory, he is wretched who reads it; hated of man below and hated of God above.

b. *Song of the Old Man*

(*Can yr Henwr*; text: *PLlH* [=*CLlH*, ll. 1–21].)

These stanzas, also part of the Llywarch Hen cycle, follow immediately on *The Sick Man of Aber Cuawg* in the earliest manuscripts and were printed as one with that poem in *PLlH*. The later textual history and the insistence of many scholars suggest they are distinct poems and they are treated so here (see *EWP*, *PWV*, *WP*). Several of the stanzas appear as "groups," linked together by the device of incremental repetition, e.g., stanzas 36–42 (see Jackson 1941 and references under a.).

33. Before I was hunched over, I was garrulous; my talents were praised; the men of Argoed always supported me.

34. Before I was hunched over, I was bold; I was welcomed in the taverns of Powys, paradise of Welshmen.

35. Before I was hunched over, I was splendid; my spear was foremost, drew first blood; now my back is bent, I am weary, I am wretched.

36. Crutch of wood, it is autumn—ferns are red, stalks yellow; I have rejected what I love.

37. Crutch of wood, this is winter—men are boisterous over beer; no one comes to greet me.

38. Crutch of wood, it is spring—red are the cuckoos, their cries clear; I am unloved by a maiden.

39. Crutch of wood, it is summer—red is the furrow, sprouts are wrinkled; staring down at you saddens me.

40. Crutch of wood, steady branch, support a wistful old man—Llywarch the babbler.

41. Crutch of wood, sturdy branch, God the Protector will welcome me; you are a loyal walking companion.

42. Crutch of wood, be kind, support me ever better; I am Llywarch a long time.

43. Old age is mocking me from my hair to my teeth—and the rod the young love.

44. Old age is mocking me from my hair to my teeth—and the rod women love.

45. Wild is the wind, white on the edges of the trees; comely the stag, the hill lacks growth; feeble the old one, ambling slowly.

46. This leaf, the wind whips it to and fro; alas for its fate—old, born this year.

47. What I loved since I was a lad is odious to me: a lusty maid and a spirited horse; they do not suit me.

48. The four things I have always hated most have befallen me all together: a cough and old age, disease and grief.

49. I am old, I am lonely, I am deformed and cold; after an honorable family I am wretched, I am terribly bent over.

50. I am old and stooped, a wayward fool, I am simple-minded, quarrelsome; those who loved me love me not.

51. Maidens do not love me, no one visits me, I am not able to move about; alas, that death does not come to me.

52. Neither sleep nor joy comes to me since Llawr and Gwen were killed; I am mean and feeble, I am old.

53. A wretched fate was allotted to Llywarch since the night he was born: long labor without release from fatigue.

c. *The Desolate Hearth of Rheged*

(*Diffaith Aelwyd Rheged*; text: *PLlH* [=*CLlH* III. 49–59].)

With the exception of the last, these ninth- or tenth-century stanzas all begin with the phrase, *yr aelwyd hon*, "this hearth." An excellent example of the linking device of incremental repetition, this allows the otherwise individual and self-contained stanzas to function as a single poem. The Owain and Elphin of stanza 152 are surely sons of Urien, sixth-century ruler of Rheged (see Bartrum); Owain himself is well-known from medieval romance: Chrétien's *Yvain*, the ME *Ywain and Gawain*, and the MW *Owein* (see Bromwich 1954 and 1961, Dillon, Jarman 1976, Lloyd, Parry, *PT*).

150. This hearth, open to the sky, more familiar in its midst were mead and mead seekers.
151. This hearth, nettles cover it; while its guardian lived it was more accustomed to suppliants.
152. This hearth, wild blue flowers cover it; with Owain and Elphin alive, its cauldron bubbled with booty.
153. This hearth, brown lichen covers it; more common at its banquets were fierce and fearless swordplay.
154. This hearth, a ridge of briars hides it; it used to have blazing logs; Rheged was accustomed to generosity.
155. This hearth, thorns cover it; its warriors were more accustomed to profit from associating with Owain.
156. This hearth, hemlock covers it; it was more accustomed to bright tapers and loyal mead mates.
157. This hearth, the dock-leaves cover it; more familiar in its midst were mead and mead seekers.
158. This hearth, a pig roots in it; it was more accustomed to the revelry of men and carousing around cups.
159. This hearth, a chick scratches in it; it suffered no need with Owain and Urien alive.
160. This pillar here and that one yonder, more familiar around them was the joy of a host and generosity.

d. *Cynddylan*

(Text: *CLlH* XI. 1–17.)

Cynddylan son of Cyndrwyn was the lord of Pengwern (probably on the site of modern Shrewsbury); he was killed about the middle of the seventh century. The poems concerning him were once thought to be the work of Llywarch Hen; the editor dates the poems to the ninth century and believes them to be part of a saga concerning the family of Cyndrwyn (see *BWP*, pp. 147–54; Jarman 1976, pp. 92–6; Williams 1944). He sees these poems as dramatic monologues, put in the mouth of Heledd, sister to Cynddylan. The reader will be struck by the similarity of style and tone to the Llywarch Hen poems. Readers of the *Mabinogi (M)* will recognize the Culhwch of stanza 10; Tren in stanza 3 and elsewhere is probably the river Tern of Shropshire (see *CLlH*), although sometimes in the poems it is clearly a region or town (cf. *The Eagle of Pengwern*, stanza 44).

1. Stand forth, maidens, and gaze upon the land of Cynddylan. The court of Pengwern is in flames; woe to the young who yearn for the native land.

2. A single timber in the wooden enclosure, and it in trouble; if it survives, it is a wonder; and what God wills shall come to pass.

3. Cynddylan, heart of wintry ice, pierced a warrior through his head; you stood up to the enemy for Tren's beer.

4. Cynddylan, heart of spring's ardor, profit to his compatriots in defending Tren—a desolate town.

5. Cynddylan, splendid supporter of the border, mail-clad, steely in battle, fought for Tren, his native town.

6. Cynddylan, renowned in wisdom, mail-clad unyielding leader of the host, fought for Tren as long as it lasted.

7. Cynddylan, heart of a greyhound, when he struck in battle's uproar, he created corpses.

8. Cynddylan, heart of a hawk, raging, ruinous bird of prey; whelp of unyielding Cyndrwyn.

9. Cynddylan, heart of a wild boar, when he struck in the forefront of battle: corpses in heaps.

10. Cynddylan, a Culhwch-like lion of a warrior, a wolf pursuing the enemy; the wild boar will not return to his native town.

11. Cynddylan, while he lived, his heart would go as gladly to battle as to beer.

12. Cynddylan, wearing the purple of Powys, a cell for celebrants, life of a lord; the whelp of Cyndrwyn is mourned.

13. Fair Cynddylan, son of Cyndrwyn; unseemly is the moustache on a man who is no better than a woman.

14. Cynddylan, you are a warrior: you anticipate that you will not reach old age; at Trebwll your shield full of holes.

15. Cynddylan, defend the hill where the English will come! Anxiety over one who will not be present.

16. Cynddylan, close the pass where the English come through Tren! A single tree does not make a forest.

17. My heart is wretched: laying the white flesh of Cynddylan, leader of a hundred hosts, on black planks.

e. *The Hall of Cynddylan*

(*Stafell Cynddylan*; text: *CLlH* XI. 18–33.)

Compare *The Desolate Hearth* and see the headnote to *Cynddylan*.

18. The hall of Cynddylan is dark tonight, without fire, without bed; I'll weep for a while, afterwards be silent.

19. The hall of Cynddylan is dark tonight, without fire, without candles; save God, who shall give me sense?

20. The hall of Cynddylan is dark tonight, without fire, without light; grief besets me over you.

21. The hall of Cynddylan, dark its roof-beam after fair hosts; alas, who visits it does no good.

22. Hall of Cynddylan, you have lost your shape; your shield is in the grave; while he lived, there were no broken gates.

23. The hall of Cynddylan is forsaken tonight, after the one that owned it; O death! Why was I left?

24. The hall of Cynddylan, it is not cozy tonight atop the mighty rock, without a lord, a retinue, or defense.

25. The hall of Cynddylan is dark tonight, without fire, without song; tears erode the cheeks.

26. The hall of Cynddylan is dark tonight, without fire, without family; copious my tears where the ruins lie.

27. The hall of Cynddylan it wounds me to see: roofless, without fire; dead is my lord, myself alive.

28. The hall of Cynddylan is ravaged tonight after steadfast warriors: Elfan, Cynddylan, Caeog.

29. The hall of Cynddylan is desolate tonight after the honor that held me: without men, without women who tended it.

30. The hall of Cynddylan is silent tonight after the loss of its leader; great and merciful God, what shall I do?

31. The hall of Cynddylan, dark its roof-beam after the destruction by English of Cynddylan and Elfan of Powys.

32. The hall of Cynddylan is dark tonight, devoid of Cyndrwyn's progeny: Cynon and Gwion and Gwyn.

33. The hall of Cynddylan pains me continuously after the garrulous gatherings I saw about your hearth.

f. *The Eagle of Eli*

(*Eryr Eli*; text: *CLlH* XI. 34–39.)

Eli is probably a place name, preserved in the name of the river Meheli in Montgomeryshire (see *CLlH* and headnote to *Cynddylan*).

34. Eagle of Eli, piercing its cry tonight; he feasted on a glut of gore, heart's blood of fair Cynddylan.
35. Eagle of Eli, it shrieked tonight, scratched away at men's blood; it in the wood, for me a wretched mood.
36. Eagle of Eli I hear tonight, besmeared with gore; I'll venture not. It in the wood, for me a wretched mood.
37. Eagle of Eli, how piteous tonight is the praiseworthy vale of Meisyr; long vexed the land of Brochfael.
38. Eagle of Eli, the seas are his preserves, but he visits not the fish in estuaries: he summons a feast of the blood of men.
39. Eagle of Eli, abroad in the wood tonight, it gorges, it feeds; who counts it, his insolence succeeds.

g. *The Eagle of Pengwern*

(*Eryr Pengwern*; text: *CLlH* XI. 40–4.)

Pengwern is probably to be equated with modern Shrewsbury (see *CLlH* and headnote to *Cynddylan*).

40. Gray-crowned eagle of Pengwern, tonight its cry is piercing: eager for the flesh I loved.
41. Gray-crowned eagle of Pengwern, tonight its screech is piercing: eager for the flesh of Cynddylan.
42. Gray-crowned eagle of Pengwern, tonight its talons are high: eager for the flesh I love.
43. Eagle of Pengwern, it calls far tonight, its vigil on the blood of men; Tren is a town of misfortune.
44. Eagle of Pengwern, it calls far tonight, vigilant over the blood of men; Tren was a splendid town.

h. *The Praise of Tenby*

(*Edmyg Dinbych*; text: *BWP*, pp. 162–6.)

On the basis of inferences made from one or two lines (see *BWP*, *EWP*), some scholars think that this late ninth-century

Welsh poem from the Book of Taliesin is a poem of reconciliation; others sharply disagree. The poet describes the fortress or court at Tenby as it once was, using the present tense as if the fortress still remained. His former role there and the pleasures of the court's retinue are described partly in the past tense, suggesting a lament for a vanished way of life. The concluding stanzas convey a strong feeling that the court and its retinue were overcome by a descendant of some Owain; the poet prays God that he (and the other survivors) will not come under this enemy's authority and that the power will return to the line of Ab Erbin (see *BWP*, *EWP*, Jarman 1976, Parry, *PWV*).

As with so many other of the poems, genre is an open question. Because metaphor and allegory abound, we cannot be sure that the apparent meaning of a word is its real meaning. Nor can we be sure that the apparent meaning of the poem coincides with the poet's intention.

1. I make a request of God, Shepherd of the people, Ruler of heaven and earth, supreme in wisdom.

2. There is a fair fort upon the sea; a splendid rise, joyful on holidays. And when the sea is extremely turbulent, the clamor of bards over cups of mead is customary. Comes a swift wave toward it, they leave the gray-green ocean to the Picts. And may I have, O God, through my prayer, when I may keep terms, reconciliation with thee.

3. There is a fair fort upon the wide water, an impregnable fortress, surrounded by sea. Ask, Britain, whose home is this? O leader of the line of Ab Erbin, let it be yours! There was a company and there was a song in the fortification and an eagle on high on the path of the white-faced. Before a splendid lord, starting up against the foe, a warrior of widespread fame, they assembled.

4. There is a fair fort upon the ninth wave; fair its folk in resting themselves. They do not make their pleasant life through shame; 'tis not their custom to be stingy. I shall not speak falsely of my welcome; better the captive of Dyfed than the yeomen of Deudraeth! A host of the free in the midst of a feast; narrow between each two of the best of people.

5. There is a fair fort, whose company fosters pleasure and praise and the cry of birds. Joy and songs on its holidays, around a ready lord, a radiant distributor. Before his going into an oaken chest, he gave me mead and wine from a glass cup.

6. There is a fair fort on the coast; pleasantly, each is given his share. I know in Tenby, pure white the seagull, the host of Bleiddudd, lord of the fort. It was my custom on holidays,

appeasement by the bright king of battle and a heather-colored mantle and courtly privilege, until I held tongue over the bards of Britain.

7. There is a fair fort, which abounds in song; the freedoms I sought were mine. I do not speak of rights: the law I kept; he who does not know this deserves no gifts. The writings of Britain were its chief concern, where the waves toss. Let it last long, the cell I visited!

8. There is a fair fort standing on high. Excellent its pleasures, its praise lofty. Fair all around it, enclosure of champions, relentless sea-spume comes to me, far-reaching its fingers, it explodes to the top of the rock; raucous the little sea-bird-. Anger forsworn, let it flee beyond the mountains. And to Bleiddudd the best prosperity there may be. I shall be burdened over beer with the task of memories. The blessing of the lord of harmonious heaven will endure, He who will not make us fellow-countrymen of the descendant of Owain.

9. There is a fair fort upon the sea-shore. Pleasantly, each is given his desire. Ask, Gwynedd, let it be yours. Rough, stiff spears they earned. On Wednesday, I saw men in conflict; on Thursday, it was reproaches they contended with. And hair was red with blood, and lamenting on harps. Weary were the men of Gwynedd the day they came, and atop the stone of Maelwy they shelter shields. A host of kinsmen fell by the descendant [of Owain?].

i. *Appeasement of Urien*

(*Dadolwch Urien*; text: *PT*, IX.)

This poem, dated sometime between the sixth and tenth centuries, is the earliest example of a kind of conventional Welsh bardic poetry (Jarman 1976). The poet, having upset his chief patron and doubtlessly being chagrined by his loss of material rewards as well as status, composes a *dadolwch* ("appeasement, reconciliation") to restore favor. He admits that Urien has treated him well, he apologizes, and having proclaimed his lord as the most generous and brave, is confident of being restored to favor. The colophon appears at the end of several of these poems to Urien, including *The Battle of Argoed Llwyfain*, *The Battle of Gwen Ystrad*, and *In Praise of Urien*. But we have omitted it in those poems because there it is purely conventional. Here, however, it seems integral to the poem, for it complements the metaphor describing the martial prowess of Urien's sons against their enemies (see *EWP*).

Chieftain most brave I shall not desert; Urien I shall approach, to him I shall sing; when my patronage comes, I shall gain admission to the best quarter, under the chief. It matters not much to me what chieftains I see: I shall not go to them, with them I shall not be. I shall not seek out petty-lords in the North. Though it were for much that I would wager, there is no need to boast: Urien will not refuse me. Lands of Llwyfenydd, mine are their riches, mine their conviviality, mine their generosity. Mine are their materials and their enrichments: mead from drinking horns and endless prosperity with the best and most generous lord I have heard of. The princes of every land all to you owe allegiance. They complain because they have to retreat from you. Though that is what I intended—teasing an old man, there was none whom I loved better before I knew him; now I see how much I have. Except to God above, I shall not give him up. Your noble sons, most generous of men, their spears make music in the lands of their enemies.

And until I degenerate into old age, in the firm grip of death, I shall not be happy unless I praise Urien.

j. "The rath in front of the oakwood"

(Ind ráith i comair in dairfhedo; text: *BLI,* p. 59.)

To group the Irish poems translated here under the heading "Elegies" is unusual and potentially misleading. The writers of such poems as "The rath in front of the oakwood," and *Créide's Lament for Dínertach* would not have grouped them under a single genre. The Welsh analogues and the ironic *Fall of Tara,* however, provide some evidence that there was a sense of genre operating in the original setting, though certainly differing from modern notions. The ninth-century poem known as "The rath in front of the oakwood" may be a traditional *ubi sunt* poem or a monastic gloat; *Créide's Lament* and *Líadan Speaks of Cuirithir* may be political or religious allegories. They do, however, share an "elegiac tone." The poem traditionally refers to *Ráth Imgain,* now Rathangan, County Kildare.

The rath in front of the oakwood: it was Bruidge's, it was Cathal's, it was Áed's, it was Ailill's, it was Conaing's, it was Cuiline's, and it was Máel-Dúin's. The rath survives each king in turn and the hosts sleep in the earth.

k. *The Fall of Tara*
(from *Félire Óengusso Céli Dé*; text: *FO*, p. 24.)

This much-quoted eighth-century poem occurs as part of the introductory material to the *Félire* of Oengus the Culdee, a long verse calendar of saints' days and other religious festivals. The poem represents a kind of attack on the nostalgic traditional poetry, paradoxically bearing witness to the power of that genre. Comparison with the preceding poem and with the MW *Cynddylan* poems gives some sense of the ironic interplay of elements here.

165. The mighty fortress of Tara died with the slumber of her royalty; with a multitude of venerable heroes [clerics] the great Height of Macha [Armagh] remains.
169. Smothered—a great disaster—the pride of ever-valiant Loegaire; the name of Patrick, shining, famous, this is on the increase.
173. The faith has increased; it will survive until the Day of Judgment; guilty pagans who are borne away, their raths are not inhabited.
177. The Rath of Crúachán is finished, along with Ailill, victory's child. Splendid sovereignty over noble men: that is in the monastery of Clonmacnois.

l. *Créide's Lament for Dínertach*
(*It é saigte gona súain*; text: *EIL*, pp. 86–8.)

This graceful poem dates from the ninth century and may be a genuine love lament or a political allegory. The modern reader may be reminded of the OE *Wulf and Eadwacer*. The poem also illustrates the characteristic feature known as *dúnad* ("closing") in Irish poetry: the final phrase or line recapitulates the opening phrase.

1. They are the arrows wounding sleep, every hour in the frigid night: love-lamenting for the companionship, after day, of a man from the border of the land of Roigne.
2. A great love of a man from another land who surpassed his peers has taken my complexion—not enough color. It does not let me sleep.
4. His speaking was more musical than songs (except for the

holy adoration of the King of heaven); brilliant flame without a word of boasting, slim, soft-sided companion.

5. When I was a child I was modest, I did not use to be on the wicked business of lust. Since I came into the uncertainty of age, my wantonness has brought me deception.

6. I have every good thing with Gúaire, with the king of cold Aidne; my thought is destined away from my people to the country which is in Irlúachair.

7. Men sing, in the country of luminous Aidne, around the sides of Cell Cholmáin, of the brilliant flame from the south of Limerick of the Graves whose name is Dínertach.

8. It torments my gentle heart, O chaste Christ, his grievous death; they are the arrows wounding sleep every hour in the frigid night.

m. *The Hag of Beare*

(*Aithbe damsa bés mora*; text; *EIL*, pp. 74–82.)

There are at least five manuscript versions of this puzzling ninth-century poem. The title *Sentainne Bérri (The Old Woman of Beare)* or *Caillech Bérri (The Hag [or Nun] of Beare)* occurs in some of them. The complicated manuscript tradition and obscure references make it difficult to tell which stanzas belong in the poem and what their proper order is. The poem's persona may originate in a local sovereignty goddess. Or, the poem may be fundamentally Christian with some accretions of pre-Christian material. The poem is so cryptic that parts of it seem gnomic. It is interesting to compare this poem to the MW Llywarch Hen poems.

1. Ebb-tide to me, just as to the sea; old age darkens me; although I may grieve over it, happy, it comes for its food.

2. I am Búi, the Hag of Beare; I used to wear a dress that was always new; today it is my state, for my scrawniness, that I could not wear even an old dress.

3. It is riches you love, it is not people; while we lived, it was people we loved.

4. Beloved were the people whose plains we rode over. It was good we used to have of them; it was little they used to boast of afterwards.

5. Today, though, you make claims well and that which you grant is not great. Although it is little that you grant, great is the amount that you boast.

6. Swift chariots and horses that would win the prize—there was, for a while, an abundance of them. A blessing upon the king who gave them.

7. With keenness my body seeks a way to the dwelling of (?). When the Son of God considers it the right time, let him come to redeem His pledge.

8. When my arms are seen, they are bony, emaciated. Delightful is the art they used to practice: being around noble kings.

9. When my arms are seen they are bony, emaciated. They are not worth raising, I say, about lovely boys.

10. The girls are happy when Beltaine comes. More fitting for me is sorrow. I am not only sad, I am an old woman.

11. I do not pour out honeyed speech, no wethers are slain for my wedding. My hair is thin, it is gray; a miserable veil over it is no sorrow.

12. I consider it no evil, though there be a white veil on my head. Many coverings of every color were on my head while I drank good ale.

13. I envy nothing old but only [the plain of] Feimen. Me, I have worn the clothes of age; yellow yet is the crop of Feimen.

14. The stone of the kings in Feimen, Ronan's fortress in Bregun, storms have reached them long since; their cheeks are not age-withered.

15. The wave of the great sea is loud. The winter has begun to raise it. Today I expect neither a nobleman, nor the son of a slave on a visit.

16. I know what they are doing: they row and they have ridden (?); the reeds of Ath Alma [are] the dwelling in which they spend the night.

17. Alas, that I do not sail over the sea of youth. Because my wantonness has been spent, many years of my beauty have perished.

18. Alas, for me today, whatever end may be, I must take my shawl, even in the sun. Age is what ails me; I know it myself.

19. I spent the summer of youth in which we have lived; [I spent] its autumn too; the winter of age that drowns each person— its first stage has reached me.

20. I have used up my youth from the beginning. I am satisfied that I decided on it. Had my leap over the wall been small, still, the cloak would not be new. [Even if I hadn't been very adventurous, the outcome would have been the same.]

21. Beautiful is the green cloak my King has spread over the hillside. The man who fulls it is a craftsman. He has put fleece upon it on the far side of the cloak.

23. I have passed my time drinking mead and wine with kings; today I drink whey-water among wrinkled crones.

24. Let a little cup of whey be my ale-feast. Let whatever distresses me be God's will. May praying to you, O living God, bring the body's blood from anger.

25. I see upon me the blotted cloak of age. My reason has deceived me; gray is the hair that grows through my skin: the husk of an old tree is like this.

26. My right eye has been taken from me to redeem my private lands, and the left eye has been taken to augment its [legal] immunity.

29. The flood wave and the following ebb, both have come to me, and so I know how to recognize them.

34. Happy is the island of the great sea. Flood comes to it after its ebb-tide. As for me, I do not expect flood to come to me after ebb-tide.

n. *Líadan Speaks of Cuirithir*

(*Cen áinius*; text: *EIL*, pp. 82–5.)

This ninth-century poem concerns the south-west of Ireland. The prose glosses in the manuscripts explain that the poem refers to a sort of Abelard-Heloise story and claim that Líadan's "haste in taking the veil" was the hurt done to Cuirithir. Carney has pointed out, however, that a similar poem may be a dialogue between an elderly monk and his psalter, and some such conceit, or a political allegory, may lie behind this poem.

1. Unpleasant is the deed that I have done. That which I have loved I have tormented.

2. It would have been madness not to have done his pleasure, if it were not for fear of the King of heaven.

3. It was no disadvantage to him, the tryst which he desired: proceeding beyond pain to paradise.

4. A thing of small account offended Cuirithir about me. My gentleness to him was great.

5. I am Líadan. I loved Cuirithir. This is as true as anything told.

6. For a short time I was in Cuirithir's company. My doing so was good for him.

7. Forest music used to sing to me when [I was] with Cuirithir, along with the sound of the scarlet sea.

8. I should have thought it would not have distressed Cuirithir with me, whatever arrangements I might make.

9. Do not conceal it: he was my heart's love, even though I used to love everyone as well.

10. A roar of flame has split my heart; one knows, it will not live without him.

B. *Deor*

1. Germanic Analogues

a. *The Lay of Vǫlundr*

(*Vǫlundarqviða*; text: *Edda*, pp. 116–23.)

Vǫlundarqviða, often considered one of the earliest of the Eddic poems (ninth century?), provides the legendary material for the opening two stanzas of *Deor* (see Hollander). In addition there are specific verbal echoes of the one poem in the other (see Hallberg). Although *Deor* deals with characters and legends besides the Vǫlundr (Weyland) story, the ancient Germanic tale is an important point of reference for the OE elegy (see Malone 1966). The meter is a free *fornyrðislag*.

About Vǫlundr

In Sweden there was a king called Níðuðr. He had two sons and one daughter: she was called Bǫðvildr. There were three brothers, sons of a Finnish king. One was called Slagfiðr, the second Egill, the third Vǫlundr. On snowshoes they stalked and hunted deer. They came to Úlfdalir and there built themselves a house. There is a body of water which is called Úlfsiár. Early one morning they found three women on the lakeshore, and they spun flax. Their swanskins were next to them. They were valkyries. There were two daughters of King Hlǫðvér, Hlaðguðr, the Swan-White, and Hervor, the All-Wise; the third was Ǫlrún, the daughter of Kiárr of Valland. They brought them home to their hall with them. Egill took Ǫlrún, and Slagfiðr, Swan-White, and Vǫlundr, the All-Wise. They lived together for seven winters. Then [the valkyries] flew away to seek battles and they did not come back. Then Egill strode out on snowshoes to look for Ǫlrún, and Slagfiðr looked for Swan-White. But Vǫlundr sat in Úlfdalir. He was the most skillful man, as men know from old tales. King Níðuðr had him seized by force, as is described here.

About Vǫlundr and Níðuðr

1. The maidens flew from the south through Myrkviðr, all-wise, young (?), to carry on battles; there by the seashore they sat down to rest themselves, the southern women. They spun precious flax.

2. One of them, the fair maid of men, clasped Egill to her bright bosom. The second was Swan-White; she wore swan feathers. But the third of these sisters embraced Vǫlundr's white neck.

3. Then they stayed together seven winters after that, but the whole eighth year they pined and in the ninth, need separated them. The maidens, all-wise, young (?), yearned for Myrkviðr, to carry on battles.

4. The weather-eyed archer [Vǫlundr] came there from the hunt; Slagfiðr and Egill found the halls deserted. They went out and in and looked around. Egill strode out on snowshoes eastward for Ǫlrún, and Slagfiðr south for Swan-White.

5. But Vǫlundr sat alone in Úlfdalir; he forged red gold against the anvil (?). Well he coiled all the arm-rings (?). Thus he waited for his fair wife, to see if she would come back to him.

6. Níðuðr, lord of the Niarar, learned that Vǫlundr sat alone in Úlfdalir. At night the men set forth. Nailed were their byrnies; their shields shone under the waning moon.

7. They stepped out of their saddles at the gable-end of the hall; from there they walked the length of the hall. They saw rings strung on the bast rope, seven hundred in all, which the man owned.

8. And they took them off and they put them back, except for one, which they kept. The weather-eyed archer came there from the hunt, Vǫlundr, roaming back from a distant way.

9. He went to roast a brown bear's flesh. The dried-out fir burned high over the kindling, the wind-dry wood before Vǫlundr.

10. He sat on the bearskin, counted the rings, the elves' fellow-countryman. He missed one; he thought that Hlǫðvér's daughter, all-wise, young, had it—that she had returned.

11. He sat so long that he fell asleep, and he awoke bereft of joys. On his hands he felt heavy bands, and fetters tied on his feet.

12. "Who are the warriors, those who laid the bast rope and bound me?"

13. Now Níðuðr, lord of the Niarar, called out: "Where, Volundr, lord of the elves, did you get our treasure in Úlfdalir?"

14. "The gold was not there in Grani's path; I thought our land was far away from the hills of the Rhine. I remember that we had more treasure, when we were a whole family at home."

15. Hlaðguðr and Hervor were born to Hloðvér; famous was Olrún, Kiárr's daughter.

16. She walked in the length of the hall, stood on the floor, and spoke in a low voice: "He is not kind now, the one who comes out of the forest."

King Níðuðr gave his daughter, Boðvildr, the gold ring that he took from the bast rope at Volundr's house. But he himself carried the sword which Volundr owned. And the queen said:

17. "He bares his teeth when the sword is shown to him and he notices Boðvildr's ring. His eyes are like the shining serpent's; cut the strength of his sinews and afterwards set him on Sævarstaðr."

So it was done. His sinews were cut at the knee-joints, and he was set on an islet, which was near to the land and was called Sævarstaðr. There he forged all kinds of treasures for the king. No man dared go to him, except the king alone.

18. Volundr said: "At Níðuðr's belt shines the sword which I whetted as best I could, and I tempered it as it seemed fittest to me. That shining sword is forever borne away from me. I will never see it borne to Volundr's smithy.

19. Now Boðvildr wears my bride's red rings. I do not expect compensation for that."

20. He sat but did not sleep and struck unceasingly with his hammer: he industriously plotted deceptions for Níðuðr. Two youths, the sons of Níðuðr, came there to see the precious works on Sævarstaðr.

21. They came to the chest, demanded the keys; evil was opened when they looked in. There was a great hoard of jewels which seemed to the youths to be red gold and precious stones.

22. "Come back alone, you two! Come back tomorrow! I will give that gold to you. Do not tell the maids nor the hall servants nor anyone else that you sought me out."

23. Quickly one man said to another, brother to brother: "Let us go see the rings!" They came to the chest, demanded the keys. Evil was opened when they peered in;

24. he cut off the heads of the boys, and he laid their legs under

the bellows' pit (?). But the skulls under their scalps he encased in silver; he gave them to Níðuðr.

25. And out of their eyes [he made] jewels; he sent them to Níðuðr's cunning wife. And out of the teeth of that pair he forged breast-rings; he sent them to Böðvildr.

26. Then Böðvildr praised the ring which she had broken: "I do not dare say this, except to you alone."

27. Völundr said: "I will repair the break in the gold so it will seem fairer to your father and much better to your mother and as good as it was before to you."

28. He bore beer to her, because he was better in cunning, so that she fell asleep on the bench. "Now I have avenged all the malicious wrongs done to me, except one."

29. "I am not," said Völundr, "very mobile (?) on the sinews that Níðuðr's warriors took away from me." Laughing, Völundr raised himself aloft; weeping, Böðvildr left the island. She bewailed her lover's departure and her father's wrath.

30. Níðuðr's cunning wife stood outside, and she walked in the length of the hall; but [Völundr] sat at rest against the hall wall: "Are you awake, Níðuðr, lord of the Niarar?"

31. "I wake unceasingly, bereft of joys. I sleep but little since my sons' deaths. Cold is my head, cold are your counsels to me. This now I wish—that I could ask of Völundr."

32. "Tell me, Völundr, lord of the elves, what happened to my healthy boys?"

33. "First you shall swear all oaths to me, by the ship's board and by the shield's rim, by the horse's shoulder and by the sword's edge, that you will not kill Völundr's wife, nor become my bride's slayer, though I may have a wife, who is known to you, and though I may have a new-born child within the hall.

34. Go to the smithy, to the one which you had built; there you will find the bellows stained with blood. I have cut off the heads of your boys, and I have laid their legs under the bellows' pit (?).

35. But the skulls under their scalps, I encased in silver; I sent them to Níðuðr; and out of their eyes [I made] jewels. I sent them to Níðuðr's cunning wife.

36. And from the teeth of that pair, I forged breast-rings; I sent them to Böðvildr. Now Böðvildr goes heavy with child, the only daughter you and your wife have."

37. "You could not speak a speech that would grieve me more, nor that I would wish worse to avenge (?) on you, Völundr. No man is so tall that he may pull you off your horse, nor so powerful that he may shoot you from below, there where you hover up in the sky."

38. Laughing, Vǫlundr raised himself aloft, but wretched Níðuðr remained there behind.

39. "Rise up, Þakráðr, the best of my thralls: tell Bǫðvildr, the white-browed maiden, to come fairly clad to speak with her father."

40. "Is what they said to me true, Bǫðvildr, that you and Vǫlundr were together on the island?"

41. "What they said to you is true, Níðuðr: Vǫlundr and I were together on the island for one brief moment (?), which never should have happened. I did not know how to resist him; I could not do anything against him."

b. *The Rök Stone* (Sweden)

(*Rökstenen*; text: *Ög*, 136.)

The Rök Stone, dated in the early part of the ninth century, is one of Sweden's most impressive runic monuments, consisting of 725 runes, mostly in prose. The lines of verse translated here are written in *fornyrðislag* and parallel ll. 18–19 of *Deor* in style and content. Most scholars take the Theodoric to be Theodoric the Great, though not all agree (see Jansson, p. 132; Malone 1934; Malone 1966, pp. 11–13; and Lönnroth 1977).

Then Theodoric [Þióðrikr] the brave ruled, the lord of the sea-warriors, over the strand of the Hreiðmarr. Now he sits armed on his Gothic horse, with shield strapped over [shoulder], the prince of the Mæringar.

IV

THE GIFTS OF MEN

Germanic Analogue

1. *The Lay of Hyndla*

(*Hyndlolióð*; text: *Edda*, p. 288.)

The theme of "the gifts of men" appears in three OE poems: *The Gifts of Men*, *The Fortunes of Men* (67–98), and *Christ II* (664–85). The obvious Christian morality of *The Gifts of Men* has led scholars to patristic sources for the origins of this theme (see Allen/Calder). However, Geoffrey R. Russom has found compelling analogues for such lists in Germanic tradition: for example, stanza 69 of *The Sayings of Hár* (q.v.) and *The Lay of Sigrdrífa* (q.v.). Here we give the first three stanzas of *Hyndlolióð*; stanza 3 contains examples of *iþrottir* ("noble skills") which closely parallel the conditions and accomplishments catalogued in the several OE examples.

1. [Freyia spoke:] "Awake, maiden of maidens! Awake my friend, sister Hyndla, who dwells in a cave! Now is the dark of darkness; we must ride to Valhǫll and to the holy temple.

2. Let us ask Heriafǫðr to favor our aim! He grants and gives gold to his followers; he gave helmet and byrnie to Hermóðr, and presented a sword to Sigmundr.

3. He gives victory to some, and treasure to others, eloquence to many and wisdom to men; he gives a fair wind to [sailing] men and song-craft to skalds; he gives manliness to many a warrior."

V

WISDOM POETRY

A. Germanic Analogues

1. *The Sayings of Hár*

(*Hávamál*; text: *Edda*, pp. 17–44.)

Poetry of wisdom and learning pervades all the early Germanic literatures and it comprehends a wide range of topics. In OE, wisdom poetry tends towards universal, abstract truth and contains much pagan and Christian cosmological material. In ON, on the other hand, wisdom poetry sometimes has more social and practical concerns, though it is not restricted to those areas. While OE may explore a broader range of topics, there is no single poem in Anglo-Saxon of such scope and poetic power as the *Hávamál*. This, the longest poem in the *Edda*, was probably compiled from various other poems, many of which "can no longer be distinguished with certainty" (Hallberg, p. 40). There are, however, at least five separate sections: (1) stanzas 1–79 give advice on mundane matters; (2) stanzas 80–90 form a transition to the second section (stanzas 91–110), dealing with man's relationship to woman; (3) stanzas 111–37 comprise the "Lay of Loddfáfnir," containing a variety of counsels; (4) stanzas 138–46 relate Óðinn's runic wisdom; and finally, (5) stanzas 147–64 form the *Ljóðatal*, a collection of eighteen charms, which complete this repository of Nordic wisdom. Dating for this, as for other ON poems, is uncertain (see Lindblad), but portions of it may have existed in the tenth century. It is written predominantly in *ljóðaháttr* meter (see Bellows, Hallberg, Hollander, and Shippey.)

1. Before a man goes ahead, he should inspect, he should examine all the doorways, because it is hard to know whether enemies wait in ambush on the hall-floor.

2. Hail the givers! The guest has come in: where shall he sit? He is in a great hurry, he who shall try his luck by the fire (?).

3. Fire he needs, he who has come in and is cold up to his knees; food and clothes a man needs, he who has journeyed over the mountains.

4. Water he needs, he who comes to a meal, a towel and a friendly welcome, good understanding (?), if he can get it for himself, speech and a receptive hearing (?).

5. Wit he needs, he who roams widely; everything is easy at home. He becomes a butt of scorn, he who knows nothing and sits among the wise.

6. A man should not be boastful about his wisdom; instead he should keep himself in check. When a wise and silent man comes to the homestead, harm seldom comes to the prudent one; because a man never finds a more reliable friend than great common sense.

7. The wary guest, when he comes to a meal, silently pays close attention, listens with his ears and looks about with his eyes; thus every wise man watches out for himself.

8. He is happy, the one who wins praise and respect for himself; it is harder to deal with what a man must have in another man's breast [to depend on others?].

9. He is happy who gets praise and wisdom for himself while he lives, because a man often receives bad counsel from another's breast.

10. A man does not bear a better burden on the road than great common sense; in a strange place that will seem better than treasures; this is a refuge (?) for the wretched.

11. A man does not bear a better burden on the road than great common sense; worse provisions for the journey he does not carry to the field than too much drinking of ale.

12. It is not so good, as it is said to be good, ale for the sons of men; because the more a man drinks, the less he knows his mind.

13. It is called the heron of forgetfullness, the bird which hovers over ale-feasts; it steals the minds of men. With the feathers of the bird I was fettered in Gunnlǫð's court.

14. Drunk I became, I became dead drunk at wise Fialarr's house; therefore is that ale-feast best from which each man recovers his mind.

15. Tight-lipped and thoughtful and bold in battle should a king's son be; glad and merry should every man be, until he meets his death.

16. The cowardly man thinks he will live forever if he avoids battle; but old age will give him no peace, though weapons may grant it to him.

17. The fool stares, when he comes to visit; he mumbles to himself or mopes. If he takes a drink, the man's mind is exposed right away.

18. He who roams widely and has travelled much about alone knows what goes on in the mind of each man who has wits.

19. A man should not hold on to the drinking cup, but should drink mead in moderation. He should speak as necessary or be silent. No man will blame you for being rude if you go to sleep early.

20. Unless he is aware of his own desires, a greedy man eats himself sick; often the belly brings ridicule on a foolish man, when he comes among the wise.

21. The herds know when they must go home, and then they leave the pasture; but the stupid man never knows the limit of his belly.

22. The wretched, bad-tempered man sneers at everything. He does not know what he ought to know, that he is not free of faults.

23. The stupid man stays awake all night long and thinks about everything. Then he is tired when morning comes; all his misery is as it was before.

24. The foolish man thinks that all are friends who laugh with him; if he sits among the wise, he does not see that they are plotting against him.

25. The foolish man thinks that all are friends who laugh with him; then he finds out that he has few defenders when he comes to the Ping.

26. The foolish man thinks he knows all, if he has refuge in a corner; he does not know how he should answer if men test him.

27. It is best for the fool to keep silent when he comes among men; no one knows that he knows nothing, unless he speaks too much. That man who knows nothing does not know if he speaks too much.

28. He seems wise who can ask and likewise reply; the sons of men can hide nothing, once it is rumored among men.

29. The man who is never silent speaks plenty of senseless words; the hasty tongue, if it is not held, often sings trouble for itself.

30. A man should not hold another up to scorn when he comes to visit; many a man then seems wise if he is not questioned and if he manages to keep his skin dry.

31. Wise he seems, the one who takes flight, the guest from the

mocking guest; he does not know exactly, the one who laughs scornfully over a meal, whether he gossips with foes.

32. Many men are devoted to one another, but quarrel at the meal; there will always be strife among men: guest fights with guest.

33. A man should often take an early meal unless he comes to a feast; [otherwise] he sits and snaps [at the food], acts as if he were starved, and can talk about little.

34. A great round-about way there is to a bad friend's house, although he may live on the road; but short cuts lie to a good friend's house, although he may have fared farther away.

35. He should go, a guest should not be forever in one place; the loved one becomes the loathed one if he sits too long in another's hall.

36. One's own home is better, although it may be little; a man is somebody at home. Although he has only two goats and a rope-roofed hall, that is still better than begging.

37. One's own home is better, although it may be little: a man is somebody at home. His heart bleeds who must beg meat for himself at every meal.

38. A man should not take a step away from his weapons on the field, because it is hard to know when he may need his spear out on the roads.

39. I have not found a man so generous or so hospitable that he would not accept a gift, or one so [liberal] with his money that a reward would be unwelcome, if he should receive one.

40. For the money he has gained, a man should not suffer want. Often he saves for his enemies, what he intended for his friends: much goes worse than expected.

41. With weapons and with clothes should friends be gladdened, as is most evident to one's self: those who both give and receive are friends the longest, if it turns out well.

42. A man should be a friend to his friend and return gift for gift; men should receive mocking laughter with the same and lying with a lie.

43. A man should be a friend to his friend, to him and to his friend. But no man should be a friend to the friends of his enemy.

44. Know this: if you have a friend whom you trust well and you want to get something good from him, you must become his confidant and exchange gifts, and travel often to seek him out.

45. If you have another whom you distrust, and you want to get something good from him, you must talk fairly with him but think falsely and return lying with a lie.

46. Here is still more about him whom you distrust and whose

intent you suspect: you shall laugh with him and speak other than you think; return like gift for gift.

47. I was young once, I travelled alone, then I lost my way. I thought myself rich when I found another: a man is a man's delight.

48. Generous, brave men live best; seldom do they nourish cares; but the cowardly man fears everything and the stingy man always complains about gifts.

49. My clothes I gave to two men made of wood in a field; they seemed like warriors when they had garments; a naked warrior is covered with shame.

50. The pine tree which stands in the thorp decays, neither bark nor needles protect it; such is the man whom no one loves: why should he live long?

51. Goodwill burns hotter than fire for five days among false friends; then it dies down when the sixth day comes, and all friendship fades.

52. A man does not have to give only a big gift; often he buys himself praise for little; with half a loaf and with a half-filled cup I got myself a companion.

53. Little sands, little seas, little are the minds of men; because all men were not made equally wise, mankind is everywhere half (?).

54. Moderately wise should every man be; never too wise should he be; those men live fairest who know just enough.

55. Moderately wise should every man be; never too wise should he be; because a wise man's heart is seldom glad, if he is all-wise who has it.

56. Moderately wise should every man be; never too wise should he be; no one should know his fate before: his mind is freest from care.

57. Brand from brand burns until it is consumed, flame is kindled by flame. A man is known to other men by his speech, but the stupid by their dullness.

58. Early shall he rise, he who wants to have another's money or life; seldom does a slumbering wolf get a thighbone or a sleeping man, victory.

59. Early shall he rise, he who has few laborers and [must] go to look after his work; much he misses who sleeps in the morning; half of riches depends on get up and go.

60. Dry sheaths and thatching bark—of these a man knows the right measure, and of the wood which will last him for a quarter or a half-year.

61. Washed and well-fed should a man ride to the Þing, though

he is not dressed too well; no man should be ashamed of his shoes and breeches, nor of his horse either, though he does not have a good one.

62. The eagle snaps and cranes forward when it comes to the ocean, to the ancient sea: thus is the man, when he comes into a crowd and has few defenders.

63. Every smart man shall ask and reply, he who wants to be called wise; one man may know but a second should not—the whole world knows if three do.

64. Every man wise-in-counsel should use his strength in moderation: for he finds out, when he comes among the brave, that no one is the boldest of all.

65. For the words which a man says to others, he often gets a reward.

66. I came much too soon to many places and too late to some: the ale was drunk, sometimes it was unbrewed. The unwelcome [guest] seldom strikes it right.

67. Here and there they would invite me home, when I didn't need meat for my meals, or two hams would hang at a loyal friend's house, where I had eaten one.

68. Fire is best among the sons of men and the sight of the sun; his health, if a man can keep it, and to live without shame.

69. A man is not completely wretched, though he may be in bad health: one is blessed in his sons, one in his kinsmen, one in his ample riches, one in his works well done.

70. It is better to live and live happily (?): the living man always gets the cow. I saw the fire burn for a rich man, but outside he was dead before the door (?).

71. A lame man rides a horse, a handless man drives herds, a deaf man fights and is bold; a blind man is better than a burned man would be: a corpse is of use to no one.

72. A son is better, even if he is born late, after a man is dead. Stone monuments seldom stand near the road, unless a kinsman raises one for a kinsman.

73. Two overpower one; the tongue is the head's slayer; I expect a fist in every fur cloak.

74. He welcomes night who trusts in his provisions; short are the berths in a ship; unstable is the autumn night; weather changes a great deal in five days, but more in a month.

75. This he does not know who knows nothing: many a man becomes a fool for money (?); one man is rich, another poor—no one should be blamed for that (?).

76. Cattle die, kinsmen die, you yourself will likewise die; but fame never dies, for the one who gets good [fame] for himself.

77. Cattle die, kinsmen die, you yourself will likewise die; I know one thing that never dies: a dead man's reputation.

78. I saw the full-stocked folds of Fitiungr's sons: now they bear beggars' staffs. Wealth is like the twinkling of an eye; it is the most fickle of friends.

79. If the foolish man acquires money or a woman's love, pride grows in him but never common sense; he heads right for haughtiness.

80. Then that is proven when you consult the runes, originated by the gods, those which the gods made, and which the great wise man [Óðinn] painted, that it is best if he is silent.

81. The day shall be praised in the evening; a woman, when she is cremated; a sword, when it is proven; a maiden, when she is given away; ice, when it is crossed; ale, when it is drunk.

82. Wood should be cut down in the wind; row out to sea in good weather, talk with young maidens in the dark: the day has many eyes. A ship should be used for a swift journey (?) and a shield for protection, a sword for a blow, and a maiden for kisses.

83. Drink ale by the fire, and skate on the ice, buy a lean steed, and a rusty sword, fatten a horse at home, and farm out a dog.

84. No one should trust in the words of a maiden, nor in what a woman says; because their hearts were made on a [potter's] turning wheel, and fickleness placed in their breasts.

85. A cracking bow, a burning flame, a gaping wolf, a screaming crow, a grunting pig, a rootless tree, a rising sea, a boiling kettle,

86. a flying spear, a falling wave, ice one-night old, a coiled snake, a woman's bed-talk or a broken sword, a bear's game or a king's son,

87. a sick calf, a self-willed thrall, the favoring words of a seeress, the newly slain,

88. a field sown early no man should trust, nor too quickly in his son; weather rules the field and the head [rules] the son: each of these is unreliable.

89. In his brother-slayer, though he is met on the road, a half-burnt house, a horse too speedy—a steed is useless if he breaks a foot—a man should not be so trustful that he trust all of these.

90. The love of women who are deceitful in spirit is like riding a smooth-shod horse on slippery ice, a spirited two-year-old which is badly tamed, or on a rudderless boat in a raging wind, or like a lame man trying to catch a reindeer on a thawing slope.

91. Now I will speak openly, because I know both: men's hearts are fickle with women; when we speak most fair, then we think most false. That deceives the heart of the wise.

92. Fairly must he speak and offer gifts, he who wants to get a woman's love; praise the figure of the fair maiden: he wins who flatters.

93. No man should ever mock another's love: seductive faces often capture the wise man when they do not capture the fool.

94. A man should never mock another for what happens to many a man: among the sons of men all-powerful love makes fools out of the wise.

95. Only the mind knows what lives near the heart; a man is alone with his own spirit. There is no sickness worse for any wise man than to have nothing to love.

96. That I proved when I sat in the reeds and waited for my love; the wise maid was body and soul to me—but still I do not have her.

97. I found Billingr's daughter in bed, sun-white, asleep: a jarl's delight seemed nothing to me unless I could live with that body.

98. "So towards evening, Óðinn, you shall come, if you want to win the maid for yourself; it is all amiss unless only we know of such shame."

99. Back I turned and seemed to be out of my head with love; I thought I would have all her heart and pleasure.

100. When I came next, the able warriors were all awake; with burning lights and brands raised high, so was my wretched path marked out.

101. And towards morning, when I had come back again, the hall retainers were asleep. Then I found the good woman's bitch bound on the bed.

102. Many a good maiden, if you look closely, is deceitful toward men; I learned that when I sought to seduce the wise woman to wantonness: the clever maid heaped scorn on me, and I got nothing from this woman!

103. At home a man should be glad, and cheerful with guests, knowing about himself, have a good memory and be fluent, if he wants to be well informed; he should often introduce good things to the discussion. A monstrous fool is he called who can say little; that is the character of the unwise.

104. I sought the old giant; now I have come back again. I got little from being silent there. With many words I spoke to my own advantage in Suttungr's hall.

105. On her golden throne Gunnlǫð gave me a drink of the precious mead; I gave her a bad reward afterwards for her loyal spirit, for her heavy heart.

106. I let the mouth of Rati [the gimlet] make space for me and gnaw through stone; over and under me stood the giant's paths

[rocks]; thus I risked my head.

107. I took advantage of a bargain appearance (?), little is lacking to the wise; because Óðrerir has now come up to Óðinn's mansion (?).

108. Doubtful it is to me that I could have come out again from the giant's court, if I had not enjoyed Gunnlǫð, the good woman, who lay in my arms.

109. The next day the frost-giants went to ask Hár's advice in Hár's hall: they asked about Bǫlverkr, whether he had come back among the gods, or whether Suttungr had sacrificed him.

110. Óðinn, I think, has sworn an oath upon the sacred ring: who shall trust in his troth? He had Suttungr cheated of his mead, and he made Gunnlǫð grieve.

111. It is time to recite from the sage's throne, at Urðr's Well; I saw and stayed silent, I saw and reflected, I listened to the speech of men; I heard and learned about runes, nor were they silent in counsels, at Hár's hall, in Hár's hall; thus I heard it said:

112. I advise you, Loddfáfnir, to take my advice; you would benefit if you took it; good will come to you if you accept it: do not rise at night unless you are on the lookout or you are seeking a place outside [to relieve] yourself.

113. I advise you, Loddfáfnir, to take my advice; you would benefit if you took it; good will come to you if you accept it: you should not sleep in the embrace of a woman skilled in magic, so that she locks you in her limbs;

114. she will make sure that you will not heed the speech of either Þing or king. You will not desire food nor mankind's pleasure; you will go sorrowfully to sleep.

115. I advise you, Loddfáfnir, to take my advice; you would benefit if you took it; good will come to you if you accept it: never entice another's wife to be your mistress.

116. I advise you, Loddfáfnir, to take my advice; you would benefit if you took it; good will come to you if you accept it: if you wish to travel over a mountain or a fjord, be sure you have ample food.

117. I advise you, Loddfáfnir, to take my advice; you would benefit if you took it; good will come to you if you accept it: never let a bad man know about your misfortune; because from a bad man you will never get a good return for your good will.

118. I saw a man deeply bitten by the word of a bad woman; her deceitful tongue was the death of him, and there was no truth to the charge.

119. I advise you, Loddfáfnir, to take my advice; you would benefit if you took it; good will come to you if you accept it: know

this: if you have a friend whom you trust well, go to visit him often; for the path that no one treads grows with brush and high grass.

120. I advise you, Loddfáfnir, to take my advice; you would benefit if you took it; good will come to you if you accept it: entice a good man to you with glad, familiar talk and learn healing charms while you live.

121. I advise you, Loddfáfnir, to take my advice, you would benefit if you took it; good will come to you if you accept it: never be the first to make a breach with your friend. Sorrow eats the heart, if you cannot tell someone your whole mind.

122. I advise you, Loddfáfnir, to take my advice; you would benefit if you took it; good will come to you if you accept it: you should never bandy words with a stupid fool,

123. because you can never get a reward for good from a bad man; but a good man can make you beloved through praise.

124. Peace and trust are exchanged when one can tell another his whole mind; anything is better than to be faithless; he is not another's friend who says only what that friend wants to hear.

125. I advise you, Loddfáfnir, to take my advice; you would benefit if you took it; good will come to you if you accept it: you should not dispute as much as three words with a man less worthy than you; often the better man is defeated when the worse attacks.

126. I advise you, Loddfáfnir, to take my advice; you would benefit if you took it; good will come to you if you accept it: be neither a shoe-maker nor a shaft-maker except for yourself alone; if the shoe is badly made or the shaft is bent, then misfortune is in store for you.

127. I advise you, Loddfáfnir, to take my advice; you would benefit if you took it; good will come to you if you accept it: where you come upon misdeeds, speak out about those misdeeds, and give your enemies no peace.

128. I advise you, Loddfáfnir, to take my advice; you would benefit if you took it; good will come to you if you accept it: never be glad in evil, but let yourself be pleased with good.

129. I advise you, Loddfáfnir, to take my advice; you would benefit if you took it; good will come to you if you accept it: you should not look up in battle—the sons of men become terror-crazed—lest men cast spells upon you.

130. I advise you, Loddfáfnir, to take my advice; you would benefit if you took it; good will come to you if you accept it: if you want to attract a good woman to you for joyful intimacy and to get pleasure from her, you should make a fair promise and hold fast to it; no one loathes the good if he gets it.

131. I advise you, Loddfáfnir, to take my advice; you would

benefit if you took it; good will come to you if you accept it: wary I
bid you be, but not too wary; with ale be the most wary and with
another man's woman, and with a third thing—that thieves do not
trick you.

132. I advise you, Loddfáfnir, to take my advice; you would
benefit if you took it; good will come to you if you accept it: never
mock or laugh at a guest or a traveller.

133. Often they do scarcely know, those who sit first in a house,
whose kinsmen they are who come [later]; no man is so good that a
fault does not come with him, nor so bad that he is of no use.

134. I advise you, Loddfáfnir, to take my advice; you would
benefit if you took it; good will come to you if you accept it: never
laugh at a hoary sage: often what an old man speaks is good; often
clear words come out of a shrivelled skin, the one which hangs
among the hides, and dangles with dried skins and swings among
the entrails (?).

135. I advise you, Loddfáfnir, to take my advice; you would
benefit if you took it; good will come to you if you accept it: do not
abuse a guest nor spit on (?) him at your gate. Treat the wretched
well.

136. Powerful is that bolt which must slide back and forth to
unlock [the door] for all; bestow a ring (?) or it will bring every evil
upon your limbs.

137. I advise you, Loddfáfnir, to take my advice; you would
benefit if you took it; good will come to you if you accept it: when
you drink ale, choose for yourself the might of earth; because
earth fights against beer, and fire disease, oak constipation, an ear
of corn against witchcraft, the elder bush against hall-strife—
against feuds one should call on the moon—alum (?) against
sickness caused by bites, and runes against misfortune, earth fights
against flood.

138. I know that I hung on a windy gallows-tree, nine nights all
together, wounded by a spear and consecrated to Óðinn, myself to
myself, on that gallows tree—no one knows where it grows up
from the roots.

139. No bread nor drinking horn did anyone hand up to me; I
peered down: I took up the runes, wailing I took them up: I fell
back down.

140. Nine mighty charms I took from the famous son of Bǫlþorr,
Bestla's father, and I got a drink of the precious mead, poured out
from Óðrerir.

141. Then I began to flourish and be wise and to grow and
thrive; one word led to another, one work led to another.

142. Runes you will find and clear staves, powerful magic

staves, great strong staves, which the great wise man [Óðinn] painted and the mighty gods made and which the foremost of the gods carved.

143. Óðinn among the Æsir, and Dáinn for the elves, Dvalinn for the dwarves, Ásviðr for the giants, and I carved some myself.

144. Do you know how to carve runes? Do you know how to interpret? Do you know how to paint? Do you know how to make trial? Do you know how to ask? Do you know how to worship? Do you know how to offer? Do you know how to sacrifice?

145. It is better that it be un-prayed for than over-worshipped; a gift always expects a gift in return; it is better that it be un-offered than over-sacrificed. Thus Þundr carved runes before there were men; where he rose up, when he came back.

146. Those charms I know which the king's wife does not know, nor any son of mankind; one is called "Help" and that will help you against charges and sorrows and all afflictions.

147. I know a second, which the sons of men need, those who want to live as healers.

148. I know a third: if I have a great need to bind my enemy, I blunt the edges of my adversaries' swords; neither weapon nor staffs cut for them.

149. I know a fourth: if men bear bonds for my limbs, I chant a spell so that I can go free; the fetters spring from my feet and the bonds from my hands.

150. I know a fifth: if I see a shaft shot in malice speeding into the host, it does not fly so forcefully that I cannot stop it, if I catch sight of it.

151. I know a sixth: if a thane wounds me with the roots of a green tree, that man who rouses me to fury will taste the harm instead of me.

152. I know a seventh: if I see flames high over the bench-mates in the hall, it does not burn so widely that I cannot quench it; I know how to chant that charm.

153. I know an eighth, which is useful for all to learn: wherever hate grows among the sons of a warrior, I can bring a quick settlement.

154. I know a ninth: if the need arises for me to save my ship on the flood, I calm the wind on the waves and lull the whole sea.

155. I know a tenth: if I see witches flying aloft, I work it so that they forget their way, their own skins, and their own desires to return home.

156. I know an eleventh: if I lead old friends to battle, I chant under the shields, and they travel with might, whole to the battle, whole from the battle, they come whole from wherever [they are].

157. I know a twelfth: if I see a gallows' corpse swinging up in a tree, I carve and paint in runes, so that the man comes and speaks with me.

158. I know a thirteenth: if I sprinkle water on a young thane, he will not fall, although he goes into battle; that man will not bow down before swords.

159. I know a fourteenth: if I number the gods before a host of men, I have knowledge of them all, of the Æsir and the elves; few fools know how to do so.

160. I know a fifteenth, which Þióðrørir, the dwarf, chanted before Dellingr's doors: he chanted power to the Æsir and prowess to the elves, understanding to Hroptatýr.

161. I know a sixteenth: if I want to have all the heart and pleasure of a wise maid, I turn the mind of the white-armed woman and I change her whole spirit.

162. I know a seventeenth: that the youthful maid will never shun me. These charms, Loddfáfnir, you will lack for a long time, though it would be good for you if you got them, useful if you learned them, needful if you accepted them.

163. I know an eighteenth, which I never teach to a maiden or a man's wife—best of all is what one knows alone; this is the end of my charms—except for the one who wraps me in her arms or who may be my sister.

164. Now are the sayings of Hár spoken, in Hár's hall, very useful for the sons of men, not useful for the sons of giants. Hail, he who spoke! Hail, he who knows! Enjoy it, he who learned. Hail, those who listened.

2. *The Lay of Grímnir*

(*Grímnismál*; text: *Edda*, pp. 56–68.)

This poem transmits primarily mythological knowledge, much of which concerns the identification of proper names. Óðinn, disguised as Grímnir, has been captured by King Geirroðr, who sets him between two fires. Geirroðr's son, Agnarr, takes pity on Óðinn, gives him something to drink, and in return receives a share of Óðinn's wisdom. The poem, which may have been composed in the tenth century, is written predominantly in *ljóðaháttr* meter (see Bellows, Hallberg, and Hollander).

About the sons of King Hrauðungr

King Hrauðungr had two sons; one was called Agnarr, the other Geirroðr. Agnarr was ten winters old and Geirroðr eight. The two of them were rowing in a boat with their fishing lines out for small fish. The wind drove them out to sea. In the darkness of night they ran aground, and they went up on shore; they found a cotter. They were there for a winter. The wife fostered Agnarr and the man [fostered] Geirroðr.

In the spring the man gave them a boat. And when he and his wife led them to the shore, the man spoke to Geirroðr alone. They had a fair wind and came to their father's harbor. Geirroðr was in the front of the boat; he jumped out upon the land and pushed the boat out and said: "Now go where the trolls may take you." The boat drifted out. But Geirroðr went up towards the houses. He was warmly welcomed. At that time his father had died. Geirroðr was then made king and became a famous man.

Óðinn and Frigg sat in Hliðskiálf and looked out upon all worlds. Óðinn spoke: "Do you see Agnarr, your foster son, where he begets children with a giantess in a cave? But Geirroðr, my foster son, is a king and now rules his land." Frigg said: "He is so stingy with food that he tortures his guests [by starvation], if he thinks too many have come." Óðinn said that that was a great lie. They wagered on the matter.

Frigg sent her child, Fulla, to Geirroðr. She bade the king be on guard so that he would not be bewitched by a wizard who had come into his land; and she said that he could be recognized by this sign: that no dog was so savage that he would attack him. But that was the greatest slander [to say] Geirroðr was not generous with his food. And yet the king had that man seized, whom the dogs would not attack. He was in a blue cloak and called himself Grímnir, but said no more about himself even though he was asked. The king had him tortured to make him talk and set him between two fires, and he sat there for eight nights.

King Geirroðr had a son, ten winters old, and he was called Agnarr after his brother. Agnarr went to Grímnir and gave him a full horn to drink, and said that the king had done wrong when he had that man tortured without cause. Grímnir drank. Then the fire came so close that Grímnir's cloak burned. He said:

1. "You are hot, fire, and much too high; go farther away, flame. My fur is singed, though I hold it aloft, the cloak is burning up.

2. For eight nights I sat between fires here, but no man offered me food, except Agnarr alone, who alone shall rule, Geirroðr's son, the land of the Goths.

3. You shall have good fortune, Agnarr, since Veratýr bids you be happy; for one drink you shall never get a better reward.

4. The land is holy, which I see lying near the Æsir and the elves; but Þórr shall be in Þrúðheimr until the gods destroy themselves.

5. It is called Ýdalir, where Ullr has built a hall for himself. The gods gave Álfheimr to Freyr in ancient days as a gift when he cut his first tooth.

6. A third home is there; the noble gods thatched this hall with silver. It is called Válaskiálf, which a god in ancient days fashioned for himself.

7. The fourth is called Sǫkkvabekkr, which the cool waves rush over; there Óðinn and Sága drink all their days, glad, out of golden cups.

8. The fifth is called Glaðsheimr, where gold-bright Valhǫll spaciously stands; there Hroptr chooses weapon-slain men every day.

9. He easily recognizes the hall when he sees it, he who comes to Óðinn: the dwelling is raftered with spears, the hall is thatched with shields, along the benches byrnies are strewn.

10. He easily recognizes the hall when he sees it, he who comes to Óðinn: a wolf hangs over the western door and an eagle hovers above it.

11. The sixth is called Þrymheimr, where Þiazi dwelled, the immensely powerful giant; and now Skaði, the bright bride of the gods, dwells there, where once was her father's home.

12. The seventh is Breiðablik, and there Baldr has built a hall for himself, in that land where I know the fewest troubles lie.

13. The eighth is Himinbiǫrg, and it is said that Heimdallr rules the temples there; there the guardian of the gods, glad, drinks the good mead in his comfortable house.

14. The ninth is Fólkvangr, and there Freyia decides who will have seats in the hall; she chooses half of the slain every day, and Óðinn has [the other] half.

15. The tenth is Glitnir; it is studded with gold and also thatched with silver; and there Forseti dwells most of his days and stills all strife.

16. The eleventh is Nóatún and there Niǫrðr has built a hall for himself; the lord of men, the sinless one, rules in his high-timbered shrine.

17. Brush, high grass, and woods grow in Víðarr's land; and

there the brave son gets down off the horse's back to avenge his father.

18. Andhrímnir has Sæhrímnir, the best of meat, boiled in Eldhrímnir, but few know on what the Einheriar feast.

19. The famed, war-trained Heriafǫðr feeds Geri and Freki; but Óðinn, glorious in arms, lives forever on wine alone.

20. Huginn and Muninn fly every day over the earth; I fear for Huginn that he will not come back, though I am more afraid for Muninn.

21. Þund roars loudly, Þióðvitnir's fish sports in the flood; the river current seems too strong for the host struggling towards Valhǫll (?) to wade in.

22. Valgrind it is called, which stands outside on the field, holy, before the holy doors; old is that gate, but few know how it is locked with a bolt.

24. Five hundred and forty rooms I think there are in Bilskírnir all together; of the dwellings whose roofs I have seen, I know my son's is the greatest.

23. Five hundred and forty doors I think there are in Valhǫll; eight hundred Einheriar depart through one door, when they go to fight Fenrisúlfr.

25. The goat is called Heiðrún which stands by Heriafǫðr's hall and bites off Læraðr's branches; she will fill the barrel with clear mead, that drink cannot give out.

26. The hart is called Eikþyrnir which stands by the hall of Heriafǫðr and bites off Læraðr's branches; and from his horns there [water] drips into Hvergelmir; from there all rivers take their course:

[27–8. Catalogue of rivers omitted.]

29. In Kǫrmt and Ǫrmt and the two Kerlaugar, Þórr shall wade every day when he travels to judge at the Ash Yggdrasill, because the bridge of the Æsir burns all in flames, the holy waters boil.

[30. Catalogue of steeds omitted.]

31. Three roots spread in three directions under the Ash Yggdrasill. Hel dwells under one, the frost giants under the second, mankind under the third.

32. The squirrel is called Ratatoskr, which will run on the Ash Yggdrasill; he will carry the eagle's words from above and tell them to Níðhǫggr below.

33. And there are four harts which gnaw the highest branches (?) with necks thrown back: Dáinn and Dvalinn, Duneyrr and Duraþrór.

34. More serpents lie under the Ash Yggdrasill than any stupid fool would think; Góinn and Móinn—they are Grafvitnir's sons—

Grábakr and Grafvǫlluðr, Ofnir and Sváfnir, I think that they will always gnaw at the twigs of the tree.

35. The Ash Yggdrasill endures trouble, more than men may know: the hart bites from above, and its trunk is rotting, and Niðhǫggr makes it ragged from below.

36. I want Hrist and Mist to bring me the horn, Skeggiǫld and Skǫgul; Hildr and Þrúðr, Hlǫkk and Herfiǫtur, Gǫll and Geirǫlul; Randgríð and Ráðgríð and Reginleif, they bring ale to the Einheriar.

37. Árvakr and Alsviðr, hungry they will draw the sun up hence; but invisibly the gracious gods, the Æsir, have placed the cool iron under their yokes.

38. It is called Svǫl which stands before the sun, a shield for the shining god; I know mountain and sea would burn if it fell away.

39. Skǫll the wolf is called which follows the bright-faced god [sun] to the protecting woods (?); but the other is called Hati; he is Hróðvitnir's son, who shall [follow] the bright bride of heaven [moon].

40. The earth was shaped out of Ymir's flesh, and the sea out of his blood, the mountains from his bones, the trees from his hair, and heaven from his skull.

41. And from his brows the gracious gods made Miðgarðr for the sons of men; and from his brain all the menacing clouds were shaped.

42. The favor of Ullr and all the gods he will have, who first will reach into the flames, because worlds will open for the sons of the gods when the kettle is heaved aside.

43. The sons of Ívaldi went in ancient days to create Skíðblaðnir, the best of ships, for bright Freyr, the noble son of Niǫrðr.

44. The Ash Yggdrasill is the best of trees, and Skíðblaðnir of ships, Óðinn of gods, and Sleipnir of steeds, Bifrǫst of bridges, Bragi of skalds, Hábrók of hawks, and Garmr of hounds.

45. I have now raised up my face before the sons of the victory-gods—for that the desired help will awake (?); that will come in from all the Æsir, on Ægir's bench, at Ægir's drinking bout.

46. I am called Grímr, I am called Gangleri, Heriann and Hiálmberi, Þekkr and Þriði, Þundr and Uðr, Helblindi and Hár.

47. Saðr and Svipall and Sanngetall, Herteitr and Hnikarr, Bileygr, Báleygr, Bǫlverkr, Fiǫlnir, Grímr and Grímnir, Glapsviðr and Fiǫlsviðr;

48. Síðhǫttr, Síðskeggr, Sigfǫðr, Hnikuðr, Alfǫðr, Valfǫðr, Atríðr and Farmatýr; I have never been called by one name since I travelled among folk.

49. They called me Grímnir in Geirroðr's hall, but Iálkr in

Ásmundr's and then Kialarr when I drew the sledge; Þrór at the Þing, Viðurr in battle, Óski and Ómi, Iafnhár and Biflindi, Gǫndlir and Hárbarðr among the gods.

50. Sviðurr and Sviðrir I was called at Sǫkkmímir's, when I deceived the old giant, and when I alone became the slayer of Miðviðnir's famous son.

51. Geirroðr, you are drunk! You have drunk too much; you have lost much, since you have lost my support, that of all the Einheriar, and Óðinn's favor.

52. I said much to you and you remembered little and your friends betray you; I see my friend's sword lying all wet with blood.

53. Now Yggr will have a sword-pierced corpse. I know your life has passed; the Norns are hostile—now you can recognize Óðinn. Approach me if you can!

54. Óðinn I am called now, Yggr I was called before, Þundr I was called before that, Vakr and Skilfingr, Váfuðr and Hroptatýr, Gautr and Iálkr among the gods, Ofnir and Sváfnir, for I think that they all derive from me alone.

King Geirroðr sat and had his sword on his knee, and drew it half out. But when he heard that Óðinn had come there, then he stood up and wanted to take Óðinn from the fire. The sword slipped from his hand, its hilt turned downwards. The king stumbled and lurched forward, and the sword pierced through him and killed him. Óðinn then vanished. And Agnarr was king there for a long time.

3. *The Lay of Sigrdrífa*

(*Sigrdrífomál*; text: *Edda*, pp. 189–97.)

As in *The Lay of Grímnir*, where Agnarr receives a store of mythological wisdom for his compassion toward Óðinn, here, Sigurðr frees a valkyrie named Sigrdrífa and in return she instructs him about runes. The poem, composed mostly in *ljóðaháttr* at an uncertain date—perhaps around 1000—is probably a mélange of other poems, since some sections seem to have no organic relationship to the underlying story (see Bellows, Hallberg, Hollander).

Sigurðr rode over Hindarfiall and pressed on south to Frankland. On the fell he saw a great light, as if a fire were burning, and it shone up to heaven. And when he came near, a shield-wall stood there, and above it a banner. Sigurðr went into the wall of shields and saw that a man lay asleep there with all his weapons. First he took the helmet off his head. Then he saw that it was a woman. The byrnie was tight, as if it were grown to the flesh. Then with Gramr he slit the byrnie down from the head-opening and also out at both arms. Then he took the byrnie off her and she awakened and sat up and saw Sigurðr and said:

1. "What bit the byrnie? How did I shake off my sleep? Who made that pale shackle fall off me?"
He answered: "The son of Sigmundr, the sword of Sigurðr, which only a short time ago tore to pieces carrion for the raven. (?)"
2. "Long I slept, long I was asleep, long are the woes of men! Óðinn decreed that I could not break the sleep-runes."

Sigurðr sat down and asked her name. Then she took a horn full of mead and gave him a drink to strengthen his memory.

3. "Hail day! Hail sons of day! Hail night and her sister (?)! With gentle eyes look on us here, and give victory to those sitting in wait!
4. Hail gods! Hail, goddesses! Hail be to bountiful earth! Speech and wisdom give us, a noble pair, and healing hands while we live!"

She said her name was Sigrdrífa and that she was a valkyrie. She said that two kings had fought; one was called Hiálm-Gunnarr; he was old and the strongest warrior, and Óðinn had promised him victory, and "the other was called Agnarr, Auða's brother, whom no one wanted to help(?)."
Sigrdrífa felled Hiálm-Gunnar in battle. And Óðinn pricked her with a sleeping-thorn in revenge for this and said that she would never after win victory in battle and he said that she would be married. "And I told him that in return I solemnly vowed not to marry any man who knew fear." He spoke and asked her to teach him wisdom, if she knew what happens in all worlds.

5. Sigdrífa said: "Beer I bring you, tree of battle [warrior], mixed with strength and great fame; it is full of charms and healing rune-staves, good spells and joyful runes.
6. You shall learn victory-runes, if you want to have victory, and carve them on the sword's hilt—some on one part of the sword, some on another, and name Týr twice.
7. You shall learn ale-runes, if you do not want another's wife to betray your trust, if you trust her; on the horn shall you carve

them and on the back of your hand and mark the 'Need' rune on your nails.

8. Bless your full cup and protect yourself from danger and cast garlic into the drink: then I know that your mead will never be mixed with poison.

9. You shall learn birth-runes, if you want to save and deliver the child from the woman; on your palms shall you write them and grasp the limbs and ask the guardian women for help.

10. You shall make sea-runes, if you want to protect the sail-mares [ships] on the sea; carve them on the prow and on the rudder and inscribe them with fire on the oars: however high the breakers or black the waves, still you will come safe from the sea.

11. You shall learn branch-runes, if you want to be a healer, and learn to take care of wounds; carve them on the bark and on the trees of the forest, those which bend their branches to the east.

12. You shall learn speech-runes, if you want no man to pay back harm with spite. These wind, these weave, these bring all together at the Þing, where men must travel to a fully attended court.

13. You shall learn mind-runes, if you want to be more strong-minded than any man. Hroptr devised them, carved them and conceived them, out of the draught that had dripped from the skull of Heiddraupnir, and out of the horn of Hoddrofnir.

14. He stood on the cliff with the edges of Brimir [sword], he had a helmet on his head; then Mímir's head spoke wisely the first word and said true runes.

15. He said to carve runes on the shield, which stands before the shining god [the sun], on Árvakr's ear, and on Alsviðr's hoof, on the wheel which turns under Hrungnir's chariot, on Sleipnir's teeth and on the runners of the sleigh,

16. on the bear's paw, and on Bragi's tongue, on the wolf's claws and on the eagle's beak, on the bloody wings and on the bridge's head, on the midwife's palms and on the footprint of the healer (?),

17. on glass and on gold and on men's charms, in wine and in unfermented beer and on the seat of joy, on Gungnir's point and on Grani's breast, on the nail of a Norn and on the owl's beak.

18. All were scraped off which had been carved on, and stirred with the holy mead and sent out and abroad; these are with the Æsir, these are with the elves, some with the wise Vanir, some human beings have.

19. There are book-runes, there are birth-runes, and all the ale-runes, and valuable, mighty-runes, for the one who can have them for himself unconfused and undamaged as a charm—you will have

benefit if you have learned them, until the gods are destroyed.

20. Now you must choose, since the choice is offered to you, tree of the sharp weapons [warrior]: speech or silence—you have to decide for yourself. All evils are meted out [by fate]."

21. "I will not flee, although you know that I am doomed. I was not born to be a coward. I want to have all your friendly advice as long as I live."

22. "First, I counsel you that you should be blameless with your kinsmen; take no revenge, although they give you cause; they say that will do you good when you die (?).

23. Second, I counsel you that you do not swear an oath, unless you know it is true; grim fate follows troth-breaking, wretched is the oath-breaker.

24. Third, I counsel you that you do not deal with foolish men at the Þing, because the unwise man often speaks worse words than he knows.

25. It is quite risky if you are silent; then you appear to have been born a coward or charged with proof; unreliable is local repute unless it be good. The next day make him forfeit his life and reward people for the hateful lies!

26. Fourth, I counsel you that if a foul witch lives on your path, it is better to go on than to be her guest, although night may be overtaking you.

27. The sons of men need forseeing eyes, where they shall fight in anger; often evil women sit by the road, those who blunt both sword and spirit.

28. Fifth, I counsel you: even though you see fair women on the benches, do not let the bought love [of a woman] disturb your sleep, do not entice women to kiss you.

29. Sixth, I counsel you: although the ale-talk among men may turn hostile, do not argue with a drunken tree of fight [warrior]; wine steals the wit of many.

30. The song [of battle] and ale have been a sorrow to many a man, a slayer to some, bad luck to some; many are the griefs of men.

31. Seventh, I counsel you: if you exchange reproaches with a man full of courage, it is better for men to fight than to be burned within your own house.

32. Eighth, I counsel you: that you protect yourself against evil and shun deceit; do not tempt a maiden, nor a man's wife, nor incite them to lust.

33. Ninth, I counsel you that you bury corpses, where you find them on the earth, whether they are men who died from sickness or from drowning or from weapons.

34. A bath shall you make for those who are dead, wash their hands and head, comb and dry them, before they are placed in the coffin, and pray that they sleep in peace.

35. Tenth, I counsel you that you never trust the vows of an outlaw's son, whether you are his brother's slayer or you have felled his father; a wolf is in the young son, although he is gladdened by gold.

36. Battles and feuds, do not think they are sleeping, nor grief either; a warrior needs to have his wits and weapons, he who will be foremost among men.

37. Eleventh, I counsel you that you guard yourself against evil in every way with friends. Long life I do not seem to see for the prince: bitter are the quarrels which have arisen."

B. Celtic Analogues

1. "Gnomes I"

(Text: *EWGP*, I.)

These Welsh gnomes, dated between the ninth and tenth centuries, are from the Black Book of Carmarthen, written at the end of the twelfth century. They were edited in part in *CLlH* VII. 1–12, and edited and translated in *PLlH* 169–86; 188–92. The form is that of the *englyn*, the generic name for a three- or four-line stanza, tightly knit together by end and internal rhyme and alliteration. Each *englyn* in this poem combines nature description with nature gnome and many conclude with a human gnome. This strange mixture is typical of early Welsh "gnomic" poetry, although Jackson suggests the present poem may belong to a different tradition (*EWGP*, p. 3; see also Dillon, Jackson 1935, Parry, and *PWV*).

1. Sharp the wind, bare the hill, difficult to find shelter; the ford floods, the lake freezes; a man can stand upon a single reed.

2. Wave upon wave covers the coast; the wind whistles high before the mountain tops; one can hardly stand outside.

3. Cold is the lake from the crunch of winter; wrinkled the reeds, stalks broken; wrathful is the wind, trees bare.

4. Cold the clan of fish in icy shade; the stag lean, reeds bearded; evening is short, trees bowed down.

5. Snow falls, its cover white; warriors do not go about their business; cold are the lakes, their color lacks warmth.

6. Snow falls, white hoarfrost; idle the shield on an old man's shoulder; fierce the wind, grass freezes.

7. Snow falls upon ice; wind sweeps the tips of thick branches; mighty the shield on the shoulder of the brave.

8. Snow falls, it covers the vale; warriors hasten to battle; I do not go, a wound prevents me.

9. Snow falls along the slope; the steed a captive, cattle lean; not like a summer's day today.

10. Snow falls, mountain edged in white; naked the masts of ships at sea; a coward hatches many a plot.

11. Gold handles on drinking horns, horns among the host; paths are cold, the sky flashing; afternoon is short, treetops bent.

12. Bees in hives, birds' cries faint: a bleak day; white-cloaked the ridge, crimson the dawn.

13. Bees in shelter, cold the ford's cover; it freezes when there is ice; despite one's evasions, death shall come.

14. Bees in captivity, the sea green; reeds wrinkled, the slope solid; cold and raw is the world today.

15. Bees sheltered from winter's wetness; green are the grasses, cow-parsnips hollow; cowardice in a man is a wretched quality.

16. Long the night, the moor bare, the slope gray; green the shore, seagull in sea's spume; rough are the seas, there will be rain today.

17. Dry is the wind, the way wet, the watercourse in turmoil; cold is the grove, the stag lean, river in flood; fair weather will come.

18. Foul weather in mountains, rivers raging, flood drenches dwelling floors; it is the sea—seeing the world.

20. The bowed stag seeks a snug glen; ice crunches the bare countryside; the brave escape from many a strait.

21. The thrush's breast is speckled; speckled is the breast of the thrush.

21. The shore crunches beneath the hoof of a lean and bowed stag; aloft, the wind whistles; hardly at all can one stand outside.

22. First day of winter, dusky brown the heather tips; sea's wave foaming, day is short; let your counsel come to pass.

23. From the shelter of a shield and spirited steed, and men bold and brave, fair is the night to pursue a foe.

.

2. "Gnomes II"

(Text: *EWGP*, II.)

Here again we find the mixing of nature description with human and nature gnomes. As with "Gnomes I," the date of composition for these particular stanzas falls somewhere in the ninth or tenth centuries, perhaps a bit later. Whatever the date, this selection clearly belongs to an ancient tradition (see *EWP* and Parry).

1. Spear-bearing is the army, ash trees in bunches; ducks in a lake, the wave pebble-white; the heart is stronger than a hundred counsels.
2. Night is long, the bog bitter; commotion in assembly is common; good and evil do not coexist.
3. Night is long, the mountain severe; the wind whistles above the tree tops; the malicious do not deceive the righteous.
7. Branches of bramble and blackberries on them; the blackbird is in its nest, and the lying are never silent.
8. Rain outside, fern is wet; white the ocean's pebbles, spray of spume, too; a bright candle is man's reason.
9. Rain outside away from shelter; gorse is yellow, the cow-parsnip withered; Lord God, why did you bring into being the cowardly?
10. Rain outside, wets my hair; whiney are the weak, the precipice steep; ocean wan, the sea salty.
11. Rain outside, wets the depths; the wind whistles above the reed tips; empty each accomplishment without its proper talent.

3. "Gnomes III"

(*Bidiau*; text: *EWGP*, VII.)

The Welsh texts of the following stanzas, written between the ninth and twelfth centuries, all begin with the word *bid*, which is either the present third person singular consuetudinal or the third person singular imperative of the verb "to be." Therefore, one could translate either "is wont to be, is customarily," or "let (x) be." In proverbial and gnomic contexts, these two possibilities invite the meanings of "is by natural law" or "must be," rather like OE *sculan*. Hence, "a cock's comb is (to be) red (if it is to be a cock's comb)." In his edition, Jackson suggests that, given the very mixed nature of these gnomes and the exclusivity of some of the possible translations of *bid*, the best general translation is "is" (see *EWGP*, pp. 61–2, and Parry).

2. Swineherds rejoice in the wind's sighs; calm is beautiful; the outcast is used to adversity.

3. An inquisitor is accusing; the warrior is savage; clothes are close-fitting; whom the poet loves is a splendid giver.

4. A lion is king and is lively, and a wolf is in his lair; he does not save face who gives not.

5. Running is swift in the mountains; care is in the breast; the unfaithful are fickle.

6. A knight is conspicuous; thieves are skulking; a woman will defraud the prosperous; a lazy shepherd is the wolf's accomplice.

7. A knight is conspicuous; a steed runs; a lad loves learning; the deceitful are unfaithful.

8. Cattle are bowed and the wolf gray; lively is the steed after barley; a cobweb binds grain in its root.

9. The deaf person is hard of hearing, a hollow thing is concave; lively is the steed in battles; a cobweb binds grain where it is buried.

10. The deaf person says "eh, eh?"; the foolish are fickle; the pugnacious are mad; happy is he whose beloved looks upon him.

11. The lake is deep; spears are sharp; the brave in battle is a sturdy lion; who praises Him is wise and blessed of God.

12. An exile is a stranger; the rash are contentious; the foolish are inclined to laugh; plains are bare; leeks are pungent.

13. A furrow is wet; bail is frequent; the sick complain, the healthy are happy; the pup snarls; a hag is venomous.

14. A cry is mournful; an army is swift; the fat are lecherous; the brave are bold and the slope icy.

15. The seagull is white; the wave is high; the stain of blood is on ash; frost is gray; the lion is courageous.

17. A hen is taloned; the brave give battle; the foolish are feisty; the heart is broken from grief.

4. *Snow on the Mountains*

(*Eiry Mynydd*; text: *EWGP*, III.)

These stanzas, which, like the Llywarch Hen and Cynddylan poetry, come from the Red Book of Hergest, are what their editor prefers to call "quasi-gnomic" (*EWGP*, p. 3). Composed between the ninth and twelfth centuries, they belong to a long tradition of Welsh nature poetry and are chiefly descriptive. We may not understand how or why nature description and human gnomes fit together, but we need not consider one or the other as irrelevant or secondary (see *EWGP*, p. 1; *CLlH*, xliii–xliv). The present text allows us to assume that this peculiar form was a well-established and highly developed art (see Parry, p. 39; Jarman 1976, pp. 111–13; *PLlH*, pp. 37–8). As in most early Welsh *englyn* poetry, the verb "to be" is often omitted (see *EWP*, Parry, and *PWV*).

1. Snow on the mountains, everywhere white; customary for the crow to caw; no good comes from oversleeping.

2. Snow on the mountains, white the deep-sided brook; trees bow down before wind's rush; many a couple love each other and yet never touch.

3. Snow on the mountains, wind wafts it; broad the full moon, dock leaves green; the mischievous person is rarely blameless.

4. Snow on the mountains, the stag nimble; bold warriors are common in Britain; a stranger must be discerning.

5. Snow on the mountains, stag in heat; ducks in water, the surface white; slow the old, easily overtaken.

6. Snow on the mountains, stag moving on; the mind rejoices in what it loves; though I be told a tale, I recognize a flaw wherever it may be.

7. Snow on the mountains, pebble-white strand; fish in the ford, its shelter snug; hated is he who harrasses.

8. Snow on the mountains, stag startled; with a warrior, fine weapons are common, and mounting a saddle and attacking spear against spear.

9. Snow on the mountains, stag lean-shanked; often have I said, I know, this is unlike a summer's day.

10. Snow on the mountains, stag hunted; the wind whistles above the tower's eaves; dire, O man, is sin.

11. Snow on the mountains, stag leaping; the wind whistles over the high white wall; quiet is usually lovely.

12. Snow on the mountains, stag in the vale; the wind whistles over the front of the roof; evil does not conceal itself where it occurs.

13. Snow on the mountains, stag on the strand; the old misses his youth; bad vision makes a person a prisoner.

14. Snow on the mountains, stag in the bush; pure black the raven, swift the roebuck; healthy and free, a wonder why he complains.

15. Snow on the mountains, stag in brush; bogs are cold, mead in casks; the injured usually moan.

16. Snow on the mountains, besprinkled the crest of the tower; animals seek shelter; woe to the woman who has an evil husband.

17. Snow on the mountains, besprinkled the face of the rock; reeds withered, cattle not plunging; woe to the man who has an evil wife.

18. Snow on the mountains, stag in ditch; bees sleeping snug; a thief and a long night go hand in hand.

19. Snow on the mountains, liverwort in the river; slow in movement, the sluggish are not quick to avenge an insult.

20. Snow on the mountains, fish in the lake; proud the hawk, chieftains fine; those who want don't always get.

21. Snow on the mountains, lords' vanguard red; fierce are numerous spears; O, how I miss my brothers!

22. Snow on the mountains, swift the wolf; he stalks the edges of devastation; the wounded are usually wretched.

23. Snow on the mountains, the stag not slow; rain falls from the sky; the disheartened nurtures sadness.

24. Snow on the mountains, deer nimble; waves wet the shore; let the skilful conceal his plan.

25. Snow on the mountains, stag in glen; summer is temperate, the lake calm; gray-bearded the frost; the clever one to the edge of the bed.

26. Snow on the mountains, besprinkled the edges of trees; strong is my arm and my shoulder; I pray that I shall not reach a hundred.

27. Snow on the mountains, bare the tips of reeds; ends of branches bowed down, fish down deep; where there is no learning, there is no real talent.

28. Snow on the mountains, fish in the ford; the lean, hunched stag seeks glen's shelter; longing for the dead does not avail.

29. Snow on the mountains, stag in the wood; the fortunate does not travel on foot; the coward fosters much harm.

30. Snow on the mountains, stag on the slope; the wind whistles above the tips of the ash; the old one's third foot: his walking stick.

31. Snow on the mountains, stag swimming; ducks in a lake, white the water lily; the perverse does not want to listen.

32. Snow on the mountains, hens' feet red; shallow is the water where it babbles; boasting increases dishonor.

33. Snow on the mountains, the stag nimble; rarely does the world concern me; a warning to the unfortunate does not avail.

34. Snow on the mountains, its fleece white; wonderful is the dear face of a kinsman, seen often.

35. Snow on the mountains, rooftops white; if the tongue told what the heart felt, such a one would have no neighbors.

36. Snow on the mountains, day has come; the wretched are all ill, the base half-covered; the foolish have every defect.

5. *Advice to a Prince*

(*Audacht Morainn*, "The Testament of Morann";
text: *AM*, pp. 4–15.)

Unlike the OE poems of wisdom and advice, the OIr "advice to princes" poems, of which *Audacht Morainn* is the prime example, do not deal with the "fates of men," but rather with the "natural laws of kingship." While there is clear Christian influence on the OE texts, the *Audacht Morainn* appears to be a remnant of a tradition as yet insulated from Christian homiletics. Both the language and the structure of the poem are extremely archaic and the oldest stratum of the text is virtually free of Latin loan words (see *AM*, p. xvi). The king is depicted here as the bringer of justice, peace, and fertility by a kind of sympathetic magic, but a magic clearly tempered by common sense. A similar archaic picture can be seen in the MW *Praise of Urien*.

Morainn is a legendary judge in whose mouth this advice is placed. Other early and late Irish examples of this genre, the *speculum principis*, indicate that such poems may have been intended to be recited at royal inaugurations. The frame material has been omitted.

4. Let him [the new king] keep my advice which here follows:
5. Declare to him before every [other] word.
6. Bring this to him along with every word:
7. Let him guard justice, it will guard him.
8. Let him elevate mercy, it will elevate him.
9. Let him take care of his tribes, they will take care of him.
10. Let him help his tribes, they will help him.
11. Let him soothe his tribes, they will soothe him.
12. Tell him: it is through the justice of the ruler that plagues, great lightnings, are warded off from the people.
13. It is through the justice of the ruler that he governs great tribes and great wealth.
14. It is through the justice of the ruler that he secures peace, ease, joy, rest, comfort.
15. It is through the justice of the ruler that he sends fighters to

the border of hostile neighbors.

16. It is through the justice of the ruler that every heir can place his house-post in [the land of] his proper inheritance.

17. It is through the justice of the ruler that the manna of the great acorns of the great wood continues to be tasted.

18. It is through the justice of the ruler that the yields of milk of great cattle continue to be maintained.

19. It is through the justice of the ruler that there continues to be abundance of every tall, high grain.

20. It is through the justice of the ruler that an abundance of fish swim in streams.

21. It is through the justice of the ruler that beautiful children are well begotten.

22. Tell him: as he is young, his rule is young.
> Let him observe the driver of an old chariot, for the driver of an old wheel-rim does not sleep.
> He looks before, he looks behind, forward, and to the right and to the left.
> He looks, he protects, he releases, so that he may not break by neglect or violence the wheel-rims that run under him.

23. Tell him: he ought not to elevate any judge unless he [the judge] should know the true legal precedents.

24. It is through the justice of the ruler that every advanced craftsman reaches the crown of wisdom. It is afterwards that he will sit to teach the good rule which he has accepted.

25. It is through the justice of the ruler that the borders of every true nobleman extend so that each cow may reach the end of its grazing.

26. It is through the justice of the ruler that every garment of clothing is obtained at a glance.

27. It is through the justice of the ruler that enclosures protecting cattle and every product extend.

28. It is through the justice of the ruler that the three immunities from violence protect every land's chief at every assembly from disturbances during his glorious rule's time:
> The first immunity: racing horses at assemblies.
> The second of the immunities: encampment.
> The third immunity: the privilege of the ale-house with companions, with great provisions of the mead-circuit, where foolish and wise, familiar and unfamiliar, are intoxicated.

29. Tell him: he ought not to redden many fore-courts, for bloodshed is a vain pouring-away of every rule, with protection of kin for a ruler (?).

30. Tell him: he should give any reciprocal service which is due from him; let him bind what he should bind; let him cancel the blushing of his cheeks [shame] with sharp edges in battles against other territories, against their oaths, against their defending.

31. Tell him: that neither fortunate gifts, nor great wealth, nor advantage should blind him to the suffering lowly [ones].

32. Tell him: he should estimate the creations of the creator who made them as they were made; anything he will not judge for its remunerations, it will not be full fruits that it gives them.

33. Let him estimate the earth by its fruits.

34. Let him estimate the yew-wood by its fitness for sale.

35. Let him estimate milk-yield by its growth.

36. Let him estimate grain by its height.

37. Let him estimate streams by clean washing.

38. Let him estimate iron by its fitness [in settling] disputes between tribes.

39. Let him estimate copper by its solidity, firmness, dense substance.

40. Let him estimate silver by its life, strength, white composition.

41. Let him estimate gold by its wonderful foreign decoration.

42. Let him estimate soil by its performance in which he may seek produce.

43. Let him estimate sheep by their fleece which is chosen for clothing for the tribes.

44. Let him estimate pigs by their fat side, for it is of every face a redeeming of decorum (?).

45. Let him judge the retinue of a true lord; for to every king is the rule of his troop. Anything he will not judge for its remunerations, it will not be full fruits that it gives them.

VI

WIDSITH

A. Celtic Analogues

1. *The Battle of the Trees*

(*Cad Goddeu*; text: *BT* 23.09–27.12.)

Or, *The Army of the Trees*. This Welsh poem, perhaps ninth century, and others like it from the Book of Taliesin are obscure both in meaning and function (see *PT*, pp. xiv–xxiii; *M*, pp. 16–21, 159–87; Williams 1944). Yet we can perceive that it deals with the concept of the poet as a "wide traveller," not only in space but also in time. Taliesin is renowned for his "eternal" character, a symbol, perhaps , of the archetypal poet/sage, co-eval with the world itself. The references to Math, Gwydion, and Dylan Eil Mor will strike a note in those familiar with the fourth branch of the *Mabinogi*, "Math fab Mathonwy."

I was in many shapes before I was released: I was a slender, enchanted sword—I believe that it was done. I was raindrops in the air, I was stars' beam; I was a word in letters, I was a book in origin; I was lanterns of light for a year and a half; I was a bridge that stretched over sixty estuaries; I was a path, I was an eagle, I was a coracle in seas; I was a bubble in beer, I was a drop in a shower; I was a sword in hand, I was a shield in battle. I was a string in a harp enchanted nine years, in the water as foam; I was a spark in fire, I was wood in a bonfire; I am not one who does not sing; I have sung since I was small. I sang in the army of the trees' branches before the ruler of Britain. I wounded swift horses, destroyed powerful fleets; I wounded a great scaley animal: a hundred heads on him and a fierce host beneath the base of his tongue, and another host is on his necks: a black, forked toad—a hundred claws on him, an enchanted, crested snake in whose skin a hundred souls are punished. I was in Caer Nefenhir where grass and trees attacked, poets sang, warriors rushed forth. Gwydion raised his staff of enchantment, called upon the Lord, upon Christ, making pleas so that He, the Lord who made him, might deliver him. The Lord replied in language and in the land: "Transform stalwart trees into armies with him and obstruct Peblig the powerful from giving battle." When the trees were enchanted, in the hope of our purpose, they hewed down trees with . . . . Three chieftains fell in grievous days' battles. A maiden uttered a bitter sigh, grief broke forth; foremost in lineage, pre-eminent maiden. Life and wakefulness gain us no vantage in Mellun: men's blood up to our thighs. The three greatest upheavals that have happened in the world: and one comes to pass in the story of the flood, and Christ's crucifying, and then Doomsday. Alder, pre-eminent in lineage, attacked in the beginning, willow and rowan were late to the army; thorny plum was greedy for slaughter; powerful dog-wood, resisting prince; rose-trees went against a host in wrath; raspberry bushes performed, did not make an enclosure for the protection of life . . . and honeysuckle, and ivy for its beauty; sea-gorse for terror. Cherries mocked; birch for high-mindedness— it was late that it armed, not because of cowardice, but because of greatness. Goldenrod held a shape, foreigners over foreign waters; fir trees to the fore, ruler in battles; ash performed excellently before monarchs; elm because of its ferocity did not budge a foot: it would strike in the middle, on the flanks and in the end. Hazel wood was deemed arms for the tumult; happy the privet, bull of battle, lord of the world . . . fir trees prospered; holly turned green, it was in battle; fine hawthorn delivered pain. Attacking vines attacked in battle; destructive fern; broom before the host were ploughed under. Gorse was not lucky, but despite that it was turned into an army, fine fighting heather was changed into a host, pursuer of men. Swift and mighty oak: before him trembled heaven and earth; fierce enemy of warriors, his name in wax tablets . . . tree gave terror in combat; he used to oppose, he opposed others from a hole; pear worked oppression in the battle-field, fearful drawing up of a flood of noble trees. Chestnut, shame of the prince of fir trees. Jet is black, mountains are rounded, trees are sharp; great seas are swifter since I heard the scream. Tips of birch sprouted for us, immutable energy; tips of oak stained for us

from *Gwarchan Maeldderw*, laughing from the hillside, a lord not
. . . Not from a mother and father was I made; as for creation, I
was created from nine forms of elements: from the fruit of fruits,
from the fruit of God at the beginning; from primroses and flowers
of the hill, from the blooms of woods and trees; from the essence
of soils was I made; from the bloom of nettles, from water of the
ninth wave. Math enchanted me before I was mobile; Gwydion
created me, great magic from the staff of enchantment. From
Eurwys and Euron, from Euron and Modron, from five fifties of
magicians and teachers like Math was I produced. The lord produced me when he was quite inflamed; the magician of magicians
created me before the world—when I had existence, there was
expanse to the world. Fair bard! Our custom is profit; I can put in
song what the tongue can utter. I passed time at dawn, I slept in
purple; I was in the rampart with Dylan Eil Mor, in a cloak in the
middle between kings, in two lusty spears that came from heaven;
in Annwfn they will sharpen in the battle to which they will come;
four-score hundred I pierced because of their lust—they are
neither older nor younger than I in their passion. The passion of a
hundred men is needed by each; I had that of nine hundred. In an
enchanted sword, renowned blood flowing in me from a lord from
his place of concealment; from a drop was the warrior killed.
Peoples were made, re-made, and made again. The brilliant one
his name, the strong hand; like lightning he governed the host.
They scattered in sparks from the tame one on high. I was a snake
enchanted in a hill, I was a viper in a lake. I was a star with a shaft;
I was this hunting-shaft. Not badly shall I prepare my cloak and
cup. Four twenties of smoke will come upon each. Five fifties of
bondmaids the value of my knife; six yellowish-brown horses—a
hundred times is better; my pale-yellow horse is swift as a seagull;
I myself am not feeble between sea and shore. I shall cause a field
of blood, on it a hundred warriors; scaley and red my shield, gold
is my shield-ring. There was not born in Adwy anyone who
attacked me except Goronwy from the dales of Edrywy. Long and
white are my fingers; long have I not been a shepherd. I lived as a
warrior before I was a man of letters; I wandered, I encircled, I
slept in a hundred islands, I dwelt in a hundred forts. Druids, wise
one, prophesy to Arthur: there is what is before, they perceive
what has been. And one occurs in the story of the flood, and
Christ's crucifying and then Doomsday. Golden, gold-skinned, I
shall deck myself in riches, and I shall be in luxury because of the
prophecy of Virgil.

2. *Taliesin's Travels*

(Text: NLW Ms. 6209E, pp. 157–8.)

Although this poem survives only in a late, post-medieval manuscript, it seems to belong to the ancient traditions of the legendary
Taliesin (*PT*, pp. xv–xix; *M*, pp. 16–21; Williams 1944). As in *The
Battle of the Trees* (q.v.), the speaker claims to have travelled far
and wide in time and space—not in the mythological world of that
poem but in one that rings with biblical and classical allusions. The
allusions to Ceridwen and Gwion Bach refer to Taliesin's earlier
state, when he first acquired magical wisdom and knowledge, was
swallowed by the witch in the shape of a hen, and was reborn as
Taliesin (for the story, see *The Tale of Gwion Bach* and *The Tale
of Taliesin* in *M*, pp. 159–81).

I was with my lord in the heavens when Lucifer fell into the
depths of hell; I carried a banner before Alexander; I know the
stars' names from the North to the South. I was in the fort of
Gwydion, in the Tetragrammaton; I was in the canon when
Absalon was killed. I brought seed down to the vale of Hebron. I
was in the court of Don before the birth of Gwydion. I was
patriarch to Elijah and Enoch; I was head keeper on the work of
Nimrod's tower; I was atop the Cross of the merciful Son of God. I
was three times in the prison of Arianrhod. I was in the ark with
Noah and Alpha; I witnessed the destruction of Sodom and
Gomorrah. I was in Africa before the building of Rome; I came
here to the survivors of Troy. And I was with my Lord in the
manger of oxen and asses; I upheld Moses through the water of
Jordan; I was in the sky with Mary Magdalen. I got poetic
inspiration from the cauldron of Ceridwen; I was poet-harper to
Lleon Llychlyn; I was in Gwynfryn in the court of Cynfelyn, in
stock and fetters a day and a year. I was revealed in the land of the
Trinity, and I was moved through the entire universe; and I shall
remain till Doomsday upon the face of the earth. And no one
knows what my flesh is, whether meat or fish. And I was nearly
nine months in the womb of the witch Ceridwen; I was formerly
Gwion Bach, but now I am Taliesin.

3. *Amargein's Song*

(From the *Lebor Gabála Érenn*, or "Book of Invasions";
text: *LGE*, pp. 110–11.)

Amargein is depicted as having been the poet of the "sons of
Mil," last of the legendary invaders of Ireland and ancestors of the
early Gaelic ruling houses. *Lebor Gabála* as we have it was compiled no earlier than the eleventh century, but this poem appears
to date ultimately from pre-Christian, possibly pagan vatic, poetry.
Amargein's Song carries more of a magical poetic claim than
Widsith's boast, and seems to stem from a tradition similar to that
revealed in the MW *Taliesin's Travels*. The final two questions
may either be glosses incorporated into the text at some stage or
an attempt to make the poem into a riddle.

I am wind on the sea. I am a storm-wave. I am ocean's roar. I
am a seven-antlered stag. I am a hawk of the cliff. I am a dew-drop
["a drop of the sun"]. I am a fair body. I am a boar for valor. I am
a salmon in a pool. I am a lake in a plain. I am a word of their
poetic art. I am a word of skill. I am a spear in cutting, which pours
out savagery. I am a god who makes antlers for the head.
Who clears the stony-places of a mountain? Who is the one who
ordains the phases of the moon? Who, also, where the sunset falls?
Who brings the cattle from the house of Tethra? Who touches the
cattle of Tethra?
Who is the troop, who the god, who sharpens their blistered
points? Wordspells about a spear? Wordspells of wind?

VII

RIDDLES

A. Germanic Analogue

1. *The Riddles of Gestumblindi*

(from *Heiðreks saga*, or *Hervarar saga*; text: *SKHW*, pp. 32–44.)

The only extant Germanic analogues to the large collection of OE Riddles in *The Exeter Book* are *The Riddles of Gestumblindi* found in *Heiðreks saga*. Christopher Tolkien notes that they are unique in two ways: 1) there are no others to be found in ON, and 2) there are no parallels to them in content throughout world literature (*SKHW*, p. xix; see also Heusler and Einarsson, S.). We note that the riddles bear some resemblances to the "contest of wits" in such other Eddic poems as *The Lay of Vafðrúðnir* (q.v.). *Heiðreks saga* is from the classical period (late thirteenth century), but the riddles seem to have existed some time before the composition of the saga.

There was a man called Gestumblindi [the blind guest], a mighty man and a great enemy of King Heiðrekr. The king sent him word that he should come meet him and come to terms with him, if he wanted to preserve his life. Gestumblindi was not a great wise man, and for that reason, since he knew he was unable to debate the king and knew also that it would be risky to depend on the judgment of wise men, because his offenses were many, Gestumblindi decided on this plan: he would sacrifice to Óðinn for help and ask him to consider his case and promise him great gifts. Late one evening there was a knock on the door, and Gestumblindi went to the door and saw that a man had come. He asked him his name; he called himself Gestumblindi and said that they should switch clothes and so they did. The master of the house now went away and hid himself, but the new arrival went in, and it seemed to all there that they recognized Gestumblindi, and the night passed by.

On the next day, Gestumblindi made his way to meet the king, and he greeted the king respectfully. The king was silent.

"Lord," he said, "I have come here because I wish to come to terms with you."

Then the king answered, "Will you suffer the judgment of my wise men?"

He said, "Are there no other ways to clear myself?"

The king said, "There are other ways, if you think yourself able to tell riddles."

Gestumblindi said, "I am little able to do this, but the alternative is likely to be hard."

"Would you," said the king, "rather suffer the judgment of my wise men?"

"I choose," he said, "to tell riddles instead."

"That is right and well fitting," said the king.

Then Gestumblindi said:

(44) "I wish I had what I had yesterday; guess what that was. A crippler of people, a stopper, but also a starter of words. King Heiðrekr, consider this riddle!"

The king said, "Your riddle is good, Gestumblindi, I have guessed it. Bring him ale. That cripples the wits of many a man, and many are the more eager to talk, when ale gets the better of them; but with some the tongue gets tangled up, so that no word comes out."

Then Gestumblindi said:

(45) "From home I travelled, from home I made a journey, I looked on the way of ways; there was a way under that and a way over, and a way on all ways. King Heiðrekr, consider this riddle!"

"Your riddle is good, Gestumblindi, I have guessed it. You travelled there over a river-bridge, and under you was the way of the river, but birds flew over your head, and on both sides of you, and that was their way."

Then Gestumblindi said:

(46) "What is that drink, which I drank yesterday, that was not wine nor water, mead nor ale, nor anything of food, and I went thirstless thence? King Heiðrekr, consider this riddle!"

"Your riddle is good, Gestumblindi—I have guessed it. You lay there in the shade, when dew had fallen on the grass and cooled your lips and quenched your thirst."

Then Gestumblindi said:

(47) "Who is that shrill one who walks on hard paths, which he has travelled before; he kisses very firmly, the one who has two mouths, and walks only on gold? King Heiðrekr, consider this riddle!"

"Your riddle is good, Gestumblindi, I have guessed it. That is the hammer which is used in the goldsmith's work; it calls out loudly when it hits on the hard anvil and that is its path."

Then Gestumblindi said:

(48) "What is that wonder which I saw outside in front of Dellingr's door; two lifeless things without breath, they boiled a wound-leek [they forged a sword?]. King Heiðrekr, consider this riddle!"

"Your riddle is good, Gestumblindi, I have guessed it. Those are the smith's bellows; they have no wind, unless they are blown, and they are as dead as the smith's other work, but with them one can forge a sword as well as other things."

Then Gestumblindi said:

(49) "What is that wonder which I saw outside in front of Dellingr's door; it has eight legs and four eyes and it bears its knees higher than its belly? King Heiðrekr, consider this riddle!"

"Those are spiders."

Then Gestumblindi said:

(50) "What is that wonder which I saw outside in front of Dellingr's door; its head points toward Hel's road, but its feet turn towards the sun? King Heiðrekr, consider this riddle!"

"Your riddle is good, Gestumblindi, I have guessed it; it is the leek; its head is fast in the ground, but it branches out as it grows up."

Then Gestumblindi spoke:

(51) "What is that wonder which I saw outside in front of Dellingr's door; harder than a horn, blacker than a raven, whiter than a shield, straighter than a shaft? King Heiðrekr, consider this riddle!"

Heiðrekr spoke, "Your riddles are becoming feebler, Gestumblindi; what need is there to sit over this longer? That is the agate, with a sunbeam shining on it."

Then Gestumblindi spoke:

(52) "Fair-haired brides, two bondmaids, carried a cask of ale to the storehouse; that was not turned by hand nor shaped by a hammer, though the one who made it was upright off the islands. King Heiðrekr, consider this riddle!"

"Your riddle is good, Gestumblindi, I have guessed it; swan-brides travel there to their nest and lay eggs; the eggshell is not made by hands nor shaped by a hammer, and the swan that was upright off the islands is the one with whom they begot the eggs."

Then Gestumblindi spoke:

(53) "What women are they on the wild mountain, woman with woman begets, maiden with maiden begets a son—and these women have no husbands? King Heiðrekr, consider this riddle!"

"Your riddle is good, Gestumblindi, I have guessed it; these are two angelicas and an angelica shoot between them."

Then Gestumblindi said:

(54) "I saw travelling a mould-dweller of the earth, a corpse sat on a corpse; a blind one rode a blind one to the surf-conveyer [the sea], the steed was without breath. King Heiðrekr, consider this riddle!"

"Your riddle is good, Gestumblindi, I have guessed it; you found a dead horse there on an ice-floe and a dead snake on the horse and they all drifted together down the river."

Then Gestumblindi said:

(55) "Who are the thanes who ride to the Þing all at peace together; they send their troops over the lands to settle a homestead? King Heiðrekr, consider this riddle!"

"Your riddle is good, Gestumblindi, I have guessed it; it is Ítrekr and Anðaðr, those who sit at their board-game."

Then Gestumblindi said:

(56) "Who are those women who fight around their defence-less king; the brown-haired ones guard him every day, but the fair go forth? King Heiðrekr, consider this riddle!"

"Your riddle is good, Gestumblindi, I have guessed it; this is the game of *hnefatafl* [a kind of chess]; the darker ones defend the *hnefi* [the king], but the white ones attack."

Then Gestumblindi spoke:

(57) "Who is that one alone, who sleeps in the hearth-pit, and who is made only out of stone; neither father nor mother does he, the "brightness-eager" one, have; there will he live out his life. King Heiðrekr, consider this riddle!"

"That is fire, stored on the hearth, and struck out of flint."

Then Gestumblindi said:

(58) "Who is that powerful one who passes over the ground; he swallows water and wood. He fears the wind, but no man, and he wages war with the sun? King Heiðrekr, consider this riddle!"

"Your riddle is good, Gestumblindi, I have guessed it; that is fog:

it passes over the ground, so that one can see nothing because of it, not even the sun; but it is gone as soon as the wind comes up."

Then Gestumblindi spoke:

(59) "What is that creature that kills men's flocks—and is encircled on the outside with iron; it has eight horns but no head, and a great many follow it? King Heiðrekr, consider this riddle!"

"That is the *húnn* [bear's cub—a gaming piece] in *hnefatafl*."

Then Gestumblindi spoke:

(60) "What is that creature which protects the Danes [warriors]; it has a bloody back, but it guards men, it meets spears, gives life to some, a man puts his body in the hollow of its hand? King Heiðrekr, consider this riddle!"

"That is the shield; it often becomes bloody in battle and it guards the men well, those who are shield-handy."

Then Gestumblindi spoke:

(61) "Who are those playmates, who pass over the lands, and puzzle their father (?); they carry white shields in winter but black ones in summer? King Heiðrekr, consider this riddle!"

"Those are ptarmigans [arctic birds]; they are white in winter and black in summer."

Then Gestumblindi spoke:

(62) "Who are those women, who go about mourning, and puzzle their father (?); to many men they have caused harm, thus they will live out their lives? King Heiðrekr, consider this riddle!"

"Those are the maids of Hlér [the waves], who are thus called."

Then Gestumblindi spoke:

(63) "Who are those maidens who go many together and puzzle their father (?); they have pale hair and white hoods, yet those women do not have husbands? King Heiðrekr, consider this riddle!"

"Those are the billows, which are thus called."

Then Gestumblindi spoke:

(64) "Who are those women who go all together, and puzzle their father (?); they are seldom kind to the race of men and they have to stay awake in the wind? King Heiðrekr, consider this riddle!"

"Those are the women of Ægir; thus the waves are called."

Then Gestumblindi spoke:

(65) "Once a goose grew great, eager for children, the one who brought building-timber together; straw-biting swords protected her, yet the roaring drink-lava field lay above her. King Heiðrekr, consider this riddle!"

"A duck had built its nest there between the jaw-bones of an ox, and the skull lay above her."

Then Gestumblindi spoke:

(66) "What is that great one, who rules much and turns half towards Hel; it guards men and strives with the earth, if it has a well trusted friend for itself? King Heiðrekr, consider this riddle!"

"Your riddle is good, Gestumblindi, I have guessed it; that is the anchor with a good rope; if its fluke is in the ground, it will keep one safe."

Then Gestumblindi spoke:

(67) "Who are those women who walk in the sea-skerries and they trek along the firth; they have hard beds, those white-hooded women, and they play little in calm weather? King Heiðrekr, consider this riddle!"

"Those are the waves, and their beds are skerries and heaps of stones, and they are little to be seen in calm weather."

Then Gestumblindi spoke:

(68) "In summer I saw a band of retainers awake at sunset. They were not cheerful at all; the warriors drank ale in silence and the ale-cask stood crying out. King Heiðrekr, consider this riddle!"

"There piglets drank from a sow, and she was squealing."

Then Gestumblindi spoke:

(69) "What is that wonder which I saw outside in front of Dellingr's door? It has ten tongues, twenty eyes, and on forty feet it goes. King Heiðrekr, consider this riddle!"

Then the king said, "If you are the Gestumblindi whom I thought, then you are wiser than I supposed; you're talking now about the sow out in the yard."

Then the king had the sow killed, and it had nine piglets inside, as Gestumblindi had said. Now the king began to suspect who the man must be.

Then Gestumblindi spoke:

(70) "Four hang, four walk, two show the way, two guard against the dogs, one lags behind and is always dirty. King Heiðrekr, consider this riddle!"

"Your riddle is good, Gestumblindi, I have guessed it; that is a cow."

Then Gestumblindi spoke:

(71) "I sat on a sail, I saw dead men bearing a blood-hollow to the bark of a tree. King Heiðrekr, consider this riddle!"

"There you sat on a wall and saw a falcon carry an eider-duck to the crags."

Then Gestumblindi spoke:
> (72) "Who are those two who have ten feet, three eyes, and one tail? King Heiðrekr, consider this riddle!"

"That is the case when Óðinn rides on Sleipnir."

Then Gestumblindi spoke, "Say then this last thing, if you are wiser than any other king:
> (73) What did Óðinn speak in Baldr's ear before he was borne to the pyre?"

King Heiðrekr said, "You alone know that, you despicable creature!"—and then Heiðrek drew out Tyrfingr and hacked at him, but Óðinn changed himself into the shape of a falcon and flew away; yet the king struck after him and cut off his tail-feathers from behind, and that is why the falcon has had such short tail-feathers ever since.

Then Óðinn spoke: "For this, King Heiðrekr, since you have attacked me and wanted to kill me without cause, the worst thralls shall be your slayers." After that they parted.

B. Celtic Analogue

1. *The Song of the Wind*

(*Canu y Gwynt*; text: *BT* 36.22–37.19.)

The title of this tenth-century (?) Welsh poem is given in the manuscript, so that scholars have not had to guess the riddle. Furthermore, the celebrated fourteenth-century poet, Dafydd ap Gwilym, wrote a riddle-poem on the wind, which echoes many of the wind's characteristics found here (see *MWL*, *PWV*). Other examples of riddles in early Welsh are hard to find (see *EWP*, Jarman 1976, Parry). The Taliesin legend does contain some pseudo-riddling scientific queries, which are old or reflect an old tradition that surely played a part in bardic contests (*M*, p. 175).

Guess who it is: He was created before the flood, a strong creature without flesh or bone, without veins and without blood, without head and without feet. He is not older nor younger than the beginning; he is not brought from his purpose by fear or death; he has no need of living creatures. Great God, the mighty winds— whence do they come in origin? Great are the miracles of Him who made him. He in the field and in the woods, without hand, without foot, without old age or longing, without suffering death. And he is the same age of the five ages of the five periods, and he is even older how many fifties of years! And he is as broad as the face of the earth. And he was not born and was not seen. On the sea and on land he sees not and is not seen. He is disloyal and does not come when wanted. On land and on sea he is indispensable; he is peerless and irresistible. He is from the four corners, he takes no advice . . . [BT 37.11–12] . . . Sometimes noisy, sometimes mute, he is untamed. He is mighty and he is bold as he travels over the land. Sometimes mute, sometimes noisy, he roars. His turbulence is the greatest on earth. He is good, he is bad, he is obscure, he is conspicuous, since no eye sees him. He is bad, he is good, he is yonder, he is here. He brings disorder and does not compensate for what he does, does not repair his damages. And he is not to blame. He is wet, he is dry, he comes often.

VIII

JUDGMENT DAY POEMS

A. Germanic Analogues

1. *The Prophecy of the Seeress*

(*Vǫlospá*; text: *Edda*, pp. 1–15.)

Apocalyptic motifs are common to the literatures of the world. *The Prophecy of the Seeress* is often regarded as the premier achievement both of its kind and of ON poetry generally. It deals with the whole sweep of human, natural, and supernatural history and appropriately begins the *Edda*. Possibly dating from the ninth or tenth century, *Vǫlospá* describes the creation of the world, the chaos that emerges in the course of history, and the destruction of the universe in *Ragnarǫk*—"the doom of the gods." Grounded in pagan tradition, this prophetic poem also includes some possible Christian influences. As Turville-Petre notes, however, "It is often difficult to know whether a motive is pagan or Christian, or whether it was common to both traditions" (1964, p. 282; see also Bellows, Hallberg, Hollander, and Nordal). *Vǫlospá* is composed in *fornyrðislag* meter.

1. Silence I ask of all the holy race, the high and the low, the sons of Heimdallr. You want, Valfǫðr, me to recount well the ancient tales of the living which I remember from the remotest past.

2. I remember the giants, born of yore, those who once reared me; nine worlds I remember, nine rafters (?), the famous world-tree beneath the earth.

3. Long ago were the times when Ymir lived: there were neither sands, nor seas, nor cool waves; the earth did not exist at all, nor the heavens above; there was a yawning gap (?) and grass nowhere.

4. Then the sons of Burr lifted up the land, they who created glorious Miðgarðr. The sun shone from the south on the earth's stones; then the ground was grown with green plants.

5. From the south, the sun, the moon's companion, cast its right hand over heaven's rim; the sun did not know where it had a dwelling; the stars did not know where they had a place; the moon did not know what power it had.

6. Then all the gods went to the tribunal, the most holy gods, and held council: they gave a name to night and the waning moon; they named morning and midday, afternoon and evening, reckoned [time] in years.

7. The Æsir met at Iðavǫllr, where they built high-timbered shrines and temples; smithies they built, treasures they forged; they shaped tongs and made tools.

8. In their enclosure they played at tables, happy they were; they lacked nothing of gold, until three giant maidens came, greatly powerful, from Iǫtunheimar.

9.–16. [Catalogue of dwarves omitted.]

17. Until three came out of the host, mighty and gracious, the Æsir, to the house: on the land they found Askr and Embla, with little strength, unfated.

18. They did possess breath, they did not have feeling, the warmth of life, movement nor good color: Óðinn gave them breath, Hœnir gave them feeling, Lóðurr gave them the warmth of life and good color.

19. I know where an ash tree stands, called Yggdrasill, a high tree, moistened with white water; dews come from there, which fall into the valleys; green it always stands above Urðr's well.

20. Maidens come from there, very wise, three from the water which stands under the tree; one is called Urðr, the second Verðandi,—they carved on wood—Skuld the third; they made laws, they measured out lives for the children of men, the fates of men.

21. She remembers that battle, the first in the world, when they pierced Gullveig with spears, and burned her in Hár's hall, thrice burned, thrice born, again and again, though she still lives.

22. Heiðr they called her, wherever she came to a house, the seeress skilled in prophecy, she practiced magic (?); she cast spells where she could, she cast spells on deluded minds, she was always a delight to wicked women.

23. Then all the gods went to the tribunal, the most holy gods,

and held council: should the Æsir pay tribute, or should all the gods share the payment?

24. Óðinn let fly [his spear] and shot into the host: that was the first battle in the world; the wall of the Æsir's fortress was broken, the Vanir, prophets of war, trod the field.

25. Then all the gods went to the tribunal, the most holy gods, and held council: who had mixed all the air with venom and who had given Óðr's wife to the giant's race?

26. Þórr alone fought there, swollen with rage; he seldom sits still when he hears about such things. Oaths were broken, words and vows, all weighty agreements, which had passed between them.

27. She knows where Heimdallr's horn is hidden, under the sunlit holy tree; she sees a river pour in a cascading (?) stream from Valfǫðr's pledge [Óðinn's one eye]—do you want to know more or not?

28. She sat outside alone, when the old one came, Yggiungr of the Æsir, and looked in her eye: "What would you learn from me? Why do you test me? I know all about where you hid your eye, Óðinn: in the famous well of Mímir. Mímir drinks mead every morning from Valfǫðr's pledge—do you want to know more or not?

29. Herfǫðr chose rings and necklaces for her; she got wise spells and a divining rod (?)—she saw far and wide through every world.

30. She saw the valkyries come from afar, ready to ride to Goðþióð; Skuld held her shield, and Skǫgul another, Gunnr, Hildr, Gǫndul, and Geirskǫgul: now are listed the maidens of Heriann, valkyries ready to ride over the earth.

31. I saw the fate hidden for Baldr, for the bloody victim, Óðinn's son: it stood fully grown higher than the fields, the frail and very fair mistletoe.

32. There came from that tree, which seemed so frail, a dangerous, grievous weapon; Hǫðr took aim. Baldr's brother was born soon after; one-night old he, Óðinn's son, began to fight.

33. He did not wash his hands nor comb his hair until he bore Baldr's enemy to the pyre; and Frigg wept in Fensalir for Valhǫll's woe—do you want to know more or not?

34. Then from Váli they twisted battle-bonds, which were very hard fetters [made] out of his guts.

35. She saw a captive lie by the grove of the kettle [hot-spring?] in shape like guileful Loki; there sits Sigyn, yet she is not very joyful about her mate—do you want to know more or not?

36. A river with knives and swords flows from the east through

poisonous valleys. It is called Slíðr.

37. There stood to the north in Niðavellir a golden hall of Sindri's race; and another stood at Ókólnir, the beer-hall of the giant, who is called Brimir.

38. She saw a hall stand far from the sun on Nástrǫnd; its doors turn to the north. Poison drops fell from its roof vents, the hall is wound with the backs of snakes.

39. There she saw men wading through heavy streams, oath-breakers and murderers, and him who seduces another's wife; there Níðhǫggr sucked the dead corpses, the wolf tore men—do you want to know more or not?

40. In the east the old one sat in Iárnviðr and raised Fenrir's race there: a certain one from all of them will become the sun's destroyer in a troll's shape.

41. He takes his fill of the life-strength (?) of doomed men; he reddens the homes of the gods with red gore; the sunshine will be black in summers after, the weather all malevolent—do you want to know more or not?

42. He sat there on a mound and struck his harp, guardian of the giantess, glad Eggþér; the bright-red cock, which is called Fialarr, sang over him in the gallows tree.

43. Gullinkambi sang over the Æsir; he wakes the men of Heriafǫðr; and another sings below the earth, a sooty-red cock, in the halls of Hel.

44. Garmr barks loudly before Gnipahellir. His fetter will break and the wolf will run free; she knows many things. Farther in the future I see the mighty fate of the gods, of the victory-gods.

45. Brother will strike brother and slay each other, sisters' sons will break kinship; hard it will be in the world, great whoredom, axe-age, sword-age, shields will be cloven, wind-age, wolf-age before the world falls; no man will spare another.

46. Mímir's sons play, and the world's end begins (?) with the old Giallarhorn; Heimdallr blows loudly, the horn is aloft, Óðinn speaks with Mímir's head.

47. The towering ashtree Yggdrasill trembles; the old tree groans and the giant is loosed. Each man takes fright on the roads to Hel, before the kinsman of Surtr [Fenrisúlfr] swallows him.

49. Garmr now barks loudly before Gnipahellir. His fetter will break and the wolf will run free; she knows many things. Farther in the future I see the mighty fate of the gods, of the victory-gods.

50. Hrymr drives from the east, he lifts his shield high; the Miðgarðr serpent twists in giant-rage, the dragon beats the waves and the eagle screams, the pale-beaked one tears the corpses; Naglfar is loosed.

51. A ship fares from the east: the people of Muspell will come over the sea, and Loki will steer; all the sons of the giant follow after the wolf, along with them comes Býleiptr's brother.

48. How are the Æsir? How are the elves? All Iǫtunheimar resounds; the Æsir are at the Þing; the dwarves groan before the stone doors, sages of the rock wall—do you want to know more or not?

52. Surtr fares from the south with switch-bane [fire], the battle gods' sun shines from the sword; the cliffs tumble, and the monsters fall, men tread the hell-path and heaven splits open.

53. Then upon Hlín comes a second grief, when Óðinn goes out to fight the wolf, and Beli's slayer [Freyr], gleaming, to fight Surtr: then will Frigg's delight [her husband] fall.

55. Then comes the great son of Sigfǫðr, Víðarr, to fight the wolf; he thrusts his sword into the heart of Hveðrungr's son: then his father is avenged.

55H. The world-serpent opens wide its jaws through the heavens; the jaws of the terrible dragon gape in the heights. Óðinn's son will confront the dragon at [the scene of] the death of the wolf, and Víðarr's kin (?).

56. Then comes [Þórr], the famous son of Hlóðyn, Óðinn's son goes to fight the wolf (?). In wrath he slays the holy guardian (?) of Miðgarðr; all men will abandon their homesteads. The son of Fiǫrgyn goes scarcely nine feet from the serpent, unafraid of shame.

57. The sun grows black, the earth sinks into the sea, the bright stars turn from heaven; steam gushes against the life-nourisher [fire], the high flame plays against heaven itself.

58. Garmr now barks loudly before Gnipahellir. His fetter will break and the wolf will run free; she knows many things. Farther in the future I see the mighty fate of the gods, of the victory-gods.

59. She sees the earth come up yet again from the sea, green once more; cataracts fall, the eagle flies over them, he who hunts for fish in the mountains.

60. The Æsir meet on Iðavǫllr and speak about the mighty world-serpent, and remember there the great event and Fimbultýr's ancient runes.

61. Afterwards there in the grass will be found the wondrous gold game pieces, which they had owned in former days.

62. Fields will grow unsown, misfortune will all be cured, Baldr will return: Hǫðr and Baldr will dwell [in peace] on Hroptr's victory-grounds, and the battle-gods—do you want to know more or not?

63. Then Hœnir will choose the lot-twigs, and the sons of both

brothers will live in the wide wind-home—do you want to know more or not?

64. She sees a hall standing, fairer than the sun, thatched with gold at Gimlé; there shall the loyal hosts dwell and forever enjoy happiness.

65. Then the mighty one comes down from above, the powerful one in divine judgment, he who rules all.

66. There from below comes the dark dragon flying, the flashing serpent, from Niðafioll; it bears corpses in its wings—it flies over the field—Níðhoggr—now will it sink down.

2. *The Last Judgment*

(*Muspilli*; text: *AHDL*, pp. 86–9.)

The beginning and end of this eschatological poem are lost, but what remains describes the struggle between angels and devils for souls, the battle between Anti-Christ and Elias, the Last Judgment, and the end of the world. Written in imperfect alliterative verse, *Muspilli* dates from the first half of the ninth century. The dialect is Bavarian. Some scholars have posited that it could be a version of a lost Anglo-Saxon poem (see Bostock and Barber). While overwhelmingly Christian in content, the poem does allude briefly to pagan accounts of the apocalypse of the world, such as that in the *Volospá*. The word *muspilli* itself, though of much-disputed meaning, seems to reflect a pagan view of the destruction of the world by fire (see Salmon, Turville-Petre 1964, and Finger).

. . . may his day come, when he must die. For when the soul lifts itself on its way and lets the body rest, one host comes from heaven's stars, another from hellfire: there they fight over [it]. The soul must be anxious, until the judgment takes its course, [announcing] to which of the two hosts it may be fetched. For if Satan's band wins, it leads the soul instantly where suffering will befall it, into fire and into darkness: that is a truly horrible thing. If, however, those who come from heaven fetch it, and it becomes the angels' property, they bring it instantly up into the kingdom of heaven: there is life without death, light without darkness, a dwelling without sorrow; there no one is sick. If, then, the man wins a dwelling in paradise, a house in heaven, there enough help will come to him. For there is great need for every man that his mind should drive him to it, that he might eagerly do God's will and fearfully avoid the fire of hell, the torment of hellfire. There age-old Satan offers hot flame. So he ought to remember this, and worry greatly, he who knows himself sinful. Woe to him who must atone for his crimes in darkness, burn in hellfire: that is a truly terrible thing, when a man prays to God and help does not come to him. The wretched soul hopes for grace; this is not heavenly God's intent, for here in the world he did not act accordingly. So when the mighty King fixes a time for the judgment, there each race must come. Then no child dare ignore the summons, [thinking that] not every man must go to the judgment. There before the Ruler he must stand to reckoning, for that which he had done in the world.

I have heard the righteous in the world tell that the Anti-Christ shall fight with Elias. The evil doer is armed; then the fight between them will begin. The warriors are so strong, the cause is so great. Elias fights on the side of eternal life; he would strengthen the kingdom [of the Lord] for the righteous: therefore the One who rules heaven will help him. The Anti-Christ stands by the old enemy, stands by Satan, who will betray him: therefore he will fall wounded on the battlefield and be without victory in that conflict. Yet many of God's servants believe that Elias will be destroyed in the battle. When Elias' blood drips onto the earth, then the mountains will catch fire, not any tree on earth will stand, rivers will dry up, the moor will swallow itself, heaven will burn slowly with fire, the moon will fall, middle-earth will burn, no stone will remain standing. Then Judgment Day comes to the land, comes with fire to punish men: for there no kinsman may give help to another before the *muspilli*. When the broad moist earth all burns up and fire and air are all swept away, where then is the border-land where man always fought with his kinsmen? The land is burnt up, the soul stands in sorrow; it does not know with what it may do penance: thus it turns towards hell. So it is good for a man when he comes to judge, that he should rightly judge each case. Then he need not be worry, when he comes to the trial. The wretched man, because he mars the right with bribes, does not know what kind of guard he has, [he does not know] that the Devil stands there concealed. He has in reckoning every evil thing that the man, early or late, did, so that he can say it all, when the man comes to trial; consequently no man should accept bribes.

When the heavenly horn is sounded and the Judge raises himself on the way, (He who shall judge the dead and the living), then the greatest of hosts raises itself with Him; that [host] is so very brave that no one can fight it. Then He will go to the judgment place, which is marked out there. There the trial will take place, as has always been told. Then the angels will go over the land, waken the people, lead [them] to the judgment. Then shall each man arise from the dust, free himself from the weight of the burial mounds: his body shall come to him again, so that he may account for himself completely and be judged according to his deeds. When He sits down, He who there shall judge and pass sentence on the dead and the living, then a host of angels, of good men, will stand around there; the court is so great. There to the judgment come so many who arise from their rest. Thus no man can escape anything there. There the hand will speak, the head tell, every limb up to the little finger, what murder he committed among men. There is never a man so cunning that he can lie about anything there, that he may conceal any deed; for all will be made known before the King, unless he might compensate for it with alms, and with fasting might do penance for crimes. Then he grows confident, he who has done penance, when he comes to the trial. Then the glorious Cross on which holy Christ was hanged will be brought forth. Then He will show the scars, which He received as a man, which He endured for the love of mankind.

B. Celtic Analogue

1. "Judgment, its destruction will not be small"

("*Bráth, ní ba beg a brisim*"; text: *PoJ*, pp. 29–33.)

The pre-Christian Celtic tradition apparently lacked the apocalyptic vision of ON. As a Christian topic, however, the Last Judgment was immensely popular in medieval Ireland, though poetic versions are less common than those in prose. This example is dated to the tenth century. The ending suggests that the poem was a prayer for protection, a "lorica" (q.v.), rather than a homiletic or heroic narrative. Or, perhaps, the poem may be related to secular praise and reconciliation poems, in which a retainer addresses his lord.

1. Judgment, its destruction will not be small the day the world will burn up. It would be fitting, O Christ with hosts, for Adam's seed to dread it.
2. Obdurate is the human race—harder than stones are their hearts—when they do not pay attention to the vastness of all the pains,

3. when the earth will spew up the host of Adam's vast progeny, when a single blaze will fill up both heaven and earth,

4. when there will come together in a single meeting—in which every dispute will be settled—the host of hell, the tribes of earth, the army of saints, the nine orders of angels,

5. when the judge will pass true, righteous judgments: heaven for those of the chosen, an increase of punishment for the evil.

6. The humble, lowly people, with pure hearts, the insignificant paupers will be in the ranks of the King of heaven.

7. The red-mouthed lawyers, the jesters, the perverted, the satirists, the proud, contentious clerics, will not get a decision of honor or welcome.

8. The envious kinslayers, the immoral chiefs without religion, the wanton, unwomanly woman will find death and destruction.

9. Hard and bitter will be their penance. They will drop tears across their cheeks: the lying, the impious, the people of all persisting sin.

10. It will be a disgrace, it will be a reproach to the host of the wicked, you see, when all of them will see the sin of each one.

11. After being for a very long time in the blazing fire of judgment, they will be thrown by the King of the sun into a place of punishment at the last.

12. Wretched will be the cry they will make; alas, vast will be their wailing, at separating from the holy angels, at going with black demons.

13. Woe to the soul which does not heed the uproar of the great Day of Judgment! Worse by seventy-seven [times] dwelling in hard, punishing hell.

14. Its extreme cold, its extreme burning, its hunger, its enormous thirst, its hammering, its heavy punishment, its horror, its gloom, its killing,

15. its terrible monsters, its wounds, its constant lamentation, its stinking, blazing sea, its awful, devilish faces,

16. woe to the one who has come into this world, woe for our bodies, woe for our souls, for anyone for whom it is his destiny to dwell long in ruthless hell.

17. From Your kindness, O kind Father, from Your gentleness, O King of heaven, do not throw me into the bitter prison in which are all groans.

18. For each noble intercession in heaven and on earth when You bring a charge against me, may You deal gently with my soul.

19. For Your Cross, for Your passion, for Your kingship, O Over-King, come strongly to my aid in all the torments of my soul.

20. For each noble intercession in heaven and on earth, I pray

to You, O Christ of my heart, that the kingdom of heaven may be for my soul.

21. For Your Cross, for Your passion, protect me from every evil, that they may not destroy me, O heavenly King, the temptations of devils or of men.

22. For Your Cross, for Your passion, come to my aid immediately; before I go from the jaundiced world, take from me every impiety.

23. Out of Your vast mercy, protect me on every occasion. Put Your great love into my soul, so that it may be filled with love for You.

24. May I be wheat in Your granary on the day the chaff is burned; may I then bear off the victory and triumph in the destruction of Judgment Day.

IX

SAINTS' LIVES

A. Germanic Analogues

1. *The Lay of St. George*

(*Lied vom heiligen Georg* [Kögel]; text: *AHDL*, pp. 133–5.)

The OHG saints' lives stand in contrast to the OE examples. While the OE lives represent a highly developed, sophisticated genre, their counterparts show only a rudimentary relationship to Latin hagiography, the inspiration for all the OE poems, with the possible exception of *Guthlac A*. *The Lay of St. George*, which may have been written in Reichenau, is an early example of the saint's life (ca. 900), relating briefly George's three-fold martyrdom and resurrection. Like *The Lay of St. Peter*, the poem's chief interest lies in its apparent independence from a direct Latin source (see Garland, Barber, and Haubrichs.)

George went to the tribunal with a great army, from the boundary land with a great troop. He went to the [assembly] ring, to the important Thing. That Thing was the most famous, dearest to God. He left the worldly kingdom, he gained the heavenly kingdom. He did that himself, the famous chief George.
Then all the many kings tempted him; they wanted to turn him [from his faith]; he would hear nothing of it from them. George was firm in mind; he would hear nothing of it from them—I swear (?), but he performed everything for which he prayed to God. That he did himself, Lord Saint George.

Then at once they sentenced him to prison. There with him then went angels, the beautiful ones. There two women pined away; he saved their lives. Then so nobly and gloriously he made the meal. There, in truth, George wrought that miracle. George then prayed; the Lord granted him all. The Lord granted him all, for which George prayed to Him. The blind he made to see, the halt to walk, the dumb he made to speak, the deaf to hear. A pillar had stood there many years. Out of it foliage suddenly sprang. There, in truth, George wrought that miracle.

The powerful man became very angry; Tacianus the tyrant flared greatly in rage about it. He said George was a sorcerer. He commanded George to be seized, commanded him to be punished, commanded him to be struck hard with a wondrously sharp sword. That I know is very true: George raised himself up there, George raised himself up there; He preached well there. George put the heathen men greatly to shame.

The powerful man became very angry. He commanded George to be bound, turned on a wheel. In truth I say this to you: they broke him in ten pieces. That I know is very true: George raised himself up there, George raised himself up there; he [preached] well there. George put the heathen men greatly to shame.

Then he commanded George to be seized, he commanded him to be scourged very harshly. They ordered him to the ground in a mill [and] all burnt to powder. They threw him into the well: he was a blessed son [of the Lord]. They rolled many large stones over it. They began to walk around him; they commanded him to rise up. A great deed George did there, as he ever truly does. That I know is very true: George raised himself up there, George raised himself up there. The glorious man sprang out [of the well] at once. George put the heathen men greatly to shame.

He ordered [a dead] man to stand up; he commanded him to come there to him, commanded him to speak at once. Then he commanded a prayer to be said, "I pray you (?) believe him." He said they were lost, all deceived by the devil. Lord Saint George himself announced that to us.

Then he went to the chamber, to the queen. He began to teach her. She began to listen to him. Elossandria was virtuous; she hastened at once to do good, to give away her money. She gave away her treasure there: that helps [her] so many years. From eternity to eternity, so will she be in grace. Lord Saint George himself gained that by prayer. George raised up his hand. Abollinus trembled. He commanded the Hound of Hell; then he went at once into the abyss.

2. *The Lay of St. Peter*

(*Petruslied*; text: *AHDL*, p. 131.)

This brief prayer, which some scholars place in the early ninth century, may be the earliest German poem to use rhyme. Musical notation accompanies it in the manuscript, and it shows Otfrid's influence, both in meter and style. The poem is probably best regarded as an intercessionary prayer, calling on St. Peter for aid (see Garland, Barber, and Schützeichel 1971).

Our Lord has given Saint Peter the power, that he may save the one who has faith in Him.
  Kyrie eleyson, Christe eleyson.
He also holds with his words the doors of heaven. There he may let in the one whom he wants to save.
  Kyrie eleyson, Christe eleyson.
Let us all very loudly together beseech God's confidant, that he might deign to show mercy to us who have sinned.
  Kyrie eleyson, Christe eleyson.

B. Celtic Analogue

1. *Fíacc's Hymn*

(*Génair Patraicc i Nemthur*; text: *TP*, Vol. II, pp. 307–21.)

This late eighth-century poem appears in the *Liber Hymnorum*, a collection containing several saints' lives told as hymns. Fíacc, bishop of Sletty and a disciple of St. Patrick's in the *Book of Armagh*, is supposed to have authored the poem, but the attribution is doubtful. Writing such poems about earlier saints is a common practice in medieval Irish literature. The biographical information about St. Patrick conforms to that found in the prose lives. The OE *Guthlac A* is probably the closest analogue to *Fíacc's Hymn*. Both show a mixture of popular-traditional and learned elements and both are related, in one way or another, to a prose version of the same biography.

1. Patrick was born at Nemthur. This is what it says in stories: a young boy of sixteen years when he was carried away in tears.

2. Sucat was his name when he was carried off; who his father was ought to be known: [Patrick was] son of Calpurnius, the son of Potitus, grandson of the deacon Odissus.

3. He was six years in servitude; he did not use to concern himself with people's vanity. There were a number of people of four households that Cothraig was serving.

4. Victor [an angel] said to Miliuc's servant [Patrick] that he should go on the waves. He [Victor] placed his foot on the flagstone; its print survives, it will not go away.

5. He led Patrick across all Britain—great God, it was a marvellous course—until he left him with Germanus southward, in the south of Letha.

6. In the islands in the Tyrhennian sea, he fasted in them, he computed: he read the canon with Germanus; that is what the writings say.

7. The angels of God kept enticing him back to Ireland. He often used to see in visions that he would be coming back again.

8. Patrick's awaited coming was an aid to Ireland. The sound of a cry had been heard far away from the youth of the wood of Fochlad.

9. They prayed that the saint might come, that he might go about amongst them, that he might convert the tribes of Ireland from sin to life.

10. The tribes of Ireland used to prophesy that a new prince of peace would come to them, that his successors would last until Doomsday; that the silent land of Tara would be deserted.

11. His druids did not conceal Patrick's coming from [King] Loegaire. The prophecy came to pass about the prince they were speaking of.

12. Patrick was zealous until he died. He was a champion at casting out wickedness: this is what exalted his rank up beyond the households of men.

13. He used to chant hymns, the apocalypse, and the three-fifties [of psalms]. He preached, he baptized, he prayed, he did not stop praising God.

14. The coldness of the season did not use to stop him from spending the night in pools. He strove for his kingdom in heaven; by day he preached in the high places.

15. In Slane, north of Benn Bairche—neither drought nor flood used to afflict it—he sang one hundred psalms each night; he was a servant for the King of angels.

16. He spent the night on bare flagstones after that, with a wet cloak around him; his pillow was a standing-stone. He did not leave his body in warmth.

17. He preached the gospel for everyone. He performed miracles everywhere. He cures the lame and lepers, the dead he would restore to life.

18. Patrick preached to the Scotti. He endured great tribulation everywhere, so that everyone he brought to life would be about him at Judgment Day.

19. The sons of Eber, the sons of Eremon, all went with the Devil; transgression let them down into the great deep pit.

20. Until the apostle came to them—even the swift wind led him—for three score years he preached the Cross of Christ to the tribes of the Féni [the Gaels].

21. Darkness was upon the tribes of Ireland. The people worshipped the pagan gods [*side*]. They did not believe in the true divinity of the true Trinity.

22. In Armagh there is kingship; it is long since it has abandoned Emain. A great church is Downpatrick; not very clear, though it be a wilderness, is Tara (?).

23. When Patrick was sick he wanted to go to Armagh. An angel met him on the way, in the middle of the day.

24. He led him southward to [the angel] Victor. It was he [Victor] who had arranged it. The bush Victor was in burned; out of the fire he spoke.

25. He said, "Pre-eminence to Armagh, give thanks to Christ. You shall soon go to heaven. Your prayers have been answered.

26. The hymn which you have chosen in your life will be a 'lorica' of protection for everyone. About you on the Day of Judgment the men of Ireland will meet doom."

27. Tassach stayed after him when he gave communion to him. He said Patrick would soon come to them. Tassach's word was not false.

28. He put a boundary upon the night so that light might not be spent during it. For the space of a year there was light; that was a long day of peace.

29. In a battle fought in Bethron against the tribe of Canaan by the son of Nun, the sun stood still on Gibeon, so the writer tells us.

30. Since the sun stood still for Joshua upon the death of the wicked, although it might be continuous, it would be fitting illumination at the death of the saints.

31. The clerics of Ireland came to watch over Patrick from every route; the sound of the chanting had prostrated them; each of them fell asleep on the road.

32. Patrick's soul was separated from his body after tribulations. God's angels on the first night looked after it ceaselessly.

33. When Patrick ascended, he approached the other Patrick.

Together they ascended to Jesus, Son of Mary.

34. Patrick, without hint of pride, much good he considered it, being in the service of the Son of Mary; it was a portent of piety in which he was born.

X

BATTLE POEMS

A. General

1. Germanic Analogues

a. *The Lay of Atli*

(*Atlaqviða in grœnlenzca*; text: *Edda*, pp. 240–7.)

Two Eddic poems, *Atlaqviða* and *Atlamál*, recount the legend of Atli (Attila the Hun). The first is generally regarded as superior both in conception and execution; some have even praised the poem as the best example of the heroic lay in the language. Both poems, only the first of which we translate here, deal with the fall of the Niflungar, whom Atli destroys out of his lust for the Niflung gold. *The Lay of Atli* probably comes from the latter part of the ninth century and may be West Germanic or Saxon in origin (see Turville-Petre 1953, p. 13). It is written in a combination of *fornyrðislag* and *málaháttr* (see Bellows, Hallberg, Hollander and Dronke).

1. Atli sent a messenger, a well-known man, riding to Gunnarr; Knéfrøðr he was called. To Gíuki's court he came, to Gunnarr's hall, to the benches surrounding the hearth and to the sweet beer.
2. There the companions drank wine in the war-hall—and silently concealed their plans—they feared the wrath of the Huns; then Knéfrøðr called out with a cold voice, the southern man; he sat on the high bench.
3. "Atli sent me riding here with his message, on the bit-champing steed, through Myrkviðr the unknown, to ask you,

Gunnarr, to come to his benches, with ring-adorned (?) helmets, to seek Atli's home.

4. There you can choose shields and smooth-shaven ash spears, gold-red helmets and a great company of Huns, silver-gilt saddle cloths, blood-red sarks, spears, darts, bit-champing horses!

5. He said he would give you the field of wide Gnitaheiðr, a ringing spear and gilded ship-prows, great treasures and home-steads on the Dnieper, the mighty forest which men call Myrkviðr."

6. Then Gunnarr turned his head and said to Hǫgni: "What do you counsel us, young man, when we hear such things? I did not know of any gold on Gnitaheiðr that we did not own as much.

7. We own seven halls full of swords, each of them has a hilt of gold. I know my steed is the best, and my sword the sharpest, my bows bench-seemly, and my byrnies of gold, helmet and shield the brightest, which come from Kiárr's hall; one of mine is better than those of all the Huns."

8. "What do you think the woman meant when she sent us a ring wrapped in a wolf's clothes? I think she wanted to give us warning; I found the hair of a wolf wound in the red ring; wolfish is our way if we ride out on this mission."

9. No kinsmen urged Gunnarr, nor friends either, counsellors nor advisors, nor those who were mighty; then Gunnarr spoke as a king should, glorious, in the mead-hall, with great spirit:

10. "Arise now, Fiǫrnir! Make the warriors' golden cups pass around on the floor into the hands of men!

11. The wolf will rule the inheritance of the Niflungar, the old, gray-coated ones, if Gunnarr is lost; black-coated bears will bite with ragged teeth, be sport for the pack hounds, if Gunnarr does not come back."

12. Loyal people, weeping, led the war-like lord of the land out of the Huns' court; then the young heir of Hǫgni said: "Fare now safely and wisely wherever your spirit takes you!"

13. The bold ones made the bit-champing steeds gallop on the mountains, through Myrkviðr the unknown. All the land of the Huns shook where the fierce ones rode; they drove on the lash-fearing [steeds] through the all-green fields.

14. They saw the land of Atli and his lofty towers, the warriors of Bikki standing on the high fortress, the hall over the southern peoples, girt with seat-beams, with bound rims, with white shields, spears, lances; and there Atli drank wine in his war-hall; the guards sat outside to watch for Gunnarr and his men, if they should come here seeking with ringing spear to rouse the prince to battle.

15. Their sister saw first that they came into the hall, both her

brothers—she had drunk little beer: "Gunnarr, now you are betrayed! What can you do, powerful one, against the vicious plots of the Huns? Get out of the hall quickly!

16. It would have been better, brother, had you come in byrnie, with ring-adorned (?) helmets to see Atli's home. You should have sat in the saddle through sun-hot days; you should have made the Norns weep for the death-pale corpses, the shield-maids of the Huns know the harrow (?); and you should have sent Atli himself into a snake-pit—now the snake-pit is destined for the two of you."

17. "It is now too late, sister, to gather the Niflungar, too far away to seek reinforcements, loyal warriors from the banks of the Rhine."

18. They seized Gunnarr and put him in fetters, the king of the Burgundians, and bound him fast.

19. Hǫgni slew seven with his sharp sword, and the eighth he threw into the hot fire; so shall a brave warrior defend himself against enemies as Hǫgni fought on Gunnarr's side.

20. They asked the brave one if he would buy his life, the king of the Goths, with gold.

21. "The heart of Hǫgni must lie in my hand, bloody, cut from the bold rider's breast, with sharp-biting sword, from the king's son."

22. They cut the heart from Hialli's breast, bloody, and put it on a platter and bore it before Gunnarr.

23. Then Gunnarr, the lord of the people, said: "Here I have the heart of Hialli the coward, unlike the heart of Hǫgni the brave; it trembles greatly while it lies on the platter: it trembled twice as much when it lay in his breast."

24. Then Hǫgni laughed as they cut out the heart of the living wound-smith; he did not think at all to cry. They laid it bloody on a platter and bore it before Gunnarr.

25. Then the glorious Gunnarr, the spear-Niflungr, said: "Here I have the heart of Hǫgni the brave, unlike the heart of Hialli the coward; it trembles little while it lies on the platter. It did not tremble as much when it lay in his breast.

26. So shall you, Atli, be as far from men's eyes, as you will be from my treasure. The whole hoard of the Niflungar is entrusted to me alone: now Hǫgni is dead.

27. I always had doubt, while both of us were alive. Now I have none, since I alone live. The Rhine, sprung from the gods, shall own the strife-gold of men, the inheritance of the Niflungar; and the war-rings glisten in the rolling water rather than gold shine on the arms of Huns!"

28. "Bring the wagon here! The prisoner is now in chains."
29. Atli the great rode on Glaumr the long-maned, surrounded by battle-thorns [swords], their brother-in-law. Guðrún, [kin] of victory-heroes (?) . . . held back tears, appeared in the battle-hall.
30. "So may it go with you, Atli, as you had often sworn oaths with Gunnarr and once pledged, by the south-inclining sun and by Sigtýr's mountain, by the horse of the bed of rest [couch] and by Ullr's ring."
28. And on from there the shaker of the bit [horse] dragged the guardian of the treasure [prince], the warrior (?), to his death.
31. A crowd of men placed the living prince in a pit that was crawling with snakes inside; but Gunnarr, alone, hate in his heart, struck the harp with his hand, the strings resounded. So must a brave ring-giver defend his gold against men!
32. Atli made his galloping horse turn toward his lands back from the murder; there was a din in the court from the press of horses, the weapon-song of the warriors; they were back from the heath.
33. Guðrún then went out towards Atli, with a gilded goblet, to give tribute to the ruler: "Now, lord, you can be served in your hall, glad by Guðrún, the dead young beasts!"
34. The ale cups of Atli rang, wine-heavy, when the Huns gathered together in the hall, long-moustached men; the troops went in.
35. The bright-faced one then strode in to bring them drink, the terrible woman, and chose ale-morsels for the warriors, with repulsion, for the pale-faced ones, and declared her scorn to Atli:
36. "Giver of swords, you chewed the bloody hearts of your sons with honey; you can digest, proud one, the dead flesh of men, eat them as ale-morsels, and cough them up in the high-seat (?)!
37. You will never call Erpr or Eitill to your knees again, those two merry with ale; you will never see the gold-givers again in the middle aisle making spear shafts, clipping manes, or riding horses."
38. Moaning was on the benches, the terrible song of men, uproar under costly cloaks; the sons of the Huns wept, except for Guðrún alone; she never wept for her bear-hard brothers and dear sons, young, inexperienced, those whom she begot with Atli.
39. The woman, bright as a young goose, scattered gold; she gave red rings to the housecarls; she made fate grow and the shining metal go, nor did the woman even spare the temple (?).
40. Unwary was Atli—he had drunk himself weary, he had no weapons, he did not guard himself against Guðrún; often the game was better, when they would frequently embrace with tenderness before the nobles.

41. With a sword-spike she gave their bed blood to drink, with her death-eager hand, and she loosed the hounds; she thrust before the hall door, the woman, a fiery brand, she wakened the housecarls. This was the payment she took for her brothers.

42. She gave to the fire all who were inside and who had come from Myrkheimr from Gunnarr's murder; the ancient timbers fell, the temple smoked, the dwelling of the Buðlungar, the shield-maids burned, inside; doomed, they sank in the hot fire.

43. Now that is fully told. Never after will any woman in a byrnie go thus to avenge her brothers. She brought the death-word to three kings, the bright-one, before she died.

b. *The First Lay of Helgi, Hundingr's Slayer*

(*Helgaqviða Hundingsbana in fyrri*; text: *Edda*, pp. 130–9.)

The first of the Helgi lays represents a clear expression of the Germanic battle ethic, concentrating, as it does, almost entirely on Helgi's warlike deeds. Like so many poems in the *Edda*, this lay seems to contain a number of accretions, which represent portions of other lost works. It has been dated to the mid-eleventh century and is written mostly in *fornyrðislag* meter (see Bellows, Hallberg and Hollander).

1. Old were the times when eagles screamed, holy waters fell from Himinfiǫll; then Borghildr in Brálundr bore Helgi, the great-hearted.

2. Night was in the dwelling, the Norns came, who shaped the ætheling's life; they decreed the prince would become most famous and be thought of as the best sovereign.

3. With strength they wove the strands of fate, when the towers in Brálundr were crumbling; they arrayed the golden cords and under the moon-hall's [heaven's] middle they made them fast.

4. East and west they hid the ends; the prince had his lands there in between; Neri's kinswoman hung a cord on the northern side and decreed it to hold forever.

5. One thing only afflicted the kinsman of the Ylfingar and the maid who bore the loved one: the raven said to the raven—it sat in a high tree, waiting for food—: "I know something.

6. Sigmundr's son stands in his byrnie, a half-day old; now the day has come. His eyes shine sharp like a warrior's, he is a friend of wolves, we shall have cause for joy."

7. The troop thought he was a [true] prince, they said a good harvest had come for men; the king himself came from the battle-tumult, to bring the young prince a noble leek.

8. He named him Helgi and gave him Hringstaðir, Sólfiǫll, Snæfiǫll, and Sigarsvellir, Hringstǫð, Hátún and Himinvangar, and an ornamented blood-snake [sword] to Sinfiǫtli's brother.

9. Then he grew amidst his friends, the noble-born elm tree, in the radiance of bliss; he rewarded and gave gold to his retainers, the ruler did not spare the blood-stained hoard.

10. For a short time the king waited for war, [only] until the prince was fifteen winters old; he slew the hardy Hundingr, who long had ruled lands and thanes.

11. The sons of Hundingr afterwards claimed riches and rings from the son of Sigmundr, because they had recompense due for that prince for great plunder and a dead father.

12. The prince did not give them compensation, nor allow the kinsmen to get wergild; he said a great storm of gray spears and Óðinn's wrath were in the offing.

13. The warriors went to the battle, which they had set at Logafiǫll; the foes broke Fróði's peace, the hounds of Viðrir went eager for slaughter about the island.

14. The king sat down, after he had slain Álfr and Eyiólfr, under Arasteinn, Hiǫrvarðr and Hávarðr, Hundingr's sons; he had killed all the warrior's race.

15. Then light burst from Logafiǫll and from that light lightning sprang; then [valkyries?] were under helmets on Himinvangar . . . their byrnies were stained with blood. And from their spears rays shot forth.

16. At early morning in wolf-wood, the prince asked the southern maids if they would come home that night with the warriors; the bows were twanging.

17. But from the horse Hǫgni's daughter—the clashing of shields grew still—said to the prince: "I think that we have other tasks than to drink beer with the ring-breaker.

18. My father has promised his daughter to Granmarr's grim son; but I have, Helgi, called Hǫðbroddr as bold a king as the son of a cat.

19. Yet the prince will come within a few nights, unless you show him the battlefield (?) or take the maiden from the prince."

20. "Do not fear the slayer of Ísungr! Sooner will the din of battle be heard, unless I lie dead."

21. The king sent messengers from there, through air and over water, to summon his troops, to offer abundant gleam of the river [gold] to the warriors and their sons.

22. "Bid them go quickly to the ships and be ready to leave Brandey!" The lord waited until men by the hundreds came there from Heðinsey.

23. And from the shores his boats, decked with gold, glided out of Stafnsnes; then Helgi asked Hiǫrleifr: "Have you mustered bold men?"

24. And the young king said to the other it would take long to count the long-prowed ships and the shield men from Trǫnoeyrr, which sailed out through Ǫrvasund.

25. "Twelve hundred true men; but there are half as many again of the king's battle-host in Hátún; we expect the din of battle."

26. The captain took down the ship's tents, so that the host of warriors awakened and the heroes saw daybreak, and the princes hoisted the sails on the mast in Varinsfiǫrðr.

27. There was a moaning of oars and a clash of irons, shield crashed against shield, the vikings rowed; the prince's fleet went rushing under the chieftains out from the land.

28. So it sounded, when the sister of Kólga [the waves] and the long keels came together, as if the surf were breaking on cliffs.

29. Helgi ordered the sails drawn higher, the crew did not shun the clash of the waves, when the terrible daughter of Ægir [a wave] wanted to sink the sea-steeds.

30. But from above battle-brave Sigrún protected them and their ship; mightily she snatched the king's beasts of the tossing sea [ships] out of Rán's hand at Gnipalundr.

31. So there in the evening the fair-decked ships floated into Unavágar; but from Svarinshaugr they made out the host with angry mind.

32. Then the god-born Guðmundr asked: "Who is the ruler, the one who leads the troops, and who brings a threatening host to the land?"

33. Sinfiǫtli spoke—he raised the red shield up on the sailyard, the rim was made of gold; there was a coast guard who knew how to answer and exchange words with chieftains—:

34. "Say in the evening when you feed the swine and bait your bitches to their swill, that the Ylfingar have come out of the east, eager for battle, from Gnipalundr.

35. There Hǫðbroddr will find Helgi, a prince unwilling to flee in the midst of his fleet, he who often has sated eagles, while you kissed slave girls at the handmill."

36. "You remember few of the ancient tales, prince, when you hurl untruths at chieftains; you have eaten the meat of wolves [carrion], and you have slain your brothers; often have you sucked

wounds with your cold mouth, you have crept into rocky dens, loathed by all men."

37. "You were a seeress in Varinsey, a deceitful woman, you made up lies; you said that you would have no man, a byrnied warrior, except Sinfiǫtli.

38. You were a loathsome, giantess, valkyrie, terrible, powerful at Alfǫðr's; all the Einheriar had to fight, obstinate woman, for your sake.

39. On Ságones we gave birth to nine wolves; I alone was their father."

40. "You were not the father of the brood of Fenris-wolves, though you are older than all, as I remember, since the giant maidens gelded you near Gnipalundr in Þórsnes.

41. You were the stepson of Siggeirr, you lay at home in lairs, used to the wolves howling out in the woods; then all possible trouble came from you, when you pierced your brothers' breasts. You won fame for yourself from dreadful crimes.

42. You were Grani's bride in Brávǫllr, gold-bridled, you were ready to race; I have ridden you weary many a mile, slim under the saddle, cow, downhill."

43. "You seemed to be an indecent young boy, when you milked Gullnir's goats, and another time you went in a tattered coat as Imðr's daughter; do you want to quarrel longer?"

44. "I would much rather sate the ravens at Frekasteinn with your corpse, than bait your bitches to their swill or feed your swine; may evil powers wrangle with you."

45. "It would be much more fitting for you, Sinfiǫtli, to wage battle and to gladden eagles, than to argue with empty taunts, even if ring-breakers do become bitter enemies.

46. Granmarr's sons do not seem good to me, though it is fitting for princes to speak the truth; they have shown at Móinsheimar that they have a mind to wield swords."

47. With force they made Svipuðr and Sveggiuðr run to Sólheimar, through dewy valleys, darkened slopes; the steed of Mist [the earth] shook where the men travelled.

48. They met the lord at the courtyard gate, they said fierce warriors had come; Hǫðbroddr stood outside, hooded with a helmet, he watched his kin riding horses: "Why do the Hniflungar look so fearful?"

49. "Quick keels are moving toward the shore, mast-stags [ships] and long sailyards, many shields, shaven oars, the noble host of warriors (?), the glad Ylfingar.

50. Fifteen bands have gone up on land, but out in Sogn there are seven thousand [more]; black sea-beasts [ships] adorned with

gold lie here at anchor off Gnipalundr. There is the greatest strength of their host; now Helgi will not put off the sword-þing [battle]."

51. "Let the bridled steeds run to Reginþing, and Sporvitnir to Sparinsheiðr, Mélnir and Mýlnir to Myrkviðr! Let no man henceforth sit idle, those who know how to wield wound-flames [swords].

52. Summon Hǫgni and Hringr's sons to you, Atli and Yngvi and Álfr the old; they eagerly wage battle, let us offer the Volsungar resistance!"

53. In one lightning movement they came together, gray-iron points at Frekasteinn; Helgi, Hundingr's slayer, was always foremost in the battle, there where men fought, furious in fight, unwilling to flee; that ruler had a stout heart.

54. Out of the heavens the helmeted ones came there from above—the clang of spears grew—, those who protected the prince; then Sigrún spoke—the valkyries flew, the giantess' horse [wolf?] ate Huginn's food [the slain]—:

55. "King, you shall have delight and prosperity among men, scion of Yngvi, and enjoy life, since you have felled the prince, unwilling to flee, who caused the death of Ægir [sea-kings?].

56. And, prince, both become you well, red rings and the noble maid; prince, hale shall you both enjoy, Hǫgni's daughter and Hringstaðir, victory and lands; now the strife is ended."

c. *The Lay of Hamðir*

(*Hamðismál*; text: *Edda*, pp. 269–74.)

The text of *Hamðismál* is very corrupt, and the story itself is full of abrupt twists and turns. But the poem's delineation of the Germanic code of vengeance makes a powerful statement. In the sixth-century *De Rebus Geticis*, Jordanes recalls that Ermanaric, the fourth-century king of the East Goths, had a young woman torn apart by wild horses because of her husband's treachery. Legend has changed the story somewhat, and the ON poem tells of Guðrún's revenge through her sons for the death of Svanhildr, her daughter by Sigurðr. The poem may be as old as the tenth century and may be West Germanic or Saxon in origin (Turville-Petre 1953, pp. 13–14; see also Bellows, Hallberg, Hollander and Dronke).

1. Woeful deeds sprouted on the threshhold, joyless dawn (?); early in the morning every grief over the ills of men quickens sorrow.

2. That was not now nor yesterday, that has long since passed; few things are older, time twice told (?), when Guðrún, born of Giúki, urged her young sons to avenge Svanhildr.

3. "Your sister was called Svanhildr, the one whom Iǫrmunrekkr had trampled with steeds, white and black on the battle-way, with the gray, pace-trained horses of the Goths.

4. The royal line has been reduced to you, and you alone remain of the strands of my race.

5. Lonely have I become, like the aspen in the forest, robbed of kinsmen, like the pine of branches, deprived of joy like a tree of its leaves, when the branch-scather [fire? storm? girl?] comes on a warm day."

6. Then Hamðir, the great-hearted one, spoke this: "Little would you then, Guðrún, have praised Hǫgni's deed, when they woke Sigurðr from sleep; you sat on the bed, and his killers laughed.

7. Your blue-white bed linens woven by artists were drenched with your husband's blood. Sigurðr died then; you sat beside his dead body, you gave no heed to joy; Gunnarr willed it for you.

8. You meant to hurt Atli by Erpr's murder and by Eitill's death, that was the worse for you; so should each wield the sore-biting sword to slay the other, but not harm himself."

9. Then Sǫrli spoke this—he had good sense—: "I do not want to quarrel with my mother; but it seems to you both that there is still a lack of words; what are you asking now, Guðrún, that would not bring you to tears?

10. You weep for your brothers and sweet sons, your close-born kinsmen, led near to combat; you shall also weep for us both, Guðrún, who sit here doomed on our steeds, we will die far away."

11. They went out of the court, ready to rage; the youths then travelled over the dewy fells, on Hunnish steeds, to avenge the murder.

14. Then Erpr spoke this one time only—nobly he carried himself on the steed's back—: "Bad it is to show the road to a cowardly man!" They called the bold one a bastard.

12. They found the wily one on the way: "How will the brown-skinned one help us?"

13. Their half-brother answered, said that he would give help to his kinsmen as one foot to another: "How may a foot help a foot, or the flesh-grown hand another?"

15. They drew their sheath-irons from the sheaths, the edges of swords, to the delight of the giantess: they decreased their strength by a third, they made their young kinsman bow to earth.

16. They shook their woolen cloaks, they girded on their swords, and the high-born men arrayed themselves in rich tunics.

17. The paths lay in front of them; they found paths of woe and their sister's son wounded on the gallows, the wind-cold wolf-trees west of the dwellings, and the crane's bait swayed without ceasing. It was not desirable to wait.

18. There was joy in the hall, the men glad with ale, and no one could hear the horses, before a bold man blew his horn.

19. They went to tell Iǫrmunrekkr, that warriors under helmets had been seen: "Take good counsel! Powerful men have come, for you have trampled to death the sister of mighty men."

20. Then Iǫrmunrekkr laughed, he stroked his beard with his hand. He wanted to do battle, he became war-like from the wine; he shook his brown locks, looked at his white shield, and turned the gold cup round in his hand.

21. "I would then think myself happy if I could see Hamðir and Sǫrli in my hall; then I would bind those boys with strong bow-strings, the good sons of Giúki, fasten them on the gallows!"

22. Then a woman, glad of their fame, said this—she stood by the door, the slender-fingered one spoke with the young thanes: ". . . can two men alone bind or kill ten hundred Goths in the high fortress?"

23. There was a clamor in the hall, the ale-cups shattered, men lay in the blood which came from the breasts of the Goths.

24. Then Hamðir, the great-hearted one, spoke this: "Iǫrmun-rekkr, you wanted us to come, brothers of the same mother, into your fortress. You see your feet, you see your hands, Iǫrmunrekkr, thrown into the hot fire."

25. Then the god-born king roared aloud, bold in his byrnie, as a bear would roar: "Stone those men, since spears will not pierce them, nor edge nor iron, the sons of Iónakr."

26. Then Hamðir, the great-hearted one, spoke this: "You did evil, brother, when you opened that bag [mouth]; often bad advice comes out of that bag!"

27. "You would have courage, Hamðir, if only you had wisdom; he lacks much who is witless."

28. "His head would now be off, if Erpr lived, our battle-keen brother, whom we slew on the road, the war-keen man—the sisters [Norns] compelled me—the man who should have stayed inviolate—they roused me to killing—.

29. I think we should not act like wolves, so that we do harm to ourselves, like the Norns' bitches, those which, greedy, are reared in the wilderness.

30. We have fought well, we stand on the slain of the Goths,

above those struck down by swords, like eagles on a branch! We have won good fame, whether we die now or tomorrow; a man does not live till evening after the Norns' decree!"

31. There Sǫrli fell at the hall's gable, and Hamðir sank at the back of the house.

d. *The Battle of Hafrsfjǫrðr*

(from *Heimskringla, Haralds saga ins hárfagra*, chap. 18;
text: *HK*, I, pp. 115–17.)

The famous battle in which Haraldr inn hárfagri ("the fair-haired") established his dominance over Norway inspired this poem. Traditionally the battle has been dated c. 872, but, as Gwyn Jones writes, "A consensus of recent opinion would place Hafrs-fiord earlier than 900, but not before 885; that is, during the second half of the reign of King Alfred in England" (p. 89). Like *The Battle of Brunanburh*, it is less a description of a battle than a celebration of one. Scholars tend to consider the poem roughly contemporaneous with the battle itself, though there is some dispute on the matter (see Kershaw).

42. You have heard how the king from the noble family fought there in Hafrsfjǫrðr against Kjǫtvi the rich; ships came from the east, lusting for battle, with gaping figureheads and carved prows.

43. They were laden with warriors and white shields, western spears and French swords; the beserks howled, Gunnr accompanied them, the wolf-skins were shrieking and swords clashed.

44. They tested the resolute ruler of the eastmen, who dwells at Útsteinn. He taught them to flee. The prince brought out the steeds of Nǫkkvi [ships] when he expected battle. Shields clanged together before Haklangr fell.

45. Then the thick-necked ruler got tired of holding his land against Lúfa [King Haraldr]; he used the island as a shield. They threw themselves under the seat-planks, those who were wounded, they stuck their rumps up in the air, they thrust their heads in the keel.

46. On their backs the prudent warriors had the glistening hall-barks of Sváfnir [shields]—they were struck with stones—the ships hastened eastwards—and by way of Jaðarr they fled home from Hafrsfjǫrðr and they thought about mead-drinking.

e. The Lay of Bjarki

(*Bjarkamál* from *Heimskringla, Óláfs saga helga*, chap. 208;
text: *HK*, II, pp. 361–2.)

Bǫðvarr Bjarki, a follower of the fifth-century Danish King
Hrólfr Kraki, died fighting for his lord. The two stanzas of his lay
printed below (ca. 950?) are the only ones preserved in the original
vernacular tongue; Saxo Grammaticus gives Latin paraphrases for
parts of the poem in the *Gesta Danorum*, II, 53 ff., written around
1200 (see *SG* and Garmonsway, p. 156). Critics have remarked on
the similarity between these stanzas and *The Fight at Finnsburg*
(see also *EM* and Hallberg).

141. Day has risen, the cock's feathers flutter, it is time for
bondsmen to labor at their chores; awake now, awake, friends one
and all, eager companions of Aðils.
142. Hár the hard-gripper, Hrólfr the archer, men of good
race—they do not flee; I do not wake you for wine nor for the
secret wisdom of women, but rather I wake you for Hildr's hard
play [battle].

f. Skaldic Poetry
1. Eyvindr Finnsson skaldaspillir, d. ca. 990
The Lay of Hákon

(*Hákonarmál*, from *Heimskringla, Hákonar saga góða*, chap. 30,
31; text: *HK*, I, pp. 186–97.)

This praise poem commemorates Hákon Aðalsteinsfóstri, King
of Norway, who routed the sons of his dead brother Eiríkr blóðøx
at the Battle of Storð around 960, but who received his death
wound in doing so. The poem is an imitation of an earlier poem
about Eiríkr (*Eiríksmál*), a fact that may account for the poet's
nickname, which means "skald-destroyer" or "plagiarist". The
description of the battle itself is in *málaháttr*; the rest of the poem
is written in *ljóðaháttr* meter (see Hallberg and Kershaw).

1. Gautatýr sent Gǫndul and Skǫgul to choose among kings,
who of Yngvi's race should fare to Óðinn and dwell in Valhǫll.
2. They found Bjǫrn's brother putting on his byrnie, the nobly

dressed king standing under his banner, battle-spears were lowered and the dart shook. Then battle was begun.

3. The single-handed slayer of the jarls called on the men from Hálogaland as well as on the men from Rogaland; he went to the battle; the noble man had a good troop of Northmen, terror of the Danes, he stood under his eagle-helmet.

4. He cast off his war-dress, thrust his byrnie on the field, the chief of the men, before he started the fight. He sported with his troop, he would defend his land, the glad-hearted prince, he stood under his gold helmet.

5. So the sword in the king's hand bit Váfuðr's clothes [his battle gear] as if it had been thrust into water. Spears cracked. Shields broke. Swords clashed on the heads of men.

6. Targes and skulls were trodden by the hard hilt-feet [swords] of the god of rings [Hákon?] and the Northmen. Battles began on the island. The kings made red the bright shield-walls with the blood of men.

7. The wound-fires [swords] burned in bloody gashes. Long-beards [battle-axes] sought the lives of the men. The wound-sea [blood] surged on the headland of swords. The flood of arrows [blood] fell on the strand at Storð.

8. Reddened shield-rims hit against one another under the heavens. Skǫgul's storm [battle] played on the cloud of rings [shield]. Spear-waves [blood] roared in Óðinn's storm [battle]. Many a man sank down in the sword's stream [blood].

9. Then the kings sat with swords drawn, with shields hacked up and with byrnies shot through. That army was not in good spirits and had to go to Valhǫll.

10. Then Gǫndul spoke, supporting herself on her spearshaft. "Now the gods' troop grows, since the gods have ordered Hákon home with a great army."

11. The ruler heard what the valkyries said, glorious on horse-back. They bore [themselves] wisely, and they sat helmeted and held their shields before them.

12. "Why did you make the battle turn out this way, Geir-Skǫgul?" said Hákon. "We were worthy of victory from the gods." "We brought it about," said Skǫgul, "that you held the field and your enemies fled."

13. "We will ride," said the mighty Skǫgul, "to the green homes of the gods to tell Óðinn, that a monarch will now come to see him himself."

14. "Hermóðr and Bragi," said Hroptatýr, "go to meet the prince because a king comes, one who looks like a hero, hence to our hall."

15. The prince then spoke, he had come from the battle, he stood all covered in gore: "Óðinn seems very grim to us. We fear his temper."

16. "You will have peace from all the Einheriar: take ale from the Æsir. Enemy-of-jarls [king], you have eight brothers within," said Bragi.

17. "Our battle-gear," said the noble king, "we want to keep ourselves. One should care for helmet and byrnie well. It is good to be prepared."

18. Then it was made known how well that king had honored the temples, when all the powers and gods bade Hákon welcome.

19. On a good day is that prince born, who has such a heart. His times will always be spoken of as good.

20. Fenrisúlfr will run unbound among the dwellings of men before a king as good will walk in his empty path.

21. Cattle die. Kinsmen die. Lands and countries are wasted. Since Hákon fared to the heathen gods, many a people is enslaved.

2. Egill Skallagrímsson, ca. 900–83

(from *Egils saga*, chap. 47; text: *ONCP*, p. 147.)

Egill raided in the Øresund ca. 930; in this verse he exhorts his followers to attack Lund.

We should let our swords shine up, tooth-colorer of the wolf [warrior]; we must perform a deed in grace of the valley fish* [summer]; each of the men should try to get to Lundr as quickly as possible; there we will make a harsh magic of spears [battle] before the seat of the sun [sunset].

*valley-fish: snakes.

3. Einarr Helgason skálaglamm, d. ca. 995

(from *Heimskringla, Haralds saga gráfeldar*, chap. 15; text: *ONCP*, p. 84.)

This stanza concerns the battle between Jarl Hákon Sigurðarson and his paternal uncle, Grjótgarðr, who supports the sons of Eiríkr (see *ONCP* and Hallberg). *Skálaglamm* means "scales-tinkle."

The strong prince felled his enemies with helmet-hail [a shower of missiles]; therefore a flood came in the river of the wine-home of Loptr's friend [mead of poetry], because three very bold sons of a jarl fell in the showers of Þróttr's fire [swords]; that gives glory to the sage of the people.

4. Sighvatr Þórðarson, ca. 995–1045

(from *Heimskringla, Óláfs saga helga*, chap. 228;
text: *ONCP*, p. 129.)

Sacrificing himself for King Óláfr, Bjǫrn dies in battle.

I heard also that Bjǫrn again made known his courage to the king's marshalls sufficiently, when he helped protect the lord; he advanced; he fell in the troops among the loyal men of the king's bodyguard at the head of the renowned prince; famed is that death.

5. Sighvatr Þórðarson

(from *Heimskringla, Óláfs saga helga*, chap. 226; text: *ScP*, p. 84.)

This stanza describes the beginning of the Battle of Stiklarstaðir, where King Óláfr died.

Widely was the earth [trodden] under the feet of men—peace-breaking was there; then the byrnied army poured into the fierce battle, when servants of the bow [warriors] rushed quickly down in bright helmets; great was the steel-gust at Stiklarstaðir.

6. Þórfinnr munnr, d. 1030

(from *Heimskringla, Óláfs saga helga*, chap. 206;
text: *ONCP*, p. 150.)

One of King Óláfr's skalds inspires his men before the Battle of Stiklarstaðir. The poet's nickname *munnr* means "the mouth."

It grows dark from the great rain of the hard wind of the shield [battle]. The troop of men from Verdalr wants to fight against the bold leader. We defend the generous ruler. We feed the happy gull of blood [raven]; we fell the men from Þrándheimr in the hail-storm of Þundr [battle]. We goad one another.

7. Haraldr harðráði, King of Norway, 1046–66

(from *Heimskringla, Haralds saga Sigurðarsonar*, chap. 91; text: *ONCP*, p. 152.)

King Haraldr ("hard-counsel") announces that he will fight without his byrnie.

We do not kneel before the noise of weapons at the din in the hollow of the shield; thus commanded faithful Hildr of the slaughter-land [lady of the battlefield]; in days gone by the necklace-bearer bade me carry the helmet-support [head] high in the clash of swords, there where the ice of battle [sword] and skulls meet each other.

8. Bragi Boddason inn gamli, fl. 875 (?)

(from *Skáldskaparmál*, chap. 52; text: *ScP*, pp. 1–2.)

The poet describes a scene on a shield perhaps given to him as a gift. The scene concerns Hamðir's and Sǫrli's attack on Iǫrmun-rekkr (see section X, c.). The poet's nickname means "the old."

Furthermore Iǫrmunrekkr woke up to the bad dream with blood-stained warriors in an eddy of swords; there was a riot in the hall of Randvér's chief kinsmen, when the raven-black brothers of Erpr avenged their wrongs.

9. Þórarinn svarti, ca. 980

(from *Eyrbyggja saga*, chap. 19; text: *ScP*, p. 56.)

Nagli, battle-companion of Þórarinn svarti ("black"), goes mad with terror in the fight.

Nagli got provisions poorly for most of the corpse-geese [ravens]; the knower of the sun of the deep* [man] ran sobbing to the hill;

but Alfgeirr went, hooded with helmet, with more courage into the song of weapons [battle]; the fire of fight [sword] rushed all over the men.

*sun of the deep: gold

10. Þorbjǫrn hornklofi, ca. 900

(from *Heimskringla, Haralds saga ins hárfagra*, chap. 18; text: ScP, p. 14.)

The poet ("horn-clawed") or a raven tells of the Battle of Hafrsfjǫrðr.

Hear how he fought over there in Hafrsfjǫrðr, the nobly born king against Kjǫtvi the rich. Ships came from the east, [men] eager for battle, with gaping prows and carved heads.

11. Þormóðr Trefilsson, ca. 1012

(from *Eyrbyggja saga*, chap. 44; text: ScP, p. 75.)

Snorri goði fights with Steinþórr of Eyrr, taking five of his enemy's men and losing two of his own.

The feeder [Snorri goði] of the swan of the resounding wave of wounds* [the raven] sated the eagle on the food of the wolf [carrion] in Alptafjǫðr; there Snorri had the life taken away from five thanes in the sword-rain [battle]; so shall a man punish his enemies.

*resounding wave of wounds: blood

g. *The Lay of Hildebrand*

(*Das Hildebrandslied*; text: *AHDL*, pp. 84–5.)

The historical and legendary events surrounding Theodoric the Great, a sixth-century king of the Ostrogoths, provide the background for this poem. Exiled from Italy for thirty years, Theodoric returns *via* his champion, Hildebrand, and an armed host. Before this army engages the enemy, Hildebrand meets the opposing champion, Hadubrand, whom he discovers to be his son (see Bostock, Salmon, and Hoffman). Preserved in a manuscript from the eighth or ninth century, *The Lay of Hildebrand* has close ties with the heroic lay in OE; they share certain narrative and metrical techniques. The *Lay* begins with an OE formulaic opening, contains a number of OE words, and some Anglo-Saxon forms occur in the manuscript. It also uses the "Hero on the Beach" type-scene (see Renoir). An ON analogue can be found in *Hildibrandr's Death Song* (q.v.).

I heard tell that single warriors clashed with one another, Hildebrand and Hadubrand, between two armies. Both father and son (?) put their armour in order. They made their war-shirts ready. They girded on their swords, the heroes, over the ring-mail, as they rode to battle. Hildebrand spoke, [Heribrand's son]: he was the older man, wiser in life. With few words he began to ask who the other's father might be in the host of men . . . "or of which family you might be. If you tell me one [name], youth, I will know the others in the kingdom. The whole race is known to me."

Hadubrand spoke, Hildebrand's son: "Our people, old and wise, those who lived in former times, told me that my father was called Hildebrand; I am called Hadubrand. Long ago he went off to the east. He fled Odoacer's hatred, away with Theodoric and many of his warriors. In his homeland he left a young bride sitting in a dwelling, a child ungrown, without inheritance. He rode away to the east. Afterwards Theodoric suffered the loss of my father; that was such a friendless man. He, that warrior truest to Theodoric, was enraged at Odoacer. He was always at the head of the army; fighting was always very dear to him; he was known . . . to bold men. I do not think he is still alive."

"I call to witness," [said Hildebrand,] "great God from heaven above, that never before have you come to an encounter with such a closely-related man!" Then he wound from his arm twisted rings, made from an imperial coin, which the king, the lord of the Huns, had given to him. "Now I give this to you as a token of good favor."

Hadubrand spoke, the son of Hildebrand: "With a spear should a man receive [such] gifts, point against point . . . Old Hun, you are very cunning. You tempt me with your words, [because] you want to throw your spear at me. Just as you are an aged man, so you have practised continual deceit. Sailors [who came] west over the winding [*or* Vandal] sea [the Mediterranean?] told me that war took him away; Hildebrand, Heribrand's son, is dead."

Hildebrand spoke, Heribrand's son: "I see clearly by your armour that you have a noble lord at home, that you never became an exile in this kingdom."—"Alas now, O ruling God," [said Hildebrand,] "what dire fate is about to occur! I have wandered sixty summers and winters outside the country. There they always assigned me to a company of spear-throwers. While no one caused my death at any fortress, now shall my own child hew me with a sword, lay me low with his blade, or I will become his slayer. However, if your strength is sufficient, you may now easily win the armour, seize the booty from such an old man, if you have any right to it." "He would now be the most cowardly," said Hildebrand, "of the East People [Huns], who would refuse battle with you, since you wish for it so much, the war between us. Let him try who may [to see] which of us today has to leave his war-garment behind or might get control of both these byrnies."

Then first they let the ash-spears fly in sharp showers; they stuck in the shields. Then they rode together, the shields resounded (?); they hewed the white shields fiercely, until their linden-shields became useless to them, hacked by weapons . . .

2. Celtic Analogues

a. *The Gododdin*

(*Y Gododdin*; text: *CA*)

This Welsh poem, written sometime between the sixth and ninth centuries, is not strictly a battle poem because it is not a narrative account of an event. Instead the poet celebrates the warriors' martial virtues, and thus the poem reminds us of the OE *Finnsburg Fragment*. Although scholars refer to it as a single long poem, *The Gododdin* is actually a collection of heroic elegies. The individual stanzas concern one or more heroes, all of whom apparently took part in an ill-fated expedition led by Mynyddog Mwynfawr against the Anglo-Saxons of Deira and Bernicia (*BWP*, pp. 50–69; *GO*, pp. 8ff.). Together they constitute some thirteen hundred lines, of which only a representative sample is translated here.

Many of the personal and place names cannot be identified unequivocally, and many of them may be descriptive epithets. This verse is characterized by a certain compactness, an absence in the original of the definite article, and a fondness for stark contrast to reveal a richness of meaning. Throughout, the poet drums on the comitatus theme: the prince or leader retained a host whom he was obliged to feed and provide with drink (signified usually by the word "mead" alone); they, in turn, in payment for their provisions and keep, were obliged by honor to fight bravely and without stint for the chief (see Jarman 1967 and 1976, and *GO*). Thus the mead/ blood image persists, the exchange of feasting for fighting, the payment for the mead being death. The stanzas (*awdlau*, sg. *awdl*) are of varying lengths, and most of them contain lines of nine or ten syllables with a single end rhyme (*CA*, pp. lxx–lxxxv; and *GO*, pp. 53–6; see also Parry).

I. The might of a man, he was a lad; courage for the fray, swift long-maned steeds under the splendid lad; a broad light shield across the crupper of the lean swift one; untarnished stately swords, golden spurs and rich cloth. There is no enmity between me and you. 'Tis better that I make a song of praise to you. Sooner his blood on the ground than his wedding feast; sooner his food for ravens than his proper burial. Dear companion Owain, 'tis wrong his being under ravens. An awful wonder to me, that region where Marro's only son was killed.

II. Wearing a diadem, in the front ranks wherever he went. Breathless before a maid, he earned his mead. Full of holes the boss of his shield wherever he heard the battle cry; he gave no quarter to those he pursued. He did not retire from battle until the blood flowed; those who did not flee he cut down like so many weeds. In princely courts the *Gododdin* recounts that when Madog returned, not one in a hundred came back with him.

III. Diademed warrior, enemy's snare; the rush of an eagle in estuaries when it feeds. His contract was a goal that was preserved; better he fulfilled his purpose, which was not withdrawn; before Gododdin's army they retreated, powerful pursuit over the land of Manawyd. He spared neither shape nor shield. No one could keep from the blows of Cadfannan, reared war-like.

IV. Wearing a diadem, in the front ranks, a wolf in battle; the fiery one seized torques from the host; a cup of mead was worthy amber. He repelled the attack, blood running down cheeks. Though the men of Gwynedd and the North came, through the advice of Ysgyrran's son, shields were broken.

V. Wearing a diadem, in the front ranks, armed in battle; before his appointed day a man mighty in battle. A leader in the forefront against armies, five fifties fell before his blades; of the men of Deira and Bernicia twenty hundred passed to perdition in a single hour. Sooner his flesh to wolves than to the wedding feast;

sooner as gain for the raven than to the altar; sooner than his proper burial, his blood to the ground. For mead in the hall, a hundred hosts. Hyfaidd the Tall will be praised as long as there are bards.

VI. The men who went to Gododdin were laughter-loving, savage in battle with spears at the ready; a short year in peace, they went into silence. Son of Bodgad, his hand wreaked slaughter. Though they went to churches to do penance, old and young, mighty and slight, the tale is true: death came for them.

VII. The men who went to Gododdin were laughing and intense, attackers in a band eager for battle. They slaughtered with blades without much fanfare. Pillars of battle, Rhaithfyw gave joy.

VIII. The men who went to Catraeth were a spirited host; bright mead their feast, and it became poison. Three hundred under orders in battle; and after the rejoicing, there was silence. Though they went to churches to do penance, the tale is true: death came for them.

X. The men went to Catraeth at dawn; their fears stirred their tranquility; a thousand hundred hurling themselves at three hundred; gore staining spears; in battle, he held his ground most firmly, before the host of Mynyddog Mwynfawr.

XI. The men went to Catraeth at dawn; their spirit cut short their lives; mead they drank—yellow, sweet, ensnaring; for a year, many a minstrel rejoiced. Red their swords, nor their blades wiped; white-faced shields and four-edged spears before the host of Mynyddog Mwynfawr.

XII. The men who went to Catraeth at daybreak humiliated armies; they made biers necessary: with full blades, no protection in the world; he made, before talk of truce, a blood bath and death for his enemies; before the army of Gododdin, when he fought, the fierce upholder accomplished bold purpose.

XIII. The men went to Catraeth at daybreak; he gulped mead-feasts midnights; was wretched, lamentation of the host, that fierce killer's expedition. No great one as high-minded in purpose over mead set out for Catraeth, none from Eidin fort who so completely dispelled enemies: Tudfwlch the Tall, out of his country and his towns; he killed Saxons every week; his bravery will endure long, and the memory of him by his fair comrades. When Tudfwlch came, his country's strength, the son of Cilydd's rank was a bloody plain.

XIV. A man went to Catraeth at dawn; safe-guarding him an enclosure of shields; savagely they attack, gather goods; like a crack of thunder the clash of shields; a proud man, a prudent man, a champion; he tore, he pierced with steel spikes; over blood he slew with blades; in battle hard iron on heads; in courts the warrior was humble; before Erthgi, armies groaned.

XV. 'Tis of the battle of Catraeth that it is reported: men fall— grieving over them was long-lasting; whether easy or difficult, they fought for the land against the sons of Godebog, an evil lot; a long line of biers carried blood-stained men; sad the fate—it had to be—that was allotted Tudfwlch and Cyfwlch the Tall; though we drank bright mead by candle light, and though its taste was fine, its bitterness was long-lasting.

XXI. The men who went to Catraeth were renowned; wine and mead from golden goblets was their drink for a year, according to honored custom; three, three score, and three hundred gold- torqued men: of those who set forth after splendid mead, only three escaped from fierce fighting: the two war hounds of Aeron and steely Cynon—and I, too, streaming with blood, because of my song.

XXIII. Weapons scattered, the once orderly invincible host in disarray, great destruction; the hero turned back the English folk; he sprayed javelins in the ribs of warriors in a spear-throwing fray; he flattened men and widowed women before his death; the passionate son of Hoywgi created bloody carnage from spears.

XXIV. Hero with a protective shield beneath his brindled brow and moving like a young horse; there was shouting on the hill of battle, there were sparks; his spears were swift, were flashing; there was food for ravens, windfall for a raven; and before he was left in the ash ford as the dew descended, beside the spreading wave, a graceful soaring eagle, the world's bards deemed him a man of heart.

XXX. When Caradog rushed into battle, like a wild boar, a triple slayer, bull of battle, in combat a hewer, he would feed wild dogs from his hand; as I am witness, Owain son of Eulad and Gwrien and Gwyn and Gwriad from Catraeth, from the killing, from Hyddwn Hill before it was taken; after bright mead at hand, not one saw his father again.

XXXI. The men who attacked rushed as one; short their lives— drinkers of clear mead; the retinue of Mynyddog, famous in battle: their lives the price of their mead-feast; Caradog and Madog, Pyll and Ieuan, Gwgon and Gwion, Gwyn and Cynfan, Peredur of the steely weapons and Aeddan; attackers in battle's din, shields scattered; and though they were killed, they killed; none returned to his land.

XXXII. The men who attacked trained together for a year over mead, high-minded; how painful to speak of them, overwhelming longing; bitter their resting-place: no one nursed them; long-felt loss and sorrow for splendid men from the land of wine-feasts; Gwlyged of Gododdin, to be ready, partook of renowned Mynyddog's feast; and dearly he bought the battle of Catraeth.

XLI. Splendid men went from us; nurtured on wine and mead from Mynyddog's feast were they; I am deeply saddened by the loss of tough men of fury; like thunder from the skies, shields exploded before the onslaught of Eithinyn.

XLVIII. Not a wearied lord am I; I do not avenge attacks; I laugh no laugh beneath sand; my knee straightened in an earthen abode, an iron chain around my knees, from the mead from drinking horns, from Catraeth's folk; whether as Aneirin or not, Taliesin of the skilled utterance knows it: I sang Gododdin before dawn the following day.

b. *In Praise of Urien*

(Text: *PT*, III.)

In this Welsh panegyric, Urien, ruler of Rheged, is celebrated for his generosity, his protection of the defenceless, his prowess in battle against the English, his subjects' respect and—perhaps most importantly—his patronage of poets. Although the poem does not describe a battle, it illustrates an aspect of the heroic background (see *EWP*, Jarman 1967, and 1976). Its date is sometime between the sixth and the tenth centuries.

Urien of Erechwydd, most generous man in Christendom, much you give to the men of the world: as you gather so do you spend; the bards of the world rejoice while you live! Greater is the joy of the renowned and the celebrated, greater is the glory, because Urien and his sons exist. And he the chief, the supreme ruler, refuge for distant travellers, keen champion. The English know him when they make reports: death they found, and frequent grief; burning their dwellings and carrying off their cloaks; and many a loss and much hardship without deliverance from Urien of Rheged. Defender of Rheged, famous lord, his country's anchor, in you I am content. From all reports, your spear was eager when you would sense battle. When you attack in battle, you slaughter; houses afire before dawn before the lord of Erechwydd. The fairest of Erechwydd, most generous of its men, common the English without protection because of the most brave lord; most brave scion, you are the best of what has been and what will be; you are peerless. When they look upon him, their terror is profound. Common is conviviality around him, around the exciting

lord. Around him conviviality and profusion of riches, gold-prince
of the North, ruler of princes.

c. *The Battle of Gwen Ystrad*
(Text: *PT*, II.)

In this poem, dated between the sixth and tenth centuries, the
poet mainly praises Urien of Rheged and his fierce band. Gwen
Ystrad, or Llech Wen, merely provides the *locus* for their bold
deeds. As Williams notes in his edition, a striking feature of the
poem is Urien's control of Catraeth, not yet fallen to the
Northumbrians. The events celebrated here, then, would antedate
the subject of the *Gododdin*, an expedition to recover Catraeth
(*PT*, p. xlviii). Also noteworthy is the conventional use of *gwelais*
("I saw") four times, always at the beginning of a line. The poet in
Celtic society was a seer, among other things, and through such
conventions, he affirms his "presence" at the events by virtue of
his special training and status, his ability to "discover" all things
(Jarman 1976, pp. 15–16; *PLlH*, pp. 6–7; see also *EWP*, Williams
1944, Williams 1971).

The men of Catraeth set out at dawn around a battle-victorious
cattle-chief: Urien is he, renowned chieftain, he restrains princes
and cuts them down; the warlike, bold one is named leader of all
Christendom. The men of Britain are destructive among hosts;
Gwen Ystrad, battle-station of the battle-grinder: neither field nor
forest gave protection from your onslaught when you came there
like the surging sea, O refuge of the people! Sharp their cries
across the land. I saw splendid men in ranks, and after morning's
combat, broken flesh. I saw the throng of three districts dead. A
lively wrathful shout was heard. Defending Gwen Ystrad were
seen weary and worn-down champions. Before the ford I saw
blood-smeared battlers laying down arms before the graying
prince. They wished peace, for they had gotten into straits; hands
crossed, the pale-faced ones, in the gravelly ford. Their chiefs
became intoxicated on the flowing wine of Idon; waves washed the
tails of their horses. I saw marauders dispirited, and blood-stained
garments, and swift passionate warriors drawn up in battle: protector in battle, it was not flight he had in mind, lord of Rheged, I
marvel that he dared. I saw a noble band about Urien when he
tangled with his enemy in Llech Wen. The router of enemies
rejoiced in battle; men's spears were borne to battle: eager for the
fray those whom Urien owns!

B. *The Battle of Maldon*

1. Germanic Analogue

a. *The Lay of Ludwig*

(*Das Ludwigslied*; text: *AHDL*, pp. 136–8.)

The Lay of Ludwig celebrates the victory of Louis III over the Danes at Saucourt on 3 August 881. The poem must have been written between that date and 3 August 882, when Louis died (see Schwarz). Whether the poem is a "Historical Poem" or a later imitation of the ancient "Praise Poem," its resemblances to *The Battle of Maldon* are striking: the absolute characterization of the natives as God's people and the Vikings as the fiendish enemy (see Murdoch 1977). Louis' victory stands quite in contrast, of course, to Byrhtnoth's defeat (see also Beck, who discusses generic similarities between *Ludwig, Maldon* and the ON *Lay of Hákon*; and Berg).

Teutonic poem about King Ludwig of pious memory, son of Ludwig, who was also a king

I know a king, he is called Ludwig, who zealously serves God. I know He rewards him for that. As a child he became fatherless. For that he was given recompense at once. The Lord called him; He became his foster-father. He gave him courage, a noble following, the throne here in the land of the Franks. May he enjoy that for a long time! That he shared at once with Carloman, his brother, the number of enjoyments. When all that was finished, God wanted to test him, to see if he, so young, could endure tribulation. He let the heathen men travel over the sea, to admonish the people of the Franks for their sins. Some were chosen [for eternal life]; some were lost at once. He who had lived sinfully suffered punishment. He who had been a thief and survived began to fast; afterwards he became a good man. One was a liar, one a robber, one full of corruption and he did penance for it.

The king was far away; the kingdom was in complete disarray. Christ was angry; painfully [the kingdom] atoned for this. Yet God took pity; He knew about all the distress. He commanded Ludwig to ride there at once. "Ludwig, my king, help my people. The Northmen have so severely oppressed them." Then Ludwig spoke: "Lord, I will do everything you command, if death does not prevent me."

Then he had God's permission to go; he raised up the war-banner and rode there into the land of the Franks against the Northmen. They thanked God, those who were waiting for him. They all said; "My Lord, we have waited so long for you." Then Ludwig the Good spoke loudly: "Take comfort, comrades, my battle-companions, God has sent me here and commanded me Himself, if it seemed advisable to you, that I should fight here, and not spare myself until I rescued you. Now I want for all of God's faithful to follow me. Our life on earth is determined to be as long as Christ wills. If He wills our death, He has the power to do that. Whoever does God's will bravely here, I will reward him for that, if he comes out [of the battle] alive; if he remains therein, [I will reward] his kin."

Then he took a shield and a spear; bravely he rode [ahead]. He wanted to proclaim the truth to his enemies. Then it was not very long [before] he found the Northmen: He gave praise to God, now he sees what he had desired. The king rode boldly [forward]; he sang a sacred song. And all together they sang "Kyrie eleison." The song was sung, the war was begun. The blood shone on the battlefield (?), the Franks pursued joyfully. There fought every thane, but none like Ludwig. Quick and brave, that was native to him. He cut through one, he pierced through another. He poured at once a bitter drink for his enemies. So woe to them forever! God's might be praised: Ludwig was victorious. And thanks be to all the saints! His was the battle-victory. Again hail, Ludwig, our blessed king. He was just as ready here as truly there was a need. May the Lord in His mercies save him.

2. Celtic Analogue

a. *The Battle of Argoed Llwyfain*
(*Gwaith Argoed Llwyfain*; text: *PT*, VI.)

The Battle of Argoed Llwyfain is perhaps the one MW poem that can properly be called an analogue to the OE battle poems, resembling in particular *The Battle of Maldon*. It can only be dated roughly between the sixth and the tenth centuries. The poem is atypical of Welsh poems about war and has closer affinities with the OE narrative technique than do other Welsh texts, such as *The Gododdin* (*WP*, p. 11). The location of Argoed Llwyfain is uncertain, but Llwyfain may represent Leeming Lane, the name of the old Roman road running south from Catterick (Catraeth; *PT*, p. xliv). Otherwise, the name is purely descriptive: *ar-goed* "against, upon, by the forest" of *llwyfain* "elms"—the battle was fought by an elm grove.

Fflamddwyn ("flame-bearer") is the enemy of Urien's host and his son Owain, and their army, gathered from the northern kingdoms of Goddau and Rheged (*PT*, pp. xxxvi–xlvii; Jarman 1976, pp. 51–67; see also Dillon, *EWP, PWV, WP*).

Saturday morning there was a great battle, from the time the sun rose till it grew dark; Flamddwyn attacked in four forces. In order to muster Goddau and Rheged, a summons from Argoed to Arfynydd; they did not get even a single day's delay. Flamddwyn called out a great boast—would they give hostages? were they ready?

Owain, scourge of the East, answered thus: They would not give, they were not ready, nor would they be. And a hound of Coel's line would be a roaring lion ere he paid a hostage to anyone. Urien, lord of Erechwydd, called out, "If there is talk of meeting for a truce, let us raise our shields on high, men, and attack Flamddwyn in his ranks, and let us kill him and his cohorts." Before Argoed Llwyfain was many a corpse; crows grew red from the gore of the dead, and the war-band charged with the chieftain. I shall sing to their victory for a year!

C. *The Battle of Brunanburh*

1. Germanic Analogue

a. *Egill's Saga*

(Text: *Es*, pp. 130–41.)

This selection from *Egill's Saga* (ca. 1220–40) describes a tenth-century battle between King Æthelstan of England and a combined force of Norse and Scots. The saga calls the battle-place "Vínheiðr," and there has been considerable debate about the equation of this locale with "Brunanburh." However, the scholarly balance now tips in favor of such an identification (see Campbell and Einarsson, B.).

Chapter 52

Óláfr, king of the Scots, gathered a large army and afterwards marched south into England, and when he came to Northumberland, he laid it all waste; and when the jarls who ruled there heard about that, they called together an army and marched against the king. And when they met each other, there was a great battle, and it ended so that King Óláfr had victory, and Jarl Goðrekr fell, and Álfgeirr fled away, along with the greatest part of the army which followed them and had escaped from the battle. Álfgeirr could then offer no resistance; then King Óláfr conquered all of Northumberland. Álfgeirr went to meet King Aðalsteinn and told him of his trouble. And as soon as King Aðalsteinn heard that such a large army had come into his country, he immediately sent out messengers and called together an army, sent word to his jarls and other powerful men. The king immediately took to the road with that army which he had gathered and marched against the Scots. But when it was reported that Óláfr, king of the Scots, had gained victory and had conquered a large part of England, he then had a much greater army than Aðalsteinn, because many of the powerful men sought him out. And when Hringr and Aðils heard about that—they had collected a large army—they joined forces with King Óláfr; then they had an immense army. And when Aðalsteinn heard all this, he had a meeting with his chiefs and counsellors, and he debated about what would be most expedient to do; he then told all the people exactly what he had heard about the activities of the Scottish king and of his great host. All there agreed that Jarl Álfgeirr had the worst part in this, and thought that it was fitting to take his honors from him; and this plan was decided upon, that King Aðalsteinn should turn back and go to southern England and then gather an army as he went northward through all his lands, because they saw that otherwise it would be slow gathering a great host, as great as was needed, if the king himself did not draw the army together. And over the army, which already had come together, the king set Þórólfr and Egill as commanders; they had to lead the army which the vikings had brought there for the king, but Álfgeirr still had command of his own army himself. Then the king appointed more company commanders as it seemed necessary to him. And when Egill came home from the meeting to his comrades, they asked what news he could tell them about the king of the Scots. He declared:

> 16. Óláfr made one prince turn his back and flee, and he
> killed another; the battle was fierce; I have heard that this

lord was "þing-hard" [difficult to deal with]; Goðrekr trod many a wrong path on the moor [i.e., he died]; the waster of England laid half of Álfgeirr's kingdom under himself.

Afterwards they sent messengers to King Óláfr and they contrived this as their errand, that King Aðalsteinn wanted to hazel a field for him and offer a battle at Vínheiðr near Vínuskógar, and he did not want them to harry his land, but rather he who had the victory in battle should rule the kingdom of England. He gave a week's notice of their battle, and the one who came first should wait a week for the other. And that was then the custom, that as soon as a field was hazelled for a king, he might not harry without shame before the battle was finished. King Óláfr did just that and he halted his army and did not harry but waited for the appointed day. Then he moved his army to Vínheiðr. A fortress stood to the north of the heath. King Óláfr settled into the fortress and held the greatest part of his army there, because large, open country was nearby, and it seemed to him better there for supplying those provisions which the army had to have. But he sent his men up on the heath, where the battlefield was agreed on. There they had to pick places for pitching their tents and prepare themselves before the army came. And when the men came to that place where the field was hazelled, hazel poles were set up everywhere as boundary markers, in that place where the battle was to be fought. It was necessary to prepare the place carefully so that it would be flat, since a great army had to be drawn up in battle. Thus it was there, where the battlefield should be, that there the heath was flat; but on one side a river flowed and on the other side there was a large forest. And where it was shortest between the forest and the river—and that was quite a long way—there King Aðalsteinn's men had pitched their tents. Their tents stood the whole distance between the forest and the river; they had pitched their tents in such a way that there were no men in every third tent and, indeed, few in any. But when King Óláfr's men came visiting them, they had a great many men in front of all the tents, and they could not go in. Aðalsteinn's men said that their tents were all full of men, so that they had nowhere near enough room for their army. But the tents stood so high, that no one could see over them, whether they stood many or few in depth; they thought that there must be an army of men. King Óláfr's men pitched their tents to the north of the hazels, and it sloped downward somewhat from there. Aðalsteinn's men said from one day to another that their king would come or had come to the fortress which was south under the heath. Troops gathered to them both day and night. And when the

appointed time which had been fixed had passed, Aðalsteinn's
men sent messengers to meet King Óláfr with these words, that
King Aðalsteinn was ready for battle and had an immense army,
but he sent these words to Óláfr: he did not wish for them to make
as great a manslaughter as then seemed likely to occur; rather he
asked him to go home to Scotland; but Aðalsteinn would give him
as a token of friendship a silver shilling for every plow throughout
his whole kingdom, and he wished that they should join together
in friendship. And when the messengers came to King Óláfr, he
was beginning to prepare his army and intending to ride to battle.
And when the messengers conveyed their message, the king
stopped his journey for the day; he then sat in council along with
the commanders of his army. Men had different opinions about
this; some strongly urged that he should accept that offer; they
said that that would then have become the greatest glorious
expedition, that they should return home having received so great
a tribute from Aðalsteinn; some resisted and said that Aðalsteinn
would offer much more a second time, if this were not accepted,
and this plan was settled on. Then the messengers asked King
Óláfr to give them more time, so that they might meet King
Aðalsteinn again and test whether he would pay a still greater
tribute so there might be peace; they asked for a truce of one day
to ride home, a second for council, and a third for riding back. The
king agreed to this. The messengers travelled home and came back
on the third day, as was arranged, saying to King Óláfr that
Aðalsteinn would give all that he had promised before and in
addition, as booty to King Óláfr's army, a shilling to every free-
born man, a [silver] mark to every company captain who commanded twelve men or more, and a gold mark to every leader of
the king's men, and five gold marks to every jarl. Then the king
had this brought up before his army; it was the same as before,
that some resisted and some urged acceptance, but finally the king
gave his decision: he said that he would accept the offer if it
included that King Aðalsteinn would let him have all of Northumberland with the tributes and taxes which went with it. The
messengers again asked for a delay of three days and also that
King Óláfr send his men to hear King Aðalsteinn's decision,
whether he would accept that offer or not; they said that they
thought King Aðalsteinn would let few things be obstacles to their
reaching an agreement. King Óláfr agreed to this and sent his men
to King Aðalsteinn; the messengers all rode together and found
King Aðalsteinn in the fortress which was nearest the heath to the
south; King Óláfr's messengers brought their errand and offer of
peace before King Aðalsteinn. And King Aðalsteinn's men related

every offer with which they had travelled to King Óláfr, and besides that this was a plan of wise men to delay the battle as long as the king had not come; King Aðalsteinn gave a quick decision in this case and spoke to the messengers thus: "Convey these words of mine to King Óláfr, that I will give him permission to return home to Scotland with his army, but he must pay back all the wealth, which he wrongfully took here in my land; afterwards let us establish peace between our lands and neither harry the other; that shall also follow, that King Óláfr shall become my liegeman and hold Scotland at my hand and be my under-king; go now," he said, "and tell him how things are."

The messengers turned at once on their way in the evening and came to King Óláfr near midnight; then they woke up the king and at once told him King Aðalsteinn's words. The king at once had his jarls and other captains called to him and had the messengers come in and relate the results of their errand and King Aðalsteinn's words. And when that was made known to the men of the army, then they were all of one voice that what lay before them was to prepare for battle; the messengers also reported that Aðalsteinn had a huge army and he had come to the fortress the same day that the messengers had come. Then Jarl Aðils spoke: "Now it has come about, king, as I said, that they would prove crafty for you, these English; we have sat here for a long time and waited, while they have gathered all their army around them, and their king could have been nowhere near when we came here; now they will have assembled a great army while we sat around. Now it is my advice, king, that my brother and I ride out at once in the night with our army; it may be, that they have no fear for themselves now, since they have learned that their king is near with a great army; the two of us shall spring an attack on them and when they are put to flight, they will lose their strength and afterwards be not so bold in the attack against us."

The king thought the plan well devised: "We will get our army ready, as soon as it is light, and go to join you." They firmly agreed to this course and so ended the meeting.

Chapter 53

Jarl Hringr and his brother Aðils readied their army and went at once in the night south to the heath. When it was light, then Þórólfr's watchmen saw where the army was going; then a blast of trumpets was blown and men dressed themselves for battle; afterwards they began to draw up their troops and they had two divisions. Jarl Álfgeirr commanded one of the divisions and a

standard was borne before him; in that division were those troops
who had served him before, and also the company which had
gathered there from the surrounding districts. That was a much
larger army than that which followed Þórólfr. Þórólfr was armed
so that he had a wide and thick shield, a very sturdy helmet on his
head; he was girded with a sword which he called Lang ["long"], a
large and good weapon. He had a battle-axe in his hand. The blade
was two ells long and a four-sided spike was mounted on top and
the upper blade was broad, the socket both long and stout; the
shaft was not so long that the hand could not reach up to the
socket, but it was extremely thick. An iron spike was in the socket
and the shaft was all wound with iron. These spears were called
"byrnie-bolts." Egill had the same gear as Þórólfr; he was girded
with a sword which he called Naðr ["Adder"]; he had taken that
sword in Kúrland; that was the best weapon; neither of them had
byrnies. They set up a standard and Þorfiðr the strong carried it.
Their whole army had Norse shields and entirely Norse battle
gear; all the Norse men who were there were in their division.
Þórólfr and Egill drew up their army near the forest, but Álfgeirr's
division went along the river. Jarl Aðils and his brother saw that
they could not come upon them unawares; then they began to
draw up their troops; they also readied two divisions and had two
standards; Aðils drew up his army opposite Jarl Álfgeirr, and
Hringr opposite the vikings. Then the battle began; each side
marched straight forward. Jarl Aðils pressed firmly ahead until
Álfgeirr retreated; but Aðils' men pressed on then doubly bold; it
was not long before Álfgeirr fled, and there is this to tell about
him, that he rode away southwards over the heath and a company
of men with him; he rode until he came near to the fortress where
the king sat. Then the jarl spoke: "I do not intend for us to go to
the fortress; we received a strong reprimand the last time we went
to the king, when we came away beaten from King Óláfr, and it
will not seem to him that our condition has been much improved
by this conduct; there will now be no need to think about honors,
as far as he's concerned." Afterwards he rode southward, and
there is this to tell about his journey, that he rode day and night
until they came west to Jarlsnes; there the jarl got himself passage
south over the sea and came to Valland [France]; there he had half
his kin; he never came again to England.

At first Aðils chased the fleeing one, but it was not long before
he turned back to where the battle was, and then made his attack.
When Þórólfr saw that, he turned to meet the jarl and commanded
the standard to be carried there, commanded his men to follow
one another bravely and to stand close together—"Let us move to

the forest," he said, "and let it protect our rear, so that they cannot come at us from all sides." They did so, moving towards the forest; then it turned into a hard battle; Egill pressed on against Aðils, and there was tough fighting between them; the odds were great, but nevertheless more fell among Aðils' host. Then Þórólfr became so furious that he threw his shield on his back and took his spear in both hands; then he dashed forward and struck and slashed on both sides; men then fled on either hand, but he killed many. He cleared the path forward to Jarl Hringr's standard and nothing then could stop him; he killed the man who carried Jarl Hringr's standard and struck down the standard-pole. Then he pierced with his spear the jarl's breast through the byrnie and the body, so that it came out through the shoulders, and he raised him upon his halberd over his head and pushed the spear-handle into the earth, and the jarl died on the spear, and everyone saw that, both his men and also his enemies. Next Þórólfr drew his sword and struck on both sides; his men pressed on then too; many Welsh and Scots fell, while some took flight. But when Jarl Aðils saw his brother's fall and the great slaughter in his army and how some fled and he thought himself hard pressed, then he took to flight and ran to the forest; he fled into the forest along with his company; then the whole army which had followed him took to flight. There was a great slaughter among the fleeing men, and those who fled were scattered widely over the heath. Jarl Aðils had dropped his own standard, and no one knew whether he or some other man had fled. Soon the night began to grow dark, and Þórólfr and Egill turned back to their war-booths with their men, and then at the same time King Aðalsteinn came there with his whole army and set up his field-tents and made them ready. A little later, King Óláfr came with his army; they pitched their tents and made them ready, where their own men had set up tents; King Óláfr was then told that both his jarls, Hringr and Aðils, had fallen, and a great many of the rest of his men.

Chapter 54

King Aðalsteinn had passed the night before in the fortress, as was told above, and there he heard that there had been a battle on the heath; then he at once made himself and the whole army ready and pressed north to the heath; then he heard a complete and clear account of how the battle had gone. Then the brothers, Þórólfr and Egill, came to meet the king; he thanked them well for their courage and for the victory, which they had won; he promised them his full friendship; they all stayed there together that night.

King Aðalsteinn woke up his army as soon as it was daybreak; he had a meeting with his captains and ordered how his army should be drawn up; he drew up his own division first, and set those troops who were sharpest in the forefront of the division. Then he declared that Egill should command that army—"but Þórólfr," he said, "shall be with his own army and the other army, which I am placing with it; that will be the second division in our army, the one which he shall be captain over, because the Scots are always loose in formation; they leap to and fro and come now here, now there; they often become battle-dangerous, if men are not on guard, but they are loose on the field, if one turns against them." Egill answered the king: "I do not want Þórólfr and me separated in battle, but it seems right to me that we be placed where there is most need and the going is toughest." Þórólfr said, "we should let the king decide, where he wants to place us; let us give him what he likes; if you wish, I will take over where you are placed." Egill said: "You will now have your way, but I will often regret this battle order." Then the men went forward in divisions, as the king had commanded, and banners were set up; the king's division stood on the open space to the river, but Þórólfr's division went higher up along the forest. King Óláfr then began arraying his army, when he saw that Aðalsteinn had arrayed his; he also made two divisions and let his banner and the division, which he himself commanded, go to meet King Aðalsteinn and his army. Each side then had an army so great that it made no difference which of the two was greater in men, and King Óláfr's second division advanced near the forest to meet the army which Þórólfr commanded; the captains there were Scottish jarls, the army was mostly Scots, and that was a great host. Then the divisions clashed together and soon there was a great battle. Þórólfr pressed strongly forward and had his banner carried forward along the forest and he intended to press so far forward that he would come to the unshielded flank of the king's division; they had their shields before them, and the forest was off to the right side; they let it protect them there. Þórólfr went so far forward that few of his men were ahead of him, and when he was least on guard, Jarl Aðils and the company who followed him lept out of the forest; at once they thrust many halberds at the same time against Þórólfr, and he fell there by the forest, and Þorfiðr, who carried the banner, moved backwards to where the troops stood thicker, but Aðils pressed towards them, and then there was a great battle. The Scots then shouted their victory-cry, when they had felled the captain. When Egill heard that cry and saw that Þórólfr's standard retreated, he knew that Þórólfr himself would not be following. Then he ran in that

direction into the middle of the divisions; he quickly became aware
of the events, which had happened there, as soon as he found his
men; then he rallied the army staunchly to the attack; he was first
in the forefront. He had his sword Naðr in hand. He pressed
forward and struck on both sides and felled many men; Þorfiðr
bore the standard directly behind him, and the rest of the army
followed the standard; there was the most bitter battle. Egill went
forward until he met Jarl Aðils; they exchanged few blows before
Jarl Aðils fell and many men with him, but after his fall, that army
which had followed him fled, and Egill and his army followed them
and killed all those they overtook, because there was no need then
to ask for peace. But the Scottish jarls stood no longer, as soon as
they saw that the rest of their comrades were fleeing; they took to
their heels at once; but Egill and his army pressed on to where the
king's division was, and came then against their unshielded flank
and quickly made a great slaughter there. Then the division broke
rank and was all scattered; many of Óláfr's men fled then, and the
vikings shouted their victory-cry. And when King Aðalsteinn began
to think that King Óláfr's army was starting to give way, then he
rallied his own troops and had his standard carried forward; he then
made so hard an attack that Óláfr's troop fell back before them and
a great slaughter took place. King Óláfr fell there and the greatest
part of the army which Óláfr had had, for those who took to flight
and were overtaken were all killed. King Aðalsteinn won a
tremendous victory there.

Chapter 55

Poem 21

Now the presser of battle, towering over the land, the
descendant of kings, has felled three princes; the country
falls under the kinsman of Ælla [Aðalsteinn]; Aðalsteinn has
done more; everything is lower than this king of glorious
race. Here we swear this, breaker of the flame of the wave*
[generous man].

Refrain: Now the highest path of the reindeer [mountain]
lies under the valiant Aðalsteinn.

---

*flame of the wave: gold
(See also III.1.k.3)

XI

RUNE POEM

A. Germanic Analogues

1. *The Norwegian Rune Poem*

(Text: *OERP*, pp. 181–3.)

The Old Norwegian rune poem is one of four such poems still extant from the Middle Ages. The other poems are the OE poem, an aberrant ninth-century OHG version translated below, and a skilled Icelandic rendition dating in manuscript from the fifteenth century. At least three of the poems were obviously intended primarily as mnemonic devices, although the gnomic assertions explaining many of the runes tie the poems to the tradition of wisdom poetry (q.v.). The date of the Norwegian poem is less certain than the others, but the manuscript in which it is found cannot be earlier than the thirteenth century (see Shippey and *OERP*).

1. *Wealth* causes strife among kinsmen; the wolf lives in the forest.
2. *Slag* comes from bad iron; often the reindeer runs over the hard-packed snow.
3. *Purs* [giant] causes sickness in women; few become happy from bad luck.
4. *River-mouth* is the way of most journeys; but a sheath is of swords.
5. *Riding* is said to be worst for horses; Reginn forged the best sword.

6. *Sore* (?) is the curse of children; death makes a corpse pale.
7. *Hail* is the coldest of grains; Christ created the world of old.
8. *Need* grants small choice; a naked man grows cold in the frost.
9. *Ice* we call the broad bridge; the blind man has to be led.
10. *Harvest* is a good for men; I say that Fróði was generous.
11. *Sun* is the light of lands; I bow down to divine judgment.
12. *Týr* is a one-handed god; often the smith must blow.
13. *Birch* is the leaf-greenest of limbs; Loki bore the fortune of deceit.
14. *Man* is an increase from the dust; great is the claw of the hawk.
15. *Water* is where a waterfall falls from the mountain; but ornaments are gold.
16. *Yew* is the winter-greenest of trees; it usually snaps when it burns.

2. *Abecedarium Nordmannicum*

(Text: *OERP*, p. 181.)

The purpose of this curious OHG poem is difficult to determine. While it bears little resemblance to the other three rune poems as Halsall points out (*OERP*, p. 35), we include it here because of its early date. In manuscript the poem appears in a grammatical context, for it follows excerpts from Isidore of Seville's *Etymologiae*.

1. *Wealth* first;
2. *Aurochs* after;
3. *Þurs* [giant] the third stave;
4. *Pagan* god follows it;
5. *Riding* write at the end;
6. *Sore* (?) then cleaves.
7. *Hail* has need,
8. *Ice, Harvest,* and *sun*
9. *Tiw, Birch,* and *man* in the middle
10. *Water* the clear;
11. *Yew* concludes all.

XII

SOLOMON AND SATURN

A. Germanic Analogues

Referring to the second of the two OE poetical dialogues called *Solomon and Saturn*, Dobbie notes that it "is a rather miscellaneous collection of proverbial wisdom, in which one sage asks riddling questions and the other answers them, much in the style of the Old Norse *Vafþrúðnismál*" (*ASPR*, VI, p. lv). *Alvíssmál*, *Hárbarðzlióð*, and *Fjǫlsvinnsmál* also belong in the same general category. The characters in *Vafðrúðnismál* and *Hárbarðzlióð*, gods and giants, engage in a *senna* or "flytyng" and in this they resemble their companion piece, *Lokasenna*, far more than the OE *Solomon and Saturn*. However, the dialogue form and the didactic purpose of *Vafðrúðnismál* do indeed resemble the OE fragment. The date of *Vafðrúðnismál* is conjectural. Some believe it is as early as the tenth century, though others maintain it is a later, perhaps skaldic, piece—even though it is written in *ljóðaháttr*. The *Alvíssmál* is too late for our purposes, dating probably from the early thirteenth century; and *Fjǫlsvinnsmál* is likewise a product of the Icelandic Renaissance at the end of the twelfth century. *Hárbarðzlióð* seems to belong in the tenth century, but apart from the dialogue form, this *mannjafnaðr* ("matching of men") contains little mythological information or wisdom poetry. *The Riddles of Gestumblindi* should also be consulted as an analogue for this poem (see Bellows, Hallberg and Hollander).

1. *The Lay of Vafðrúðnir*

(*Vafðrúðnismál*; text: *Edda*, pp. 45–55.)

1. [Óðinn said]: "Counsel me now, Frigg, since I want to go to visit Vafðrúðnir. With great curiosity I want to match myself against that all-wise giant in ancient wisdom."

2. [Frigg said]: "I would convince Heriafǫðr to stay home in the courts of the gods, because I know no giant who is an equal match for Vafðrúðnir.

3. "Much have I travelled, much have I tried, much have I put the gods to test: I want to know what Vafðrúðnir's household is like."

4. "Good luck as you go. Good luck as you return. Good luck on your journey. May your wisdom suffice, wherever, Aldafǫðr, you spar in words with the giant."

5. Then Óðinn went to test the word-wisdom of the all-wise giant; he came to the hall which Ímr's father owned: Yggr went in at once.

6. [Óðinn said]: "Hail, now, Vafðrúðnir. Now I have come to your hall to see you yourself; first I want to know if you are merely wise or all-wise, giant."

7. [Vafðrúðnir said]: "Who is that man who jibes at me in my own hall? You will never get out from our hall unless you are the wiser [of us two]."

8. "I am called Gagnráðr; now I have come thirsty from my journey to your hall, I need an invitation—I have travelled far—and your hospitality, giant."

9. "Gagnráðr, why do you speak from the floor? Take a seat in the hall. Then we shall test who knows more, the guest or the old sage."

10. "When he comes to the rich, a poor man should say what is necessary or keep silent; I think too much talking will bring him ill, the one who comes to a cold-hearted host."

11. "Tell me, Gagnráðr, since you will try your luck from the floor: what is the horse called that draws each day to the sons of men?"

12. "Skinfaxi he is called that draws the bright day to the sons of men; the best of horses he seems to heroes, the steed's mane always shines."

13. "Tell me that, Gagnráðr, since you will try your luck from the floor: what is the stallion called that draws night from the east to the worthy gods?"

14. "Hrímfaxi he is called that draws each night to the worthy gods; every morning he lets foam fall from his bit, from there comes dew in the dales."

15. "Tell me that, Gagnráðr, since you will try your luck from the floor: what is the river called, that divides the ground between the sons of giants and the gods?"

16. "Ifing the river is called that divides the ground between the sons of giants and the gods; it will run open forever, there will be no ice on the river."

17. "Tell me that, Gagnráðr, since you will try your luck from the floor: what is the field called, where Surtr and the beloved gods will meet in battle?"

18. Óðinn said: "Vígríðr is the field called, where Surtr and the beloved gods will meet in battle. The field has been marked out for them for a hundred miles in every direction."

19. Vafðrúðnir said: "You are wise, guest. Go to the giant's bench and let us talk together on the seat! Guest, on our wisdom we will wager our heads in the hall."

20. Óðinn said: "Tell me first, Vafðrúðnir, if your wisdom suffices and you know it: whence came the earth and the heavens in the beginning, O wise giant?"

21. Vafðrúðnir said: "Out of Ymir's flesh the earth was shaped, and the mountains out of his bones, the heavens from the rime-cold giant's skull, and the sea out of his blood."

22. Óðinn said: "Tell me next, Vafðrúðnir, if your wisdom suffices and you know it: whence came the moon, which fares over men, and the sun also?"

23. Vafðrúðnir said: "He is called Mundilfœri, he who is Máni's father, and also Sól's; every day they must turn round the heavens to tell time for men."

24. Óðinn said: "Tell me third, Vafðrúðnir, since men call you wise and you should know it: whence comes day that fares over men, or night with the waning moon?"

25. Vafðrúðnir said: "He is called Dellingr, he who is Dagr's father, but Nótt was born to Nǫrr; the worthy gods created the new and waning moon to tell time for men."

26. Óðinn said: "Tell me fourth, Vafðrúðnir, since men call you wise and you should know it: whence did winter come or warm summer in the beginning for the wise gods?"

27. Vafðrúðnir said: "Vindsvalr is he called; he is the father of Vetr, and Svásuðr is Sumar's."

28. Óðinn said: "Tell me fifth, Vafðrúðnir, since men call you wise and you should know it: who was the eldest of the gods or of Ymir's giant kin in days of yore?"

29. Vafðrúðnir said: "Bergelmir was born countless winters before the earth was shaped; Þrúðgelmir was his father, and his grandfather Aurgelmir."

30. Óðinn said: "Tell me sixth, Vafðrúðnir, since men call you wise and you should know it: whence did Aurgelmir come among the sons of giants in the beginning, O wise giant?"

31. Vafðrúðnir said: "Poisonous drops sprinkled down from Élivágar and grew until they became a giant; (there our race came all together—therefore we are always far too terrible.)"

32. Óðinn said: "Tell me seventh, Vafðrúðnir, since men call you wise and you should know it: how did that headstrong giant beget children, he who had not sported with any giantess?"

33. Vafðrúðnir said: "They say that under the arms of the ice-giant grew maiden and son together; leg with leg, the wise giant begat a six-headed son."

34. Óðinn said: "Tell me eighth, Vafðrúðnir, since men call you wise and you should know it: what do you first remember or what farthest back do you know; you are all-wise, giant?"

35. Vafðrúðnir said: "Bergelmir was born countless winters before the earth was shaped; this I first remember, that the wise giant was laid in a bin (?)."

36. Óðinn said: "Tell me ninth, Vafðrúðnir, since men call you wise and you should know it: whence comes the wind that fares over the waves, but men never see it itself?"

37. Vafðrúðnir said: "Hræsvelgr he is called, who sits at heaven's end, giant, in the shape of an eagle; from his wings the wind is said to come over all men."

38. Óðinn said: "Tell me tenth, Vafðrúðnir, since you know all the fates of the gods: whence came Niǫrðr among the sons of the gods; he rules innumerable cairns and fanes, and he was not begot by the gods?"

39. Vafðrúðnir said: "The wise ones [Vanir] created him in Vanaheimr and gave him as a hostage to the gods. At the end of the world he will come back, home among the wise Vanir."

40. Óðinn said: "Tell me eleventh: where do men on the courtyard fight each other every day?"

41. Vafðrúðnir said: "All the Einheriar at Óðinn's courtyard fight each other every day. They choose who must fall and ride from the battle; afterwards they sit at peace together."

42. Óðinn said: "Tell me twelfth, Vafðrúðnir: how do you know all the fates of the gods? About the giants' runes and all the gods you speak most truthfully, O all-wise giant."

43. Vafðrúðnir said: "About the giants' runes and all the gods, I know how to speak the truth, because I have visited every world;

nine worlds I visited under Niflhel where doomed men go after death (?)."

44. Óðinn said: "Much have I travelled, much I have tried, much have I put the gods to test: who will be alive after the great Fimbulvetr has passed among men?"

45. Vafðrúðnir said: "Líf and Lífðrasir, they will hide themselves in Hoddmímir's wood; they will have morning dews as food for themselves, thereby they will rear men."

46. Óðinn said: "Much have I travelled, much have I tried, much have I put the gods to test: whence comes the sun back into the smooth sky when Fenrir has overtaken it?"

47. Vafðrúðnir said: "Álfrǫðull will bear a daughter before Fenrir overtakes her; when the gods die, that maiden will ride her mother's roads."

48. Óðinn said: "Much have I travelled, much have I tried, much have I put the gods to test: who are the wise-minded maidens who travelling glide over the sea?"

49. Vafðrúðnir said: "Three throngs of maidens attack (?) Mǫgðrasir's thorp; guardian spirits are they for those who are at home, although they are reared among giants."

50. Óðinn said: "Much have I travelled, much have I tried, much have I put the gods to test: which Æsir will rule the gods' estates, when Surtr's fire is slaked?"

51. Vafðrúðnir said: "Víðarr and Váli will dwell in the gods' shrines, when Surtr's fire is slaked; Móði and Magni shall have Miǫllnir when Þórr fights no more."

52. Óðinn said: "Much have I travelled, much have I tried, much have I put the gods to test: what will be Óðinn's death when the gods are destroyed?"

53. Vafðrúðnir said: "Úlfr will swallow Aldafǫðr, Víðarr will avenge him; he will cleave its cruel jaws when he kills Fenrisúlfr."

54. Óðinn said: "Much have I travelled, much have I tried, much have I put the gods to test: what did Óðinn himself whisper into his son's ear before he was laid on the pyre?"

55. Vafðrúðnir said: "No one knows what you whispered into your son's ear in days of yore. With a doomed mouth I spoke about my ancient lore and about the destruction of the gods. Now I have tested my wisdom against Óðinn: you are always the wisest of men."

XIII

CÆDMON'S HYMN

A. Germanic Analogue

1. *The Wessobrun Prayer*

(*Das Wessobruner Gebet*; text: *AHDL*, pp. 85–6.)

One of the oldest documents in OHG poetry, dating from the last half of the eighth century, *The Wessobrun Prayer* has often been treated as a translation of OE or OS poetry. More recent scholarship questions such transmission, but the resemblances between *Cædmon's Hymn* and the poetic first section of the prayer are strong (see Garland and Seiffert).

That have I learned among men, the greatest of wonders, that the earth was not, nor heaven above, nor tree . . . and the mountain was not, nor any . . . , neither did the sun shine, nor the moon give off light, nor [did] the splendid sea [exist]. Then there was nothing of boundaries or limits, and then was the one almighty God, most merciful of Men, and there were also with Him many divine spirits. And holy God . . .

God almighty, you created heaven and earth, and you gave men so many goods, grant me in your grace true faith and good will, wisdom and knowledge and strength to withstand the devils and to avoid evil and to do your will.

B. Celtic Analogue

1. "Let us adore the Lord"

(Adram in Coimdid; text: *EIL*, pp. 4–5.)

Although *Adram in Coimdid* does not show the same deep roots in traditional poetic style as *Cædmon's Hymn*, it does illustrate the same eloquence disguised as simplicity. The poem is ninth-century.

Let us adore the Lord, with his marvellous works of creation: bright and great heaven with its angels, the sea, white-waved upon earth.

XIV

THE METRICAL CHARMS

A. Germanic Analogues

Apart from the Runic Inscriptions (see below) and some later examples (often imitations of OHG Charms), few analogues for the OE Metrical Charms survive in Scandinavian. As S. Einarsson notes: "It may be that Skírnir's curse . . . and Sigrún's curse (in *Helgakviða Hundingsbana* II) represent the only true magic poetry in the Eddic poems. But there is a list of such songs, *Ljóðatal*, in *Hávamál* as well as one of magic runes, *Rúnatal*, in *Sigrdrífumál*" (p. 38). The *Ljóðatal* constitutes the last section of *The Sayings of Hár* (q.v.); the *Rúnatal*, stanzas 5–19 of *The Lay of Sigrdrífa* (q.v.). These lists are more allusions to spells than accounts or enactments of them (see Storms).

1. *Skírnir's Journey*

(*For Scírnis*; text: *Edda*, pp. 74–6.)

In this poem, the god Freyr has fallen in love with the giant-maiden Gerðr. He sends his servant Skírnir to win her hand. Gerðr's resistance provokes this series of curses from Skírnir and they have their effect: Gerðr agrees to meet Freyr and become his bride. Most authorities place the poem in the early tenth century; it is composed in variations on *ljóðaháttr* (see Bellows, Hallberg, Hollander and Crossley-Holland).

25. Skírnir said: "Do you see, maiden [Gerðr], the slender, inlaid sword which I hold in my hand here? Before this blade the old giant will bow; your father is doomed.

26. With a magic wand I strike you, for I will tame you, maiden, according to my desire; you shall go where the sons of men will never see you again.

27. On the eagle's hill you shall sit forever, turned away from the world, looking towards Hel; your food will be more loathesome to you than the flashing snake is to any man among mankind.

28. May you be a wonder to see when you come out; may Hrímnir glare at you, may everyone stare at you! May you become more widely known than the guardian of the gods [Heimdallr], may you gape out through your prison bars!

29. Raving and shrieking (?), charms (?) and unbearable pain, may your tears grow with grief! Sit down, for I will tell you a heavy grief and a double woe.

30. Fiends will pinch you the whole day in the giants' courtyards; everyday you shall crawl joyless to the halls of the frost-giants, crawl without joy; in return you shall have weeping for your pleasure and live amidst tears of grief.

31. You will always dwell with three-headed giants, or be without a husband; may desire grip you, may pining waste you! Be like the thistle, which was crushed in the last part of the harvest (?).

32. I walked to the wood and to the green forest to get a magic wand: I got a magic wand.

33. Óðinn is angry with you, the first of the gods is angry with you; Freyr will hate you, abominable woman! You have won the powerful wrath of the gods.

34. Hear ogres, hear frost-giants, sons of Suttungr, [hear] the troops of gods themselves: how I prohibit, how I forbid the delight of men to the maid, the enjoyment of men to the maid.

35. Hrímgrímnir the giant is called who shall have you, far beneath the gates of the dead; there slaves will give you the stale of goats under the roots of a tree! No other drink will you ever get, maiden, for your desire, maiden, by my desire.

36. A '*Purs* [giant] rune' I will cut for you and three staves, lust and madness and unbearable pain; so I will cut them out as I cut them in, if they are not needed."

2. *The Second Lay of Helgi, Hundingr's Slayer*

(*Helgaqviða Hundingsbana ǫnnor*; text: *Edda*, p. 157.)

Sigrún's famous curse on her brother Dagr comes after Dagr has slain Helgi to avenge the killing of Hǫgni, their father. This second version of the Helgi legend is a patchwork of fragments, and Sigrún's curse can legitimately stand on its own as an integral piece. The poem may belong to the early tenth century and is composed mainly in *fornyrðislag* (see Bellows, Hallberg and Hollander).

Helgi took Sigrún to wife and they had sons. Helgi did not live to be old. Dagr, Hǫgni's son, sacrificed to Óðinn for vengeance for his father. Óðinn gave Dagr his spear. Dagr found Helgi, his sister's husband, at a place called Fiǫturlundr. He thrust the spear through Helgi. There Helgi died. And Dagr rode to the fells [Sevafiǫll] and told Sigrún the news:

30. "I am sad, sister, to tell you woes, because I have not wanted to make my sister weep: the prince fell this morning at Fiǫturlundr, he who was the best on earth and who stood on the necks of warriors."
31. [Sigrún said]: "May every oath destroy you, those which you have given Helgi, by the shining water of Leiptr and by Unnr's cold, dank millstone.
32. That ship will not sail which sails under you, although a favorable wind follows after you. The steed will not run which runs under you, although you might have to escape your enemies.
33. The sword will not bite which you draw, unless it sings around your own head! I would be avenged on you for Helgi's death; if you were a wolf out in the woods, deprived of riches and all pleasure, you would have no food, unless you should gorge on corpses!"

3. Old High German Charms

The OHG Charms (*Zaubersprüche*) preserved in manuscripts dating from the ninth to the twelfth centuries represent the most significant Germanic analogues for the OE Metrical Charms. Scholars are sharply divided about the age and status of these works. A few definitely seem to stem from ancient magical tradition, but most have been obviously reworked and "Christianized." The two Merseburg Charms are perhaps the only "pure" pagan examples, although the form of the "Worm Charms" and the "Lorsch Bee Charm" may indicate that remnants of much earlier spells are imbedded in our specimens (see Eis, Garland, Heusler, Wolff, Fuller and Stuart).

a. *The Tobias Lorica*

(*Tobiassegen*; text: *DDPP*, pp. 183–92.)

The good Saint Tobias, who was God's prophet, sent his son so far into a foreign land, that he expected he would never see him again. His son was very dear to him; he parted from him with difficulty. He felt great sadness for him. He sent him on a forty days' journey. When he saw him standing before him, a charm was made over him, which was good from the heart, because it left nothing out.

"To the God from whom nothing is hidden, and whose personal servant you are, who abandons no man, provides well for his poor, who can protect you through fatherly goodness over field and through forest, from all various hardships, from hunger and from thirst, from worthless pleasure, from heat and from cold. May God grant your prayer and keep you safe from sudden death, whether you sleep or wake, in forest or under roof. May your enemies be brought low. May God send you back sound here again with a very upright spirit, with life and also with property. Blessed be the way over road and over path for you, first going and then coming back. By the sacred five wounds, on both sides of you, may the heavenly thane stand by you and take care of your journey and may he join to you good companions. May you travel in God's peace, may the Holy Spirit preserve you. May your heart be of stone, may your lip be of bone, may your head be of steel. May heaven be your shield. May hell be closed before you: may all evil go astray before you. May paradise be open to you. May all weapons be broken before you, so that they must shun you, so that they do not wound you. May the moon and also the sun shine upon you with joy. May the holy twelve powers honor you before God, so that the Sovereign may joyfully see you. May all good fortune happen to you. May the good Saint Stephen, who saw God standing in heaven at his Father's right hand, when he overcame his battle, always stand by you, whenever you have need and necessity of him. May Saint John the Baptist take care to set you straight, the four evangelists direct you the best of all. May your protection be the Virgin, my lady Saint Mary, against all trouble and for all cares of your body, of your soul and of your worldly honor. May Saint Gall tend to your food, may Saint Gertrude give you shelter; blessed be your life. May man and woman be loyal to you. May good counsel be yours and may you die a righteous death: may you be blessed to God."

Thus he blessed his son and sent him to a place there in a land which was called Media; the city was called Rages. Afterwards he was very glad for this. Thus must you be blessed. May the three names help with this, may the holy one help with this, my Lady Saint Mary. May all the children help with this, those who are in the heavenly kingdom. Amen.

*

May God bless you today with Abel's blessing: his sacrifice pleased God so well and it was the joy of his heart; and with the blessing of Enoch, who was so rightfully dear to God that He took him into paradise, with body and soul there he came; with the blessing of Noah, who was so true to God, that He protected him from the flood; with the perpetual blessing which He gave Abraham, because he was obedient to Him—with his son he came to the mountain; with the blessing of Isaac, with the blessing of Jacob, with the blessing of Joseph, and may He guard your life, as he was protected by Him when he was sold for money; with the perpetual blessing that was given to David, when he was taken away from the sheep and came to the royal kingdom; and with the perpetual blessing which He gave Solomon . . . which the Angel Gabriel gave to Mary, the Virgin, here.

Now may God bless you today with the blessing which the angels brought from heaven at Christ's birth. Now may God bless you today with the blessing which came from heaven upon God's son in baptism. Now may God bless you today with the blessing by which holy Christ was brought to His martyrdom. Now may God bless you today with the blessing with which He went away to heaven after His Resurrection. May the holy Cross be over you, may the holy Cross be at your right hand and at your left hand, and may there be for you a guard and a shield against all misfortune and against all blasphemy and against all your enemies, as the case may be: may the strength of God help you in this, and the Father and the Son and the Holy Spirit. Amen.

b. "The Merseburg Charms"

(*Die Merseburger Zaubersprüche*; text: *AHDL*, p. 89.)

1. For a Prisoner

The goddesses sat once, they sat here and there. Some fastened fetters, some hindered armies. Some picked apart the chains: escape from the fetter-bands! Escape from the foes!

2. For a Sprain

Phol and Wodan rode into the forest; there Balder's foal sprained its foot. Then Sinthgunt sang a charm about it, and Sunna, her sister; then Friia sang a charm about it, and Volla, her sister. Then Wodan sang a charm about it, as well as he could: as with bone-wrenching, so with blood-wrenching, so with limb-wrenching: bone to bone, blood to blood, limb to limb, as if they were stuck together.

c. "Worm Charms"

(Text: *AHDL*, p. 90.)

1. Old Saxon (*Contra vermes*)

Go out worm, with nine little worms, out from the marrow into the bone, out from the bone into the flesh, out from the flesh into the skin, out from the skin into this arrow. O Lord, may this come to pass.

2. Old High German (*Pro Nessia*)

Go out Worm, with nine little worms, out from the marrow into the veins, out from the veins into the flesh, out from the flesh into the skin, out from the skin into this arrow. *Three Our Fathers.*

d. "First Trier Charm"

(*Erster Trierer Spruch*; text: *AHDL*, p. 92)

For catarrh say:

Christ was wounded, then He became both healed and healthy. The blood was staunched; you do thus, blood! *Three Amens. Three Our Fathers.*

e. "Bamberg Blood Charm"

(*Bamberger Blutsegen*; text: *AHDL*, pp. 90–1.)

a. Christ and Judas played with a spear. Then the holy Christ became wounded in His side. Then he took his thumb and pressed it forward. Thus you stop flowing, blood, just as the River Jordan stopped when the holy John Baptized the savior Christ in it. That is a remedy for you.

b. Christ was wounded here on earth. That then became known in heaven. It did not bleed, nor smart. Nor did it bear any poison. That was a very good moment. May you be whole, wound. *In the name of Jesus Christ*. That is a remedy for you. *Three Our Fathers. And add this also three times:* I beseech you by the five holy wounds, may you be whole, wound. *And through the Father and the Son and the Holy Spirit. May it be done, may it be done.* Amen.

f. "For a Stiff Horse"

(*Ad equum erręhet*; text: *AHDL*, p. 91.)

A man was walking along the way, leading his horse by hand; then my Lord met him with His mercy: "Why are you walking, man? You're not riding thither?" "What can I ride? My horse is stiff." "Now pull it then to the side, whisper into its ear, step on its right foot: so it will be cured of stiffness." *Our Father. And then clean off his legs and feet, saying:* "Thus let this horse be cured quickly of its stiffness—*whatever its color may be,* red, black, white, dun, gray, dappled—just as God cured it Himself."

g. "The Lorsch Bee Charm"

(*Lorscher Bienensegen*; text: *AHDL*, pp. 89–90.)

Christ, a swarm of bees is out. Now fly you, my creature, here with divine peace in God's protection to come home sound. Settle, settle, bee: Saint Mary commanded you. Do not have leave to go. Do not fly to the woods, neither do you get away from me, nor do you escape from me. Settle very still, work God's will.

h. "For the Marking of a House against the Devil"

(*Ad signandum domum contra diabolum*; text: *AHDL*, p. 90.)

Well, demon [this is] so that you know, that you are called a demon, [and] so that you do not know how to, nor can you, pronounce "destruction."

i. "A Journey Charm"

(*Weingartner Reisesegen*; text: *DDPP*, pp. 18–19.)

I look after you, I send you off with my five fingers, five and fifty angels. May God send you home sound. May the victory-door be open to you, may the sail-door be the same for you; may the wave-door be closed to you, may the weapon-door be the same for you. May this blessing of good Saint Ulrich's be done in front of you and behind you and over you and beside you; thus may you dwell and thus may you be, that there be as good a peace as there was when my Lady Saint Mary was delivered of holy Christ.

4. Runic Inscriptions

In the Scandinavian runic inscriptions we find strong connections with Germanic poetry. Several of the rune carvings preserve the native alliteration and are written in the strophic pattern of *fornyrðislag*; they also share a common vocabulary and formulae with the poetic tradition. For example, *iǫrmungrund* ("spacious earth") appears in the Swedish Karlevi Stone, *The Lay of Grímnir* (20), and *Beowulf*, l. 859 (see Tigerstedt, p. 15), and we find a formula from the seventh-century (?) OE charm "For an Unfruitful Land" cropping up in a thirteenth-century Swedish runic inscription (see Jansson, p. 143). These runic inscriptions can definitely be associated with the magical potency of the Germanic charms, though this is not true of all runes (see Baeksted).

a. *The Whetstone from Strøm* (Norway)

(*Strøm runebryne*, ca. 600; text: *N*, II, 683.)

The meaning of this inscription has raised much debate; the translation we offer here, then, is basically that of Aag. The whetstone, moistened from the drinking horn, sharpens the scythe, which can then cut the hay. But the runemaster hopes that the stone will not be used to sharpen weapons of war (see *RäF*, p. 12, and Høst, p. 30).

The horn wets this stone. May it harm the hay! May it lie [still] in battle!

b. *The Noleby Stone* (Sweden)

(*Nolebystenen*, ca. 600; text: *Vg*, p. 96.)

Like the Eggjum grave cover, the Noleby stone was probably
made to be placed inside a grave. Its inscription, strongly rhythmic
though not in strict meter, is "undoubtedly of religio-magical
character" (*Vg*, p. 99).

I write runes stemming from the counsel-givers [the divine
powers]. I set them in stillness (?). The runes may make sharp the
hawk-like [the runemaster with the hawk-sharp glance?].

c. *The Björketorp Stone* (Sweden)

(*Björketorpstenen*, ca. 675; text: *DR*, 360.)

The largest and most impressive of a small cluster of such stones
in the Swedish province of Blekinge, the Björketorp stone represents a clear example of Germanic charm poetry, both in content
and form. It is composed in *galdralag*, a modification of *fornyrðislag*
found also in the OE charms and the OHG Merseburg Charms (see
Lindquist).

I, master (?) of the rune-row, have hidden powerful runes here.
Unceasingly [beset] by evil, doomed (?) to death through magic
spells (?) [shall be] the one who breaks this [monument]! I prophesy
destruction!

d. *The Eggjum Grave Cover* (Norway)

(*Eggjumstenen*, ca. 700; text: *N*, III, 90.)

The inscription on this grave cover does not fall into any clearly
defined Germanic verse form. It does, however, have a strong
alliterative pattern and shows some relationship to the ON charm
tradition represented in the *Ljóðatal* section of *The Sayings of Hár*
(q.v.; see Jacobsen).

It is not sought by the sun and the stone is not cut with an iron
knife. No man shall lay it bare, while the waning moon moves
[across the sky]. Confused men may not steal it. The man
[runemaster] splashed it with the lake of the body [blood], scraped
the thole with it [the blood?] in the bore-tired (?) boat. In what
form did the Warrior-God [Óðinn] come here from the land of the

warriors [*or*, land of the steeds?]. As the fish swimming out of the terrible (?) stream, the bird, screeching in the enemy troop (?). Warning against the evil-doer!

B. Celtic Analogues

Verbal charms seem native to both OE and OIr cultures. The Irish charms printed here appear as Christian prayers, but contain material that has been, in some cases, poorly integrated into its new Christian framework.

1. "God be with me against every trouble"

(*Día lim*; text: *EIL*, pp. 22–7.)

This first, possibly tenth-century example, most closely resembles a straightforward Christian prayer. It lacks the arcane references of the earlier examples below.

1. God be with me against every trouble, noble Three-that-is-one: Father and Son and Holy Spirit.
2. The holy, bright King of the sun, who is beautiful beyond justification, is a marvellous refuge for me against the host of black demons.
3. The Father, the Son, the brilliant Holy Spirit: these three for my protection against the clouds of the plagues.
4. Against swift death, or sudden, against the plunderings of robbers, may high Jesus protect me, and from the red malady.
5. Against demons at any time, it is the Son of God who protects me and against sickness, against wounding, against thunder, against fire.
6. Against heavy smiting, against every other injury, may the Son of Mary graciously bless my body.
7. Against judgments in Doomsday, Christ be with me against every evil: against weapons, against fear, against bitterness of the winds,
8. against peril, against betrayal, against secret charms, against pestilence in every form which it may manifest in the world.
9. Every blessing without hurt, every pure prayer, every ladder that reaches heaven: may it be helpful to me.

10. Every good saint who has suffered on the surface of the earth below, every holy disciple who believed in Christ,

11. everyone kind, everyone quiet, everyone sincere, everyone pure, every confessor, every soldier that exists under the sun,

12. every venerable patron saint who could assist me toward right, everyone simple, every noble, every saint who has suffered a cross,

13. every glorious pilgrim, every wealthy person—splendid power—every pauper, every saint who has abandoned his land,

14. every tongue, without fail, upon which grace has been put, every heart throughout the world which would not ever be capable of treachery,

15. every honorably righteous person under the expanse of bright heaven, from the sunset to the west to Mt. Zion, eastwards,

16. may they protect me from this time on against the demons of the mist, these companions of the Son of the King from the lands of the living.

17. May God be guarding me, glorious Lord of angels, so that he may find safe the talents which came from him.

18. May my King protect me, may he always help me; in every need may I be under the shadow of God's hand.

2. St. Patrick's Lorica

(*Atomruig indiu*; text: *TP*, Vol. II, pp. 354–8.)

The poem generally known as *St. Patrick's Lorica* ("breast-plate") may have been composed as early as the eighth century. The unusual poetic form resembles that of the *Audacht Morainn*. An early tradition ascribes a special protective hymn to St. Patrick (see *Fíacc's Hymn*), but this could hardly have been it. However, the poem is fundamentally Christian in its outlook, if not in form, and is generically related to the *Tobias Lorica* (q.v.).

1. I bind myself today with a mighty strength, the invocation of the Trinity, belief in threeness, confession of oneness, on the way to meeting the Creator.

2. I bind myself today with the power of the birth of Christ and His baptism; the power of His crucifixion and His burial; the power of His resurrection and ascension; the power of His descent for the Last Judgment.

3. I bind myself today with the power of the order of cherubim, in obedience of angels, in the attendance of the archangels, in the hope of resurrection to reward, in prayers of patriarchs, in prophecies of prophets, in preachings of apostles, in faiths of confessors, in innocence of holy virgins, in deeds of just men.

4. I bind myself today with the power of heaven, the light of the sun, the lustre of the moon, the splendor of fire, the swiftness of lightning, the speed of wind, the depth of the sea, the steadiness of the earth, the stability of rock.

5. I bind myself today with the power of God to steer me, the might of God to uphold me, the wisdom of God to guide me, the eye of God to look ahead for me, the ear of God to hear for me, the word of God to speak before me, the path of God to go before me, the shield of God to shelter me, the retainers of God to protect me from the ambushes of demons, from the temptations of vices, from the inclinations of nature, from every man who may wish ill to me, near and far, alone and in company.

6. I invoke today on my behalf all these powers against every sharp, merciless strength that may be against my body and soul, against the incantations of false seers, against the dark laws of paganism, against the false laws of heresy, against the deception of idolatry, against the spells of women and smiths and druids, against all knowledge that corrupts the body and soul of man.

7. Christ be my guard today against poison, against burning, against drowning, against wounding, so that I may have a multitude of rewards.

8. Christ with me, Christ before me, Christ behind me, Christ within me, Christ below me, Christ above me, Christ at my right, Christ at my left, Christ in lying down, Christ in sitting, Christ in rising up, Christ in the heart of every man who may examine me, Christ in the mouth of every one who may speak to me, Christ in every eye that sees me, Christ in every ear that hears me.

9. I bind myself today with a mighty strength, the invocation of the Trinity, belief in threeness, confession of oneness, on the way to meeting the Creator.

3. "Lorica II"

(*Ad-muiniur secht n-ingena trethan*; text: *GT*, pp. 33–5.)

This second *lorica* has no connection with St. Patrick. Greene suggests that the poem reflects an early period when Christianity and native poetic tradition were imperfectly integrated. It is not so obviously Christian as the other Irish *lorica*, and contains several obscure references.

1. I invoke the seven daughters of the stormy sea who magically spin the threads of the sons of long-life. Let the three deaths be taken from me, the three lives be given to me, the seven waves of abundance pour over me. Let not evil spirits harm me on my journey in my shining, immaculate lorica. Let my good name not be pledged for fraud. Let age come to me; let death not come to me until I am old.

2. I invoke my silver-warrior [official champion?] who has not died, who will not die. Let time of the excellence of bronze be bestowed on me. Let my form be gilded (?). Let my law be ennobled. Let my strength be made greater; let my grave not be prepared. Let death not come to me on a journey; let my coming be assured. Let not the two-headed serpent seize me, nor the scaly-gray worm, nor the senseless beetle. Let theft not despoil me, nor a band of women, nor a band of warriors. Let extra time come to me from the King of everything.

3. I invoke Senach, [who lived] seven lifetimes, whom other-world women nursed on breasts of good fortune. Let my seven candles not be extinguished. I am an impregnable fortress; I am an immovable cliff; I am a precious stone; I am a sign of seven treasures. Let me be a centenarian: hundreds of years, one hundred after another.

4. I call my good fortune to me. May the grace of the Holy Spirit be on me. *Salvation is the Lord's. Salvation is Christ's. Over all people is God's blessing.*

BIBLIOGRAPHY

The following list contains primary and secondary sources referred to in this book. It also includes material not mentioned—and therefore not given an abbreviation—but which the reader may find useful for additional background information.

Primary Texts

AE   *The Irish Adam and Eve Story from "Saltair na Rann."* Ed. David Greene and Fergus Kelly. Vol. I. Dublin, 1976.

AHDL   *Althochdeutsches Lesebuch.* Ed. Wilhelm Braune. 16th ed. rev. by Ernst A. Ebbinghaus. Tübingen, 1979.

AM   *Audacht Morainn.* Ed. Fergus Kelly. Dublin, 1976.

ASPR   *The Anglo-Saxon Poetic Records.* Ed. George P. Krapp and Elliott Van Kirk Dobbie. 6 vols. New York, 1931–42.

BLI   *Bruchstücke der älteren Lyrik Irlands.* Ed. Kuno Meyer. Berlin, 1919.

BP   *Bethu Phátraic: The Tripartite Life of St. Patrick.* Ed. Kathleen Mulchrone. Dublin, 1939.

BT   *The Book of Taliesin.* Ed. Gwenogvryn Evans. Llanbedrog, 1910.

BWP   *The Beginnings of Welsh Poetry: Studies by Sir Ifor Williams.* Ed. Rachel Bromwich. 2nd. impression. Cardiff, 1972.

CA   *Canu Aneirin.* Ed. Sir Ifor Williams. 2nd. impression. Cardiff, 1961.

CGH   *Corpus Genealogiarum Hiberniae.* Ed. M. A. O'Brien. Dublin, 1962.

CLlH   *Canu Llywarch Hen.* Ed. Sir Ifor Williams. 2nd. impression. Cardiff, 1953.

DDPP   *Denkmäler deutscher Poesie und Prosa aus dem VIII–XII Jahrhundert.* Ed. K. Müllenhoff and W. Scherer. 3rd ed. rev. by E. Steinmeyer. Vol. I. Berlin, 1892.

DR   *Danmarks runeindskrifter.* Ed. Lis Jacobsen and Erik Moltke. Copenhagen, 1942.

Edda   *Edda.* Ed. Gustav Neckel. 4th ed. rev. by Hans Kuhn. Heidelberg, 1962.

EIL   *Early Irish Lyrics*. Ed. Gerard Murphy. Oxford, 1956.

EM   *Eddica Minora*. Ed. Andreas Heusler and Wilhelm Ranisch. Dortmund, 1903.

Es   *Egils saga Skalla-Grímssonar*. Ed. Sigurður Nordal. Reykjavík, 1933.

EWGP   *Early Welsh Gnomic Poems*. Ed. Kenneth H. Jackson. 3rd impression. Cardiff, 1973.

EWP   *The Earliest Welsh Poetry*. Trans. Joseph P. Clancy. New York, 1970.

FO   *Félire Óengusso Céli Dé: The Martyrology of Oengus the Culdee*. Ed. Whitley Stokes. London, 1905.

GO   *The Gododdin: The Oldest Scottish Poem*. Trans. Kenneth H. Jackson. Edinburgh, 1969.

GT   *A Golden Treasury of Irish Poetry, AD 600–1200*. Ed. David Greene and Frank O'Connor. London, 1967.

HG   *Heliand und Genesis*. Ed. Otto Behaghel. 8th ed. rev. by Walther Mitzka. Tübingen, 1965.

HK   Sturluson, Snorri. *Heimskringla*. 3 vols. Ed. Bjarni Aðalbjarnarson. Reykjavík, 1941–51.

LA   *Liber Ardmachus*. Ed. J. Gwynn. Dublin, 1913.

LH   *The Irish "Liber Hymnorum"*. Ed. J. H. Bernard and R. Atkinson. London, 1898.

M   *The Mabinogi and Other Medieval Welsh Tales*. Trans. Patrick K. Ford. Berkeley and Los Angeles, 1977.

MWL   *Medieval Welsh Lyrics*. Trans. Joseph P. Clancy. New York, 1965.

N   *Norges indskrifter med de ældre runer*. Ed. Sophus Bugge. Christiana, 1891–1903.

NLW   National Library of Wales. Ms. 6209E.

OERP   *The Old English 'Rune Poem': A Critical Edition*. Ed. Maureen Halsall. Toronto, 1981.

Ög   *Östergötlands runinskrifter*. Ed. Erik Brate. Stockholm, 1911.

ONCP   Frank, Roberta, *Old Norse Court Poetry: The 'Dróttkvætt' Stanza*. Ithaca, 1978.

PLlH   *The Poetry of Llywarch Hen*. Trans. and ed. Patrick K. Ford. Berkeley and Los Angeles, 1974.

PoJ   "A Poem on the Day of Judgment." Ed. J. G. O'Keefe. *Ériu*, 3 (1907), 29–33.

PoBl   *The Poems of Blathmac Son of Cú Brettan*. Ed. James Carney. Dublin, 1964.

PT   *The Poems of Taliesin*. Ed. Sir Ifor Williams, English version by J. E. Caerwyn Williams. Dublin, 1968.

PWV   *The Penguin Book of Welsh Verse*. Trans. Anthony Conran. Harmondsworth, 1967.

RäF — *Die Runeninschriften im älteren Futhark*. Ed. Wolfgang Krause. Göttingen, 1966.

ScP — *Scaldic Poetry*. E.O.G. Turville-Petre. Oxford, 1976.

SG — *Saxo Grammaticus: History of the Danes*. Trans. Peter Fisher and Hilda Ellis Davidson. 2 vols. Cambridge, 1980.

SKHW — *The Saga of King Heidrek the Wise*. Ed. Christopher Tolkien. London, 1960.

SnR — *Saltair na Rann*. Ed. Whitley Stokes. *Anecdota Oxioniensia* (Medieval and Modern Series). Vol. 1, pt. 3. Oxford, 1883.

TP — *Thesaurus Palaeohibernicus*. Ed. Whitley Stokes and John Strachan. 2 vols. Cambridge, 1901.

Vg — *Västergötlands runinskrifter*. Ed. Hugo Jungner and Elisabeth Svärdström. Stockholm, 1958–70.

WP — *Welsh Poems, Sixth Century to 1600*. Trans. Gwyn Williams. London, 1973.

Secondary Texts

Aag — Aag, Finn-Henrik. "Strøm runebryne." *Maal og Minne* (1980), 144–9.

Allen/Calder — Allen, Michael J. B. and Daniel G. Calder, trans. *Sources and Analogues of Old English Poetry: The Major Latin Texts in Translation*. Cambridge and Totowa, N.J., 1976.

Andersson — Andersson, Theodore M. *The Legend of Brynhild*. Ithaca and London, 1980.

Andrieu — Andrieu, Michel. *Les Ordines Romani du Haut Moyen Âge*. Vol. 5. Louvain, 1961.

Bæksted — Bæksted, Anders. *Målruner og troldruner. Runemagiske studier*. Copenhagen, 1952.

Barber — Barber, Charles C., ed. *An Old High German Reader*. Oxford, 1964.

Bartrum — Bartrum, P. C. *Early Welsh Genealogical Tracts*. Cardiff, 1966.

Beck — Beck, Heinrich. "Zur literaturgeschichtlichen Stellung des althochdeutschen Ludwigsliedes und einiger verwandter Zeitgedichte," *Zeitschrift für deutches Altertum und deutsche Literatur*, 103 (1974), 37–51.

Bellows — Bellows, Henry Adams, trans. *The Poetic Edda*. New York, 1923.

Berg — Berg, Elizabeth. "Das Ludwigslied und die Schlacht bei Saucourt." *Rheinische Vierteljahrsblätter*, 29 (1964), 175–99.

Blair   Blair, Peter Hunter. *An Introduction to Anglo-Saxon England*. Cambridge, 1977.

Bostock   Bostock, J. Knight. *A Handbook of Old High German Literature*. 2nd ed. rev. by K. C. King and D. R. McLintock. Oxford, 1976.

Bouman   Bouman, A. C. *Patterns in Old English and Old Icelandic Literature*. Leiden, 1962.

Bromwich 1954   Bromwich, Rachel. "The Character of Early Welsh Tradition." In *Studies in Early British History*. Ed. N. K. Chadwick. Cambridge, 1954. Pp. 83–136.

Bromwich 1961   ———. *Trioedd Ynys Prydein*. Cardiff, 1961.

Brønsted   Brønsted, Johannes, *et al. Kulturhistorisk leksikon for nordisk middelalder*. 22 vols. Copenhagen, 1956–78.

Caesar   Caesar, Gaius Julius. *De Bello Gallico*. Ed. H. J. Edwards. Cambridge, Mass., 1917.

Campbell   Campbell, Alistair, ed. *The Battle of Brunanburh*. London, 1938.

Carney   Carney, J. "A Chrínóc." *Éigse*, IV (1944), 280 ff.

Crossley-Holland   Crossley-Holland, Kevin, trans. *The Norse Myths*. New York, 1980.

Davidson   Davidson, H. R. Ellis. *Gods and Myths of Northern Europe*. Harmondsworth, 1964.

de Vries   de Vries, Jan. *Altnordische Literaturgeschichte*. 2nd ed. Vol. II. Berlin, 1967.

Dillon   Dillon, Myles and Nora K. Chadwick. *The Celtic Realms*. London, 1967.

Dumville   Dumville, David N. "Biblical Apocrypha and the Early Irish: A Preliminary Investigation." *Proceedings of the Royal Irish Academy*, 73/C (1973), 73 ff.

Dronke   Dronke, Ursula, ed. *The Poetic Edda. Volume I. Heroic Poems*. Oxford, 1969.

Duckett   Duckett, Eleanor Shipley. *Anglo-Saxon Saints and Scholars*. New York, 1947.

Einarsson, B.   Einarsson, Bjarni. *Litterære forudsætninger for Egils saga*. Reykjavík, 1975.

Einarsson, S.   Einarsson, Stefan. *A History of Icelandic Literature*. Baltimore, Md., 1957.

Eis   Eis, Gerhard. *Altdeutsche Zaubersprüche*. Berlin, 1964.

Finger   Finger, Heinz. *Untersuchungen zum "Muspilli."* Göppingen, 1977.

Fuller   Fuller, Susan D. "Pagan Charms in Tenth-Century Saxony? The Function of the Merseburg Charms." *Monatshefte*, 72 (1980), 162–70.

Garland   Garland, Henry and Mary. *The Oxford Companion to German Literature*. Oxford, 1976.

Garmonsway   Garmonsway, G. N. and Jacqueline Simpson, trans. *Beowulf and Its Analogues.* New York, 1971.

Gordon   Gordon, E. V. *An Introduction to Old Norse.* 2nd ed. rev. by A. R. Taylor. Oxford, 1974.

Greene   Greene, David. "Linguistic Considerations in the Dating of Early Welsh Verse." *Studia Celtica*, 6 (1971), 1–11.

Greenfield 1972   Greenfield, Stanley B. *The Interpretation of Old English Poems.* London, 1972.

Greenfield 1966   Greenfield, Stanley B. "The Old English Elegies." In *Continuations and Beginnings: Studies in Old English Literature.* Ed. E. G. Stanley. London, 1966. Pp. 142–75.

Hallberg   Hallberg, Peter. *Old Icelandic Poetry: Eddic Lay and Skaldic Verse.* Trans. Paul Schach and Sonja Lindgrenson. Lincoln, Neb., 1975.

Harris   Harris, Joseph. "Elegy in Old English and Old Norse: A Problem in Literary History." (Forthcoming).

Haubrichs   Haubrichs, Wolfgang. *Georgslied und Georgslegende im frühen Mittelalter: Text und Rekonstruktion.* Königstein, 1979.

Henry   Henry, P. L. *The Early English and Celtic Lyric.* London, 1966.

Heusler   Heusler, Andreas. *Die altgermanische Dichtung.* Wildpark-Potsdam, 1926.

Hoffmann   Hoffmann, Werner. "Das Hildebrandslied und die indogermanischen Vater-Sohn-Kampf-Dichtungen." *Beiträge zur Geschichte der deutschen Sprache und Literatur*, 92 (1970), 27–42.

Hollander   Hollander, Lee M., trans. *The Poetic Edda.* 2nd ed. rev. Austin, Texas, 1962.

Høst   Høst, Gerd. *Runer. Våre eldste norske runeinnskrifter.* Oslo, 1976.

Jackson 1941   Jackson, Kenneth H. "Incremental Repetition in the Early Welsh *Englyn*." *Speculum*, 16 (1941), 304–21.

Jackson 1935   ———. *Studies in Early Celtic Nature Poetry.* Cambridge, 1935.

Jacobsen   Jacobsen, Lis. *Eggjum-stenen. Forsøg paa en filologisk tolkning.* Copenhagen, 1931.

Jansson   Jansson, Sven B. F. *Runinskrifter i Sverige.* Stockholm, 1963.

Jarman 1976   Jarman, A. O. H. and Gwilym Rees Hughes, eds. *A Guide to Welsh Literature I.* Swansea, 1976.

Jarman 1967   Jarman, A. O. H. "The Heroic Ideal in Early Welsh Poetry." In *Beiträge zur Indogermanistik und Keltologie.* Ed. Wolfgang Meid. Innsbruck, 1967. Pp. 193–211.

Jones	Jones, Gwyn. *A History of the Vikings*. New York, 1968.
Kartschoke	Kartschoke, Dieter. *Bibeldichtung: Studien zur Geschichte des epischen Bibelparaphrase von Juvencus bis Otfried von Weissenburg*. Munich, 1975.
Kelleher	Kelleher, John V. "The *Taín* and the Annals." *Ériu*, 22 (1971), 107–27.
Kenney	Kenney, James F. *The Sources for the Early History of Ireland: Ecclesiastical*. New York, 1929; rpt. 1980.
Kershaw	Kershaw, N. K., ed. *Anglo-Saxon and Norse Poems*. Cambridge, 1922.
Lehmann	Lehmann, Winfred P. *The Development of Germanic Verse Form*. Austin, Texas, 1956; rpt. New York, 1971.
Lindblad	Lindblad, Gustaf. "Centrala eddaproblem i 1970-talets forskningsläge." *Scripta Islandica*, 28 (1977), 3–26.
Lindquist	Lindquist, Ivar. *Galdrar. De gamla germanska trollsångernas stil; undersökt i samband med en svensk runinskrift från folkvandringstiden*. Gothenburg, 1923.
Lloyd	Lloyd, J. E. *A History of Wales from the Earliest Times to the Edwardian Conquest*. 2 vols. 3rd ed., new impression. London, 1948.
Lönnroth 1971	Lönnroth, Lars. "Hjálmar's Death-Song and the Delivery of Eddic Poetry." *Speculum*, 46 (1971), 1–20.
Lönnroth 1977	———. "The Riddles of the Rök-Stone: A Structural Approach." *Arkiv för Nordisk filologi*, 92 (1977), 1–57.
MacCana	MacCana, Proinsias. *The Learned Tales of Medieval Ireland*. Dublin, 1980.
Macnamara	Macnamara, M. *The Apocrypha in the Irish Church*. Dublin, 1975.
Malone 1934	Malone, Kemp. "The Theodoric of the Rök Inscription." *Acta Philologica Scandinavica*, 9 (1934), 76–84.
Malone 1966	———. *Deor*. 4th ed. London, 1966.
Malone 1962	———. "Two English *Frauenlieder*." *Comparative Literature*, 14 (1962), 106–17.
Melia	Melia, Daniel F. Rvw. of James Travis, *Early Celtic Versecraft*. *Speculum*, 51 (1976), 548–51.
Murdoch 1976	Murdoch, Brian. *The Irish Adam and Eve Story from "Saltair na Rann."* Vol. II (commentary). Dublin, 1976.
Murdoch 1977	———. "Saucourt and the *Ludwigslied*: Some Observations on Medieval Historical Poetry." *Revue Belge de Philologie et d'Histoire*, 55 (1977), 841–67.

Nerman, Birger. *The Poetic Edda in the Light of Archeology.* Coventry, 1931.

Nordal   Nordal, Sigurður. "Three Essays on *Vǫluspá.*" Trans. B. S. Benedikz and J. S. McKinnell. *Saga-Book of the Viking Society,* 18 (1970–1), 79–135.

Olrik, A. *Ragnarǫk.* Trans. W. Ranisch. Berlin and Leipzig, 1922.

Paasche, Frederik. *Norges og Islands litteratur inntil utgangen av middelalderen.* 2nd ed. rev. by Anne Holtsmark. Oslo, 1957.

Pálsson/Edwards   Pálsson, Hermann and Paul Edwards, trans. *Gautrek's Saga and Other Medieval Tales.* New York, 1968.

Parry   Parry, Thomas. *A History of Welsh Literature.* Trans. H. Idris Bell. Oxford, 1955.

Pilch   Pilch, H. "The Elegiac Genre in Old English and Early Welsh Poetry." *Zeitschrift für Celtische Philologie,* 29 (1964), 209–24.

Renoir   Renoir, Alain. "The English Connection Revisited: A Reading Context for the *Hildebrandslied.*" *Neophilologus,* 63 (1979), 84–7.

Russom   Russom, Geoffrey R. "A Germanic Concept of Nobility in *The Gifts of Men* and *Beowulf.*" *Speculum,* 53 (1978), 1–15.

Salmon   Salmon, Paul. *Literature in Medieval Germany.* New York, 1967.

Schlauch 1934   Schlauch, Margaret. *Romance in Iceland.* Princeton, 1934; rpt. New York, 1973.

Schlauch 1931   ———. "Wīdsīth, Víthförull, and Some Other Analogues." *PMLA,* 46 (1931), 969–87.

Schmidt   Schmidt, Herman A. P. *Hebdomada Sancta.* Vol. 2. Rome, 1957.

Schützeichel 1962   Schützeichel, Rudolf. *Das alemannische Memento Mori.* Tübingen, 1962.

Schützeichel 1972   ———. "Die Macht der Heiligen: Zur Interpretation des Petrusliedes." In *Festschrift Matthias Zender: Studien zu Volkskultur, Sprache und Landesgeschichte.* Ed. Edith Ennen and Günter Wiegelmann. Bonn, 1972. Vol. I. Pp. 309–20.

Schwartz   Schwartz, W. "The 'Ludwigslied', a Ninth-Century Poem." *Modern Language Review,* 42 (1947), 467–73.

Scott   Scott, Mariana, trans. *The Heliand.* Chapel Hill, N.C., 1966.

Seiffert   Seiffert, L. "The Metrical Form and Composition of the *Wessobruner Gebet.*" *Medium Aevum,* 31 (1962), 1–13.

Shippey   Shippey, T. A. *Poems of Wisdom and Learning in Old English.* Cambridge and Totowa, N.J., 1976.

Sieper   Sieper, Ernst. *Die altenglische Elegie*. Strassburg, 1915.

Sievers   Sievers, Eduard. *Der Heliand und die angelsächsische Genesis*. Halle, 1875.

Smith   Smith, A. H. "The Early Literary Relations of England and Scandinavia." *Saga-Book of the Viking Society*, 11 (1928/36), 215–32.

Storms   Storms, Godfrid. *Anglo-Saxon Magic*. 's-Gravenhage, 1948.

Stuart   Stuart, Heather. "*Das ist der rechte und wahrhafte Tobiassegen*: The *Tobiassegen* of Vienna Codex 2817." *Euphorion*, 74 (1980), 95–112.

Tigerstedt   Tigerstedt, E. N., ed. *Ny illustrerad svensk litteraturhistoria*. Vol. I. Stockholm, 1967.

Timmer   Timmer, Benno J., ed. *The Later Genesis*. Oxford, 1948. Rev. ed., 1954.

Turville-Petre 1964   Turville-Petre, G. *Myth and Religion of the North*. New York, 1964; rpt. Westport, Conn., 1975.

Turville-Petre 1953   ———. *Origins of Icelandic Literature*. Oxford, 1953; rpt. 1967.

Watkins   Watkins, Calvert. "Indo-European Metrics and Archaic Irish Verse." *Celtica*, 6 (1963), 194–249.

Williams 1944   Williams, Ifor. *Lectures on Early Welsh Poetry*. Dublin, 1944.

Williams 1971   Williams, J. E. Caerwyn. "The Court Poet in Medieval Ireland." *Proceedings of the British Academy*, 57 (1971), 1–51.

Wolff   Wolff, Ludwig. "Die Merseburger Zaubersprüche." In *Die Wissenschaft von deutscher Sprache und Dichtung*. Ed. Siegfried Gutenbrunner, *et al*. Stuttgart, 1963. Pp. 305–19.

INDEX OF PROPER NAMES

The following index lists all the proper names contained in the individual texts. Beside each entry we have indicated where the name first appears in each piece, and we have also briefly explained those names that may be unfamiliar or that are not otherwise explained in the texts themselves. We have alphabetized the entries according to English, not Scandinavian, conventions: the letter "æ" is alphabetized as "ae," "ǫ" as "oe," and "ð" and "Þ" as "th," except at the beginning of a word. In such cases they have a separate entry, following "A," "O," and "T," respectively. The abbreviations for the Germanic poems are those of Neckel and Kuhn or follow the principles laid down in their edition of the *Edda*. The abbreviations for the Celtic poems are our own.

Ab Erbin (PrT 3): "Son of Erbin"; Erbin was an ancestor in the royal line of Dyfed

Abel (AE 1933; TL):

Aber Cuawg (Sic 4): The estuary (*aber*) of the Cuawg, a river possibly near Machynlleth in Montgomeryshire

Abollinus (LaG): Apollyon, angel of the bottomless pit, probably the same as the Hound of Hell; see Revelations ix, 11

Abraham (Ex 78; Gen III; TL):

Absalon (TrT): Absalom, the third son of David (see II Sam. xiii–xix)

Adam (AE 9; Gen I; Gen II; Ju 1):

Adwy (Bat): Place name

Aed (Rath): A king of the Uí Berraidi

Aeddan (Gdd XXXI): British warrior who fought at Catraeth

Aeron (Gdd XXI): Place name (Ayr?), probably in Urien's kingdom of Rheged

Africa (TrT):

Agnafit (Hi 5): Coastal area in the Stockholm archipelago where modern Stockholm lies

Agnarr (Grm prose): Hrauðungr's son

Agnarr (Grm 2): Geirroðr's son

Agnarr (Sd prose): Auða's brother

Agðir (Vk 1): Province in southern Norway

Aidne (Cré 6): Area in south County Galway

Ailill (FT 177): Legendary king of Connacht, west of the Shannon; appears in the epic tale, "The Cattle Raid of Cooley" [*Táin Bó Cúailnge*].

Ailill (Rath): A king of the Uí Berraidi

Aldafǫðr (Vm 4): "Father of Men"; Óðinn

Alexander (TrT): King of Macedonia, fourth century B.C.

Álfgeirr (Sk. II 9): A Hebredian trader

Álfgeirr (Es chap. 52): Unknown; possibly a wrong name for Ealdred of Northumbria

Álfheimr (Grm 5): "Elf-World"

Alfǫðr (Grm 48; HH 38): "All-Father"; Óðinn

Álfr (HH 14): Hundingr's son

Álfr (HH 52): Hringr's son

Álfrǫðul (Vm 47): "Elf-Beam"; a kenning for the sun

Alpha (TrT): Used (with Omega) to represent God and Christ

Álptafjǫrðr (Sk. II 11): A fjord on the southeast coast of Iceland

Alsviðr (Grm 37; Sd 15): "Very-Swift"; one of the horses of the sun

Amargein (AmS): Poet to the "Sons of Míl," the legendary Gaelic invaders of Ireland

Án (Vk 7): Follower of Víkarr

Anatole (AE 1053): See Archon

Andaðr (Gest 55): A giant

Andhrímnir (Grm 18): "Soot-Face"; cook in Valhǫll

Aneirin (Gdd XLVIII): Renowned poet of the late sixth century (Nennius, *Historia Brittonum*)

Angantýr (Hi 2): A berserker; son of Arngrímr
Annwfn (Bat): Welsh name for the Otherworld
Anti-Christ (Gen II; LaJ):
Arasteinn (HH 14): "Eagle-Stone"
Archon (AE 1053): The names of this star and of Dissis, Anatole, and
   Missimbria apparently originated in the apocryphal tradition that
   "Adam" was an acronym for the cardinal points (in Greek); the star
   names appear originally to have been a mnemonic which became a
   separate tradition; see Murdoch 1976, pp. 64–6.
Arfynydd (Arg): "[Land] opposite (or against) the Mountain"; place
   name in Urien's kingdom
Argoed (Arg; SoM 33): "[Land] opposite (or against) the Forest"; place
   name in Powys and in Urien's kingdom
Argoed Llwyfain (Arg): Llwyfain is possibly formed from the same root as
   Llwyfenydd, both perhaps representing a district in the land of Urien
Arianrhod (TrT): One of the children of the Welsh goddess Don; brother
   of Gwydion and Gilfaethwy
Armagh (FíH 22; FT 165): "The Height of Macha" [*Árd Macha*];
   traditional ecclesiastical center of Christianity in Ireland; Macha may
   have been a local female deity
Arthur (Bat): Legendary British warrior-king
Árvakr (Grm 37; Sd 15): "Early-Awake"; one of the horses of the sun
Ásgarðr: Home of the Æsir
Askr (Vk 3): Farm on the Norwegian island of Fenhringr
Askr (Vsp 17): "Ash-Tree"; name of the first man whom Óðinn, Víli, and
   Véi made from a fallen tree
Áslákr (Hrók 12): A powerful landowner
Ásmundr (Hrók 21): A Norwegian king
Ásmundr (Grm 49): Óðinn
Ásviðr (Háv 143): "All-Wise"; a giant
Ath Alma (Hag 16): Unknown; presumably in west Munster
Aðalsteinn (Es chap. 52): Æthelstan, king of England (924–39)
Aðils (Bj 141): "Eadgils" in *Beowulf*; a Swedish king
Aðils (Es chap. 52): Welsh earl; follower of Óláfr
Atli (Akv; Gðr. I 25; Gðr. II 26; Gðr. III prose: Hm 8; Od prose): Buðli's
   son (Attila the Hun)
Atli (HH 52): Hringr's son
Atríðr (Grm 48): "The Attacker by Horse" (?); Óðinn
Aurgelmir (Vm 29): Giant; see Ymir
Auða (Hlr 8; Sd prose 3): Agnarr's sister

Ægir (Gest 64; Grm 45; HH 29; Los 8): The sea god
Ælla (Es Chap. 55): Usurped throne of Northumbria; killed by sons of
   Ragnar loðbrók in 867; see Blair
Æsir (Grm 4; Hák 16; Háv 143; Sd 18; Vm 50; Vsp 7): Race of gods who
   lived in Ásgarðr; ruled by Óðinn

Balder (MeC 2): Baldr (?)

Baldr (Grm 12; Vsp 31): The son of Óðinn and Frigg

Báleygr (Grm 47): "Fiery-Eyed"; Óðinn

Beare (Hag): A peninsula jutting into the Atlantic from the west of present-day County Cork

Beli (Vsp 53): A giant

Beltaine (Hag 10): Roughly equivalent to May-Day; major festival for pre-Christian Celts that celebrates the beginning of summer

Benn Bairche (FíH 15): A peak in the mountains of Mourne, north of Dundalk

Bergelmir (Vm 29): A giant

Bernicia (Gdd V): Anglo-Saxon kingdom north of the Humber

Bersi (Hrók 17): One of Hálfr's warriors

Bestla (Háv 140): A giantess; mother of Óðinn, Víli, and Véi

Bethron (FíH 29): Beth-horon, at north end of the Dead Sea where Joshua defeated the five kings

Biflindi (Grm 49): Óðinn

Bifrǫst (Grm 44): Rainbow bridge between Ásgarðr and Miðgarðr

Bikki (Akv 14): Follower of Iǫrmunrekkr

Bileygr (Grm 47): "One-Eyed" or "Shifty-Eyed"; Óðinn

Billingr (Hav 97): Unknown

Bilskírnir (Grm 24): Þórr's hall in Ásgarðr

Biǫrn (Hrók 17): One of Hálfr's warriors

Bjarki (Bj): Danish hero of the sixth century

Bjǫrn (Hák 2): Hákon's brother; son of Haraldr inn harfagri

Bjǫrn (Sk. II 4): King (Saint) Óláfr's chief marshal

Bleiddudd (PrT 6): "Wolf-Lord"; a lord of Tenby in South Wales

Bodgad (Gdd VI): His son fought at Catraeth

Bǫlþorr (Háv 140): A giant; father of Bestla

Bǫlverkr (Háv 109; Grm 47): "Evil-Doer"; Óðinn

Bǫlverkr (Hrók 12): One of Hálfr's warriors

Bǫrkr (Hrók 12): One of Hálfr's warriors

Bǫðvildr (Vkv prose): "War-Maid"

Borghildr (HH 1): Sigmundr's first wife

Borgný (Od prose): Unknown

Bragi (Hák 14; Grm 44; Sd 16): God of poetry; son of Óðinn

Brálundr (HH 1): Home of Borghildr

Brandey (HH 22): "Brand Isle" in Norway

Brávǫllr (HH 42): "Brow Field"; southeastern Sweden (?)

Bregun (Hag 14): A place on the plain of Feimen

Breiðablik (Grm 12): "Far-Shining"; seat of Baldr

Brimir (Sd 14): A sword

Brimir (Vsp 37): A giant

Britain (FíH 5; Gwy; PrT 3; SnM 4):

Brochfael (EaE 37): A common personal name, here, meaning Brochfael Ysgithrog, a ruler of Powys; d. 662

Bruidge (Rath): A king of the Uí Berraidi

Brynhildr (Gðr. I 22; Gðr. II 27; Hlr prose; Od 16): A valkyrie, originally the human daughter of Buðli; Sigurðr woos her for Gunnarr

Culhwch (Cyn 10): Culhwch son of Cilydd, a legendary character, first cousin to Arthur; see *M*, pp. 119–57

Cyfwlch (Gdd XV): Warrior who fought at Catraeth

Cynddylan (Cyn 1; EaE 34; EaP 41; HaC 18): Seventh-century ruler of Powys

Cyndrwyn (Cyn 12; HaC 32): Father of Cynddylan of Powys

Cynfan (Gdd XXXI): Warrior who fought at Catraeth

Cynfelyn (TrT): Legendary or mythological ruler

Cynon (HaC 32): One of the sons of Cynddylan

Cynon (Gdd XXI): One of the three British warriors who escaped the battle of Catraeth

Dagr (Hrók 14): One of Hálfr's warriors

Dagr (HH. II prose): Sigrún's brother; Hǫgni's son

Dagr (Vm 25): Day, son of Dellingr and Nótt

Dáinn (Grm 33): A deer? a dwarf?

Dáinn (Háv 143): An elf

Danes (Gest 60; Hrók 14):

David (TL):

Dead Sea (Gen III): Inland sea in Palestine

Deira (Gdd V): Anglo-Saxon kingdom north of the Humber

Dellingr (Gest 48; Háv 160; Vm 25); Husband of Nótt; father of Dagr

Denmark (Gðr. I prose; Gðr. II 14; Hild 1):

Deudraeth (PrT 4): Place name, possibly in Meirionethshire

Dinbych: See Tenby

Dínertach (Cré 7): Identified in the manuscript headnote as the son of Gúaire of the tribe of the Uí Fhidgeinte (County Limerick); otherwise unknown

Dissis (AE 1053): See Archon

Dnieper (Akv 5): Russian river in the Ukraine flowing into the Black Sea

Don (TrT): Welsh goddess, sister of Math fab Mathonwy; see *M*, pp. 89–109

Downpatrick (FíH 22): Early monastic center in present-day County Down; often called *Dun-leth-glas* ("Fortress of the broken fetters") in early church documents

Drótt (Hild 1): Mother of Hildibrandr

Druid (Bat): Member of "priestly" caste among early Celtic peoples

Duneyrr (Grm 33): A deer

Duraþrór (Grm 33): A deer

Dvalinn (Grm 33; Háv 143): A deer? a dwarf?

Dvína (Sk 3): Russian river flowing north and emptying into the White Sea

Dyfed (PrT 4): Region in southwest Wales

Dylan Eil Mor (Bat): Son of Arianrhod, twin brother of Lleu Llaw Gyffes; see *M*, pp. 89–109

Eber (FíH 19): Eber and Eremon were legendary "Sons of Míl Espaine" who conquered Ireland for the Gaels according to the pseudo-historical "Book of Invasions" [*Lebor Gabála*]

Edrywy (Sic 16; Bat): Place name in Dyfed (?)

Eggþér (Vsp 42): "Sword-Bearer"; a giant

Egill (Hrók 12): One of Hálfr's warriors

Egill (Vkv prose): Vǫlundr's brother

Egill Skallagrímsson (Es chap. 53): One of the most important Old Icelandic poets

Egypt (Ex 77):

Eidin (Gdd XIII): Site of the fort from which Mynyddog Mwynfawr's army set out for Catraeth; modern Edinburgh

Eikþyrnir (Grm 26): "Oak-Antlers" (?); a deer

Einheriar (Grm 18; Hák 16; HH 38): Chosen warriors of Valhǫll

Eithinyn (Gdd XLI): Warrior who fought at Catraeth

Eitill (Akv 37; Hm 8): Son of Guðrún and Atli

Eldhrímnir (Grm 18): "Sooty-from-Fire"; a kettle

Elfan (HaC 28): Warrior of Powys

Eli (EaE 34): Place name, perhaps reflected in the name of the river Meheli in Montgomeryshire

Elias (LaJ): See Elijah

Elijah (TrT): Hebrew prophet whose career is recounted in the Books of Kings

Élivágar (Vm 31): "Stormy-Waves"; mythical rivers springing from Hvergelmir; poison drops from the rivers, which froze into banks above Ginnungagap (Vsp. 3), formed the giant Ymir

Elossandria (LaG): Alexandra, Tacianus' queen

Elphin (Des 152): Son of Urien, king of Rheged

Emain (FíH 22): Royal inaugural center of the legendary kings of Ulster; near modern Navan Fort in County Armagh

Embla (Vsp 17): "Elm Tree" (?) or "Vine" (?); the first woman, whom Óðinn, Víli, and Véi made from a fallen tree

English (Cyn 15; Es chap. 52; PrU):

Enoch (Gen II; TL; TrT): Old Testament figure to whom three pseudepigraphical works are attributed

Erechwydd (Arg; PrU): A district in the land of Urien, perhaps in Yorkshire; Urien was called "Lord of Erechwydd"

Eremon (FíH 19): See Eber

Erlingr (Hrók 12): One of Hálfr's warriors

Ernon (Ex 89): The River Arnon, which flows into the Dead Sea

Erpr (Akv 37; Hm 8; Sk. II 8): Son of Guðrún and Atli

Erpr (Hm 14): Iónakr's son and Guðrún's stepson

Erthgi (Gdd XIV): Warrior who fought at Catraeth

Eulad (Gdd XXX): His son Ywain fought at Catraeth

Euron (Bat): Welsh goddess/magician

Eurwys (Bat): Welsh goddess/magician

Eve (AE 9; Gen I; Gen II):

Eyiólfr (HH 14): One of Hundingr's sons

Eymóðr (Gðr. II 19): One of Atli's messengers

Fáfnir (Hlr 10; Od 17): Reginn's brother; he transformed himself into a dragon at Gnitaheiðr

Farmatýr (Grm 48): "God of Boat-Loads"; Óðinn

Feimen (Hag 13): A plain in County Tipperary

Félire (FT): A book of feasts, a calendar of saints

Féni (FíH 20): Name designating free men in the early Irish Law tracts

Fenrisúlfr (Grm 23; Hák 20; HH 40; Vm 53): "Fenris Wolf"; son of Loki who will remain bound until the end of the world

Fensalir (Vsp 33): "Water-Halls"; halls where Frigg dwells in Ásgarðr

Fflamddwyn (Arg): "Flame-Bearer"; either a nickname or a personal name; Urien's enemy

Fíacc (FíH): Legendary Bishop of Slebte (Sletty, County Leix); supposed to have composed the hymn *Genair Patraicc* ("Patrick was born") and to have been an associate of St. Patrick

Fialarr (Háv 14): Probably another name for Suttungr

Fialarr (Vsp 42): A rooster

Ficconicia (AE 2205): Name of the "third heaven"; origin unknown

Fimbultýr (Vsp 60): "The Great God"; Óðinn

Fimbulvetr (Vm 44): "The Great Winter"; the terrible three-year winter preceding the end of the world

Fión (Gór. II 16): Danish island of Fyn

Fiǫlnir (Grm 47): "The Concealer"; Óðinn

Fiǫlsviðr (Grm 47): "Broad-in-Wisdom"; Óðinn

Fiǫrgyn (Vsp 56): Iǫrð or Earth; mother of Þórr

Fiǫri (Vk 1): Son of Jarl Freki

Fiǫrnir (Akv 10): Gunnarr's cupbearer

Fiǫturlundr (HH. II prose): "Fetter-Grove"

Fitiungr (Háv 78): "Nourisher"; earth

Fochlad, (FíH 8): The name of a wood (anglicizable as "Voclut"), legendarily located near Killala, in Tirawley, County Mayo; according to St. Patrick's own "Confessio," the place of his captivity in Ireland; more plausibly located at Killultegh between Loch Neagh and Belfast

Fólkvangr (Grm 14): "Battlefield"

Forseti (Grm 15): "The Presiding One"; god born of Baldr and Nanna

Frankland (Sd prose): Land of the Gíukungar in southern Germany

Franks (Lud):

Frekasteinn (HH 44): "Stone of the Wolf"

Freki (Grm 19): A wolf

Freki (Vk 1): Jarl of Hálogaland in northern Norway

Freyia (Grm 14; Hdl 1; Od 9; Sk 10): Daughter of Niǫrðr; chief among the female Vanir and a fertility goddess

Frigg (Grm prose; Los 2; Od 9; Vm 1; Vsp 33): Óðinn's wife

Friia (MeC 2): Frigg

Fróði (HH 13; R 10): Name of several Danish kings whose reigns were peaceful; possible Danish equivalent of Freyr

Fulla (Grm prose): Frigg's chambermaid

Fýri (Vk 1): Son of Jarl Freki

Gabriel (AE 1357; TL): Archangel
Gaels (FíH 20): The final, Gaelic speaking invaders of Ireland
Gagnráðr (Vm 8): "Counsel-Giver"; Óðinn
Gangleri (Grm 46): "Travel-Weary"; Óðinn
Gall, Saint (TL): Irish born saint who founded St. Gall Monastery on the
    Steinach river; d. 635
Garmr (Grm 44; Vsp 44): Hound at the gate of Gnipahellir
Garðar (Sk 10): Name of Swedish-Russian realm
Gautar (Los 21): Goths
Gautatýr (Hák 7): "God of the Goths"; Óðinn
Gauti (Hrók 14): One of Hálfr's warriors
Gautr (Grm 54): "God of the Goths"; Óðinn
Geirmundr (Od 29): Unknown
Geirolul (Grm 36): A valkyrie
Geirroðr (Grm intro.): "Spear-Peace" (?); Hrauðungr's son
Geir-Skogul (Hák 12; Vsp 30): Another name for Skogul, the valkyrie
Geirþiófr (Vk 19): King of the Norwegian Upplands
George, Saint (LaG): The obscure saint who probably lived under
    Diocletian in the fourth century and was later credited with slaying a
    dragon; patron saint of England
Geri (Grm 19): A wolf
Germanus (FíH 5): Bishop of Auxerre, 418–48 (?); visited Britain and
    fought the Pelagian heresy in the early British church
Gerðr (Skm 25): A frost giantess
Gertrude, Saint (TL): Abbess of the monastery at Nivelles and patroness
    of travelers; fl. 626–59
Gestill (Sk 4): A sea king
Giaflaug (Gðr. I 4): Giúki's sister
Giallarhorn (Vsp 46): "Loud-Horn"; the horn of Heimdallr, which could
    be heard throughout the nine worlds
Gibeon (FíH 29): Town near Jerusalem; became subject to the Hebrews
    under Joshua
Gimlé (Vsp 64): "Gem-Roof" or "Fire-Shelter"
Ginnungagap: "Yawning-Gap"; the void that existed before creation
    between Muspell and Niflheim; see Élivágar
Giúki (Akv 1; Gðr. I 4; Gðr. II 1; Gðr. III 2; Ghv 9; Hlr 4; Hm 2; Hrók 11;
    Od prose): Burgundian king; father of Guðrún, Gunnarr, and Hogni
Glapsviðr (Grm 47): "Swift-in-Deceit"; Óðinn
Glaðsheimr (Grm 8): "Home-of-Joy"; sanctuary for the gods
Glaumr (Akv 29): Atli's horse
Glitnir (Grm 15): "The Shining One"; Forseti's home
Gnipahellir (Vsp 44): "Cliff Cave"; entrance to the realm of the dead
Gnipalundr (HH 30): "Cliff Grove"
Gnitaheiðr (Akv 5): Heath where the dragon Fáfnir had his lair
Goddau (Arg): A district bordering Rheged; perhaps modern Selkirkshire
Godebog (Gdd XV): [Coel Hen] Godebog, early fifth-century king and
    legendary founder of some of the northern dynasties, including Urien's

Gododdin (Gdd II): A historical tribe and its region, which reached from the Firth of Forth south to the Wear in Durham, including Lothian; the name of the poem attributed to Aneirin celebrating heroes who fought at Catraeth

Gǫll (Grm 36): "The Screaming One"; a valkyrie

Gǫndlir (Grm 49): "Wand-Bearer"; Óðinn

Gǫndul (Hák 1; Vsp 30): A valkyrie

Góinn (Grm 34): A snake

Gomorrah (TrT):

Goronwy (Bat): A legendary warrior

Gothormr (Gðr. II 7): Giúki's son

Goðrekr (Es chap. 52): Unknown; possibly a wrong name for Uhtred, brother of Ealdred

Goths (Akv 20; Ghv 2; Grm 2; Hm 3): Usually used in an honorific sense meaning "warriors"

Goðþióð (Vsp 30): The land of men

Grábakr (Grm 34): "Gray-Back"; a snake

Grafvitnir (Grm 34): "Gnawing-Wolf"; a snake

Grafvǫlluðr (Grm 34): "Field-Gnawer"; a snake

Gramr (Sd prose): Sigurðr's sword

Grani (Gðr. I 22; Gðr. II 4; HH 42; Hlr 11; Od 21; Sd 17; Vkv 14): Sigurðr's horse

Granmarr (HH 18): A powerful king who lived at Svarinshaugr; see HH. II prose after stanza 13

Grettir (Vk 7): One of Víkarr's warriors

Grímildr (Gðr. II 17; Od 15): Guðrún's mother; wife of Giúki

Grímnir (Grm): "The Hooded One"; Óðinn

Grímr (Grm 46): Short form of Grímnir

Gúaire (Cré 6): Seventh-century king of Aidne

Gullinkambi (Vsp 43): "Golden-Comb"; the rooster that wakes the gods

Gullnir (HH 43): A giant (?)

Gullrǫnd (Gðr. I 12): Giúki's daughter

Gullveig (Vsp 21): One of the Vanir (?); a witch (?)

Gungnir (Sd 17): Óðinn's spear, made by the dwarves

Gunnarr (Akv 1; Gðr. I 21; Gðr. II 7; Gðr. III 8; Ghv 3; Hm 7; Od prose): Giúki's son and Guðrún's brother; a Burgundian king

Gunnlǫð (Háv 13): Daughter of the giant Suttungr; Óðinn won the mead of poetry from her

Gunnlǫð (Hrók 13): Wife of Álfr, Jarl of Hǫrðaland

Gunnólfr blesi (Vk 8): Gunnólfr "blaze"; one of Víkarr's warriors

Gunnr (Haf 43; Vsp 30): A valkyrie

Guðmundr (HH 32): One of Granmarr's sons

Guðrún (Akv 29; Gðr. I, II, III; Ghv; Hm 2; Od 27) Giúki's daughter and Gunnarr's sister; she had three husbands: Sigurðr, Atli, and Iónakr

Gwarchan Maeldderw (BT): Sixty-eight line poem in the Book of Aneirin; see *CA*, pp. 55–7

Gwen (SoM 52): A son of Llywarch Hen

Gwen Ystrad (Gwy): Unknown site of a battle won by Urien

Gwgon (Gdd XXXI): Warrior who fought at Catraeth
Gwion (Gdd XXXI): Warrior who fought at Catraeth
Gwion (HaC 32): Son of Cyndrwyn, brother of Cynddylan
Gwion Bach (TrT): Name of the youth who stole the drops of poetic
  inspiration brewed by Ceridwen, later reborn of her as Taliesin; see *M*,
  pp. 159–64
Gwlyged (Gdd XXXII): Warrior who fought at Catraeth
Gwriad (Gdd XXX): Warrior who fought at Catraeth
Gwrien (Gdd XXX): Warrior who fought at Catraeth
Gwydion (Bat; TrT): Son of Welsh goddess Don, nephew of King Math;
  see *M*, pp. 89–109
Gwyn (Gdd XXXI): Warrior who fought at Catraeth
Gwyn (HaC 32): Son of Cyndrwyn, brother of Cynddylan
Gwynedd (Gdd IV; PrT 9): Region of North Wales, including Anglesey
Gwynfryn (TrT): "White-Mound"; a place (of unknown location) sacred
  in Welsh mythological tradition; see *M*, pp. 70, 72, 192

Hábrókr (Grm 46): "The High-Legged One"; a hawk
Haddingiar, the land of (Gðr. II 22): Land of the dead (?); the sea (?); see
  Turville-Petre 1964
Hadubrand (Hdbr): Son of Hildebrand
Hafrsfjǫrðr (Haf; Sk. II 10): "Hafsfjord"; fjord located on the west coast
  of Rogaland in Norway
Haki (Hrók 1): A famous sea king
Haki (Hrók 12): One of Hálfr's warriors
Haklangr, Þórir (Haf 3): Opponent of Haraldr in the Battle of Hafrsfjǫrðr
Hákon (Gðr. I end; Gðr. II 14): Unknown
Hákon (Hák): Hákon the First ("the Good"); son of Haraldr inn hárfagri;
  early tenth century
Hálfdanr (Hrók 14): One of Hálfr's warriors
Hálfr (Gðr. II 13): Sigurðr's stepfather
Hálfr (Hrók 3): Hrókr's fallen king
Hálogaland (Hák 3; Hrók 6): District in northern Norway
Hamðir (Ghv 8; Hm): Son of Guðrún and Iónakr
Hámundr (Hrók 1): A brave warrior
Hár (Grm 46; Háv; Vsp 21): "The High One"; Óðinn
Hár (Bj 142): One of Hrólfr Kraki's warriors
Haraldr (Vk 1): King of Agðir in Norway
Hárbarðr (Grm 49): "Gray-Beard"; Óðinn
Hati (Grm 39): A mythical wolf that will swallow the moon at the end of
  the world
Hátún (HH 8): "High Town"; a place in Denmark (?)
Haukr (Hrók 15): One of Hálfr's warriors; Valr's brother
Hávarðr (HH 14): Hundingr's son
Hebron (TrT): Ancient Judaean city where, in Welsh apocryphal tradition,
  creation occurred and where seed for food was first brought to Adam
Heiddraupnir (Sd 13): "Light Dropper"; apparently a name for Mímir
Height of Macha (FT): *Árd Macha*; modern Armagh

Heimdallr (Grm 13; Skm 28; Vsp 1): Watchman of the gods; as King Rig, he fathered the three estates of slaves, freemen, and nobles

Heiðr (Vsp 22): "The Bright One" (?); a witch

Heiðrekr (Od prose): Borgný's father

Heiðrekr (Gest): Legendary king noted for his wisdom

Heiðrún (Grm 25): The goat that feeds on the branches of the tree Læraðr

Hel (Grm 31; Skm 27; Vsp 43): The realm of the dead

Helblindi (Grm 46): "Hell-Blinder"; Óðinn

Helgi (HH and HH. II): Danish hero; son of Sigmundr and Borghildr; conqueror of Hundingr and Hǫðbroddr

Hell, House of (AE 957):

Herborg (Gðr. I 6): Unknown

Herbrandr (Vk 7): Follower of Víkarr

Herfiǫtur (Grm 36): "War-Fetter"; a valkyrie

Herfǫðr (Vsp 29): "War-Father"; Óðinn

Hergrímr (Vk 23): One of Starkaðr's victims

Heriafǫðr (Grm 19; Hdl 2; Vm 2; Vsp 43): "Father of Warriors"; Óðinn

Heriann (Grm 46; Gðr. I. 19; Vsp 30): "Lord of Hosts"; Óðinn

Heribrand (Hdbr): Father of Hildebrand

Herkia (Gðr. III 2): Atli's maidservant

Hermóðr (Hdl 2): "War-Brave"; either the son of Óðinn, who went to Hel to rescue Baldr, or a king of the Danes

Hermóðr (Hák 14): The messenger god

Herteitr (Grm 47): "War-Glad"; Óðinn

Herþiófr (Vk 2): King of Hǫrðaland in Norway

Hervor (Vkv prose): "Guardian of the Host"; Hlǫvér's daughter; a valkyrie

Heðinsey (HH 22): "Hethin's Isle"; probably Hiddense in the Baltic Sea near Denmark

Hialli (Akv 22): A thrall in Atli's court

Hiálmberi (Grm 46): "Helmet-Bearer"; Óðinn

Hiálm-Gunnarr (Hlr 8; Sd prose 3): A king of the Goths slain by Sigrdrífa

Hildebrand (Hdbr): Theodoric's champion

Hildigrímr (Vk 7): Follower of Víkarr

Hildr (Grm 36; Hrók 11; Sk. II 7; Vsp 30): "Battle"; a valkyrie

Himinbiǫrg (Grm 13): "Heavens' Mountains"; Heimdallr's dwelling, where he keeps watch for intrusions of the giants

Himinfiǫll (HH 1): "Heavens' Fells"

Himinvangar (HH 8): "Heavens' Fields"

Hindarfiall (Sd prose): "Hind's Fell" or "Mountain of the Hind"

Hiǫrleifr (HH 23): One of Helgi's men

Hiǫrvarðr (HH 14): Hundingr's son

Hlaðguðr (Vkv prose): "The Necklace-Adorned Warrior-Maiden"; Hlǫvér's daughter; a valkyrie

Hlér (Gest 62): Another name for Ægir

Hlésey (Od 30): "Hlés Island"; the island of the sea god Hlér; probably Læsø in the Kattegat

Huginn [and Muninn] (Grm 20; Gðr. II 29; HH 54): "Thought" [and "Memory"]; one of Óðinn's two ravens that eat the flesh of those killed in battle

Hundingr (HH): King of Hundland, slain by Helgi

Huns (Akv 2; Gðr. I 6; Ghv 12; Hdbr; Od 4):

Hvergelmir (Grm 26): "Cauldron-Roaring"; a spring in Niflheimr, under the third root of Yggdrasill

Hveðrungr (Vsp 55): Loki (?)

Hyddwn Hill (Gdd XXX): The name "Hyddwn" occurs in *M*, p. 97, as one of the offspring of the shape-shifted nephews of Math

Hyfaidd (Gdd V): Warrior who fought at Catraeth

Hyndla (Hdl): A giantess

Iafnhár (Grm 49): "Even-High"; Óðinn

Iálkr (Grm 49): Óðinn

Iarizkárr (Gðr. II 19): A Slavic prince (?)

Iarizleifr (Gðr. II 19): A Slavic prince (?)

Iárnviðr (Vsp 40): "Iron Wood"

Idon (Gwy): A river in Cumberland, probably the modern river Eden

Ieuan (Gdd XXXI): Warrior who fought at Catraeth

Ífing (Vm 16): Mythical river

Ímr (Vm 5): A giant

Imðr (HH 43): A giantess

Ingibiǫrg (Hi 6): Hiálmarr's beloved, daughter of a Swedish king

Ingvi (Sk 2): A sea king

Iǫrmunrekkr (Ghv 2; Hm 3; Sk. II 8): Ermanaric, king of the Goths; died ca. 376; see Turville-Petre 1964

Iǫtunheimar (Los 2; Vsp 8): "World of the Giants"

Iónakr (Ghv 14; Hm 25): Guðrún's third husband and the father of Hamðir, Sǫrli, and Erpr

Irlúachair (Cré 6): In northeast County Kerry

Isaac (TL):

Ísungr (HH 20): Unknown; slain by Hǫðbroddr

Iðavǫllr (Vsp 7): "Field of Deeds" (?) *or* "Shining-Field" (?); central field in Ásgarðr, where the gods meet in council

Iðunn: Wife of Bragi; she has the golden apples of youth in her protection; see Þiazi

Itrekr (Gest 55): Possible name for Óðinn

Ívaldi (Grm 43): Father of the two craftsman dwarves, who made the ship Skíðblaðnir and other treasures for the gods

Jacob (TL):

Jarlsnes (Es chap. 53): Place in Wales

Jaðarr (Haf 46): A district in southern Norway

Jehosaphat, the valley of (AE 2001): In the Vale of Kidron, east of Jerusalem; traditionally a place of judgment

Jericho (Ex 89):

Jerusalem (AE 2233):
Jesus (BBC; FíH 33; GT 4):
Jews (Ex 77):
John the Baptist (BBC; TL)
Jordan, River (AE 1585; Ex 89; Gen. III; TrT):
Joseph (TL):
Joshua (FíH 30):
Judas (BBC): Judas Iscariot as a child possessed by Satan; see the apocryphal *Arabic Gospel of the Infancy*, xxxv

Kerlaugar (Grm 29): Mythical rivers
Kialarr (Grm 49): Óðinn
Kiárr (Akv 7; Vkv prose): Two kings, possibly identical; in Vkv, king of Valland
Kjǫtvi (Haf 1; Sk. II 10): One of Haraldr's opponents at the Battle of Hafrsfjǫrðr
Knéfrǫðr (Akv 1): Atli's messenger
Kǫrmt (Grm 29): A mythical river
Kólga (HH 28): Daughter of Ægir; a wave
Kúrland (Es chap. 53): Area of Europe roughly corresponding to the portion of the U.S.S.R. just north of Poland

Læraðr (Grm 25): Apparently another name for Yggdrasill
Lang (Es chap. 53): "Long"; Þórólfr's sword
Langobard men (Gðr. II 19): "Long-Beards" (?); Langobards (?); Lombards (?)
Leiptr (HH. II 31): Mythological river
Letha (FíH 5): "Letavia," Brittany; often later confused with "Latium"
Líadan (Lía): Female voice, identified in the manuscripts as a poetess of the "Corcu Duibne," a tribe of Kerry; otherwise unknown
Líf (Vm 45): "Life"; man who will repeople Earth
Lífþrasir (Vm 45): "Longing for Life" (?); woman who will repeople Earth
Limerick of the Graves (Cré 7): Limerick; perhaps so-called for a well-known monastic graveyard
Listi (Sk 6): Place in most southern part of Norway; now Lister
Llawr (SoM 52): A son of Llywarch Hen
Llech Wen (Gwy): Place name, perhaps a mistake for Llech Velen "Yellow Stone"; in that case it is OE *geolu stan*, Mount Galston
Lleon Llychlyn (TrT): A legendary figure (?); *Llychlyn*, "Scandinavia"
Llwyfenydd (ApU): Place name; perhaps reflected in the name of the river Levennet, between Catterick and Carlisle; see Argoed Llwyfain
Llywarch [Hen] (SoM 40): In the genealogies, a first cousin to Urien; subject of a body of poetry belonging to the ninth and tenth centuries
Loddfáfnir (Háv 112): The name of a *þulr* (sage or singer)
Loegaire (FT 169): Fifth-century king whom St. Patrick attempted to convert; the legends differ on his success
Logafjǫll (HH 13): "Mountain of Flames"; a mythical mountain

Loki (R 13; Vsp 35): The trouble-making god; son of two giants; he causes the death of Baldr

Loptr (Sk. II 3): Loki

Lorica (Lor. II; SPL; TL): Latin for "breastplate"; used figuratively as a name for a charm or prayer to ward off evil

Lot (Gen. III):

Lóðurr (Vsp 18): Unknown; perhaps Óðinn

Lucifer (AE 833; TrT):

Ludwig (Lud): "Famous in Battle"; Louis III, joint ruler of France with his brother, Carloman (c. 863–82)

Lúfa (Haf 45): "Shock-Hair"; Haraldr

Lundr (Sk. II 2): Town in southern Sweden; modern Lund

Madog (Gdd II): Warrior who fought at Catraeth

Máel-Duin (Rath): A king of the Uí Berraidi

Maeldderw (Bat): Subject of *gwarchan* (song) attributed to Taliesin but found in the Book of Aneirin

Maelwy (PrT 9): Place name; unknown

Mæringar (RöS): "Border-Dwellers"; Ostrogoths

Magdalen, Mary (TrT):

Magni (Vm 51): "Might"; one of Þórr's two sons who will inherit his hammer Miǫllnir

Mamre (Gen. III): "Fatness"; plain where Adam lived

Manawyd (Gdd III): Place name, perhaps related to Manaw, a district in Gododdin

Máni (Vm 23): The moon

Marro (Gdd I): His son fought at Catraeth

Mary (FíH 33; GT 6; JC; LBC; TL):

Math (Bat): Son of Mathonwy, brother of Welsh goddess Don; see *M*, pp. 89–109

Media (TL): Ancient country in the Near East

Mediterranean (Hdbr):

Meisyr (EaE 37): A sister of Cynddylan

Mellun (Bat): Site of a legendary or mythological battle (?)

Mélnir (HH 51): "Bit-Bearer"; a horse

Michael (AE 1917): Archangel

Miliuc (FíH 4): According to the early biographies, the pagan master whom Patrick served in his captivity

Mímir (Los 23; Sd 14; Vsp 28): A wise god, whom the Æsir sent to the Vanir to settle their truce; the Vanir killed him, and Óðinn placed his head by the Well of Wisdom under one of Yggdrasill's roots

Mímr (Los 23): Mímir

Miǫllnir (Vm 51): Þórr's hammer

Missimbria (AE 1053): See Archon

Mist (Grm 36; HH 47): A valkyrie

Miðgarðr (Grm 41; Vsp 4): "Middle-Earth"; the world of men

Miðviðnir (Grm 50): A giant

Modron (Bat): "Divine Mother"; Welsh goddess

Mǫgðrasir (Vm 49): "Desiring-Sons"; a giant
Móinn (Grm 34): A snake
Móinsheimar (HH 46): A battle-field, perhaps on the Danish island of Mǫn
Mornaland (Od 1): Unknown
Moses (TrT):
Móði (Vm 51): "Wrath" or "Courage"; one of Þórr's two sons who will inherit his hammer Miǫllnir
Mundilfœri (Vm 23): Father of the sun and the moon
Muninn [and Huginn] (Grm 20; Gðr. II 29; HH 54): See "Huginn"
Muspell (Vsp 51): "Realm of Fire"; see Surtr
Mýlnir (HH 51): "Biter" (?); a horse
Mynyddog Mwynfawr (Gdd X): "Mynyddog the Wealthy"; British chieftain whose army fought at Catraeth
Myrkheimr (Akv 42): "Dark-World"; probably identical with Myrkviðr
Myrkviðr (Akv 3; HH 51; Hlr. 25; Vkv 1): "Dark-Wood"

Naglfar (Vsp 50): Ship made out of dead men's nails; it will ferry the giants to the battle of Ragnarǫk
Nagli (Sk. II 9): A Hebridean trader
Náinn (Los 3): A dwarf
Nástrǫnd (Vsp 38): "Shore of the Dead"; shore on which Níðhǫggr eats corpses
Naðr (Es chap. 53): "Adder"; Egill's sword
Nemthur (FíH 1): Unknown; Patrick's actual birthplace is much debated
Neri (HH 4): A giant (?)
Niarar (Vkv 6): An unidentified people
Niflheimr: See Niflhel
Niflhel (Vm 43): "Dark-Hell"; Niflheimr or the realm of the dead
Niflungar (Akv 11; Od 21): The "Nibelungen"; owners of the Rhinegold; kinsmen of Giúki (Burgundians); see Hniflungar
Nimrod (TrT): Ruler mentioned in Genesis X, 8–12; his kingdom included Babel
Niǫrðr (Grm 16; Vm 38): One of the Vanir; father of Freyia and Freyr
Niðafiǫll (Vsp 66): "Dark Mountains"
Niðavellir (Vsp 37): "Dark Fields"
Níðhǫggr (Grm 32; Vsp 39): "Corpse-Tearer"; dragon in Niflheimr that gnaws at the roots of Yggdrasill
Niðuðr (Vkv prose): "Grim Warrior"
Noah (TL; TrT):
Nóatún (Grm 16): "Ship's Haven"; home of Niǫrðr
Nǫkkvi (Haf 44): A sea king (?)
Nǫrr (Vm 25): A giant; father of Nótt
Noker (MM 19): A scribe, variously identified; see Schützeichel 1962, pp. 93–6
Norns (Akv 16; Grm 53; Gðr. II 38; Ghv 13; HH 2; Hm 28; Sd 17): The Nordic Fates
Northmen (Hák 3; Lud):

Northumberland (Es chap. 52):
Nótt (Vm 25): "Night"; daughter of Nǫrr
Nun (FíH 29): Father of Joshua

Oddrún (Od): Atli's sister; lover of Gunnarr
Odissus (FíH 2): Great-grandfather of St. Patrick
Odoacer (Hdbr): Theodoric's enemy; in much-distorted legend, he seized
    Theodoric's kingdom and sent him into exile
Ofnir (Grm 34): "The Entangler" (in questions); Óðinn
Ókólnir (Vsp 37): "The Un-cold"; site of the giant Brimir's hall
Óláfr (Sk 5): Saint Óláfr of Norway
Óláfr, King of the Scots (Es chap. 52): OE Anlaf, son of Guðfrið
Ómi (Grm 49): Óðinn
Óski (Grm 49): Óðinn
Óðinn (Gest prose intro; Grm prose; Hák 1; Háv 80; HH 12; HH. II
    prose; Hlr 8; Los 1; Sd 2; Sk 3; Skm 33; Vm 5; Vsp 18):
Óðr (Vsp 25): Freyia's vanished husband
Óðrerir (Háv 107): "Exciter of the Heart" (?); the vessel in which the
    mead of poetry is stored
Owain son of Eulad (Gdd XXX): Warrior who fought at Catraeth
Owain (Gdd I): Warrior who fought at Catraeth
Owain (Arg; Des 152): Son of Urien of Rheged
Owain (PrT 8): Father of Morgan (d. 974), king of Morgannwg in South
    Wales

Ǫlrún (Vkv prose): "The One who Knows Ale Runes"; Hlǫðvér's
    daughter; a valkyrie
Ǫrmt (Grm 29): Mythical river
Ǫrvasund (HH 24): "Arrow Sound"; probably the Danish Øresund near
    Zealand

Paradise (AE 961; MM 4):
Patrick, Saint (FT 169): Traditionally, the first Christian missionary to
    Ireland; fl. 450
Patrick, the other (FíH 33): Obscure reference to a legendary "Old
    Patrick" who preceded St. Patrick to Ireland
Peblig (Bat): "The Lively One" or personal name
Pengwern (Cyn 1; EaP 40): Place name, probably modern Shrewsbury;
    ruled by Cynddylan
Peredur (Gdd XXXI): Warrior who fought at Catraeth
Pharaoh (Ex 84):
Phol (MeC 2): A fertility god (?)
Picts (PrT 2): People of unknown origins who dwelt north of the Antonine
    Wall; their kingdom endured until about the end of the ninth century
Potitus (FíH 2): Grandfather of St. Patrick
Powys (Cyn 12; HaC 31; SoM 34): Region of central Wales
Promise, Land of (Ex 90):
Pyll (Gdd XXXI): Warrior who fought at Catraeth

Rages (TL): City in Media
Ragnarǫk (Vsp headnote): "The Destruction of the Gods"; see Turville-Petre 1964
Rán (HH 30; Los 7): Goddess of the sea and the wife of Ægir
Randgríð (Grm 36): "Shield-Bearer"; a valkyrie
Randvér (Sk. II 8): Iǫrmunrekkr's son
Ratatoskr (Grm 32): "Swift-Tusk"; squirrel that runs up and down Yggdrasill to carry insults between the eagle at the top and Níðhǫggr at the bottom
Rath (Rath): Fortified, circular dwelling sites in medieval Ireland
Rathangan, County Kildare (Rath): Place in Ireland
Ráðgríð (Grm 36): "Counsel-Breaker" (?); a valkyrie
Rati (Háv 106): The drill Óðinn uses to bore through the mountain into Suttungr's cave
Red Sea (Ex 83):
Reginleif (Grm 36): "Gods' Kin" (?); a valkyrie
Reginn (R 5): A dwarf; son of Hreiðmarr, a magician; brother of Fáfnir
Reginþing (HH 51): "Great-Council"; a meeting-place
Rhaithfyw (Gdd VII): Warrior who fought at Catraeth
Rheged (Arg; Des 154; Gwy; PrU): Northwestern British kingdom lying along the coastlands of the Solway Firth and extending northwards to Strathclyde; ruled by Urien
Rhine (Akv 17; Gðr II 7; Vkv 14):
Rogaland (Hák 3): District in Norway
Roigne (Cré 1): Unknown
Ronan (Hag 14): Unknown

Sæhrimnir (Grm 18): "Sooty-Black"; a mythical boar
Sævarstaðr (Vkv 17): "Sea-Stead"
Sága (Grm 7): "Seeress"; another name for Frigg
Ságones (HH 39): "Sága's Ness"; a point of land
Sámsey (Hi 7): "Samsø"; an island between Jutland and Zealand in Denmark
Sanngetall (Grm 4): "Truth-Finder"; Óðinn
Satan (AE 9; LaJ):
Saðr (Grm 47): "Truthful One"; Óðinn
Saxi (Gðr. III 6): "The Saxon"; a German priest
Scotti (FíH 18): Latin term for the Irish
Senach (Lor. II 3): "The Old One"; unknown legendary person or deity
Seth (AE 1965; Gen II):
Sevafiǫll (HH. II prose): "Seva Fells"
Sigarr (Gðr. II 16): One of the Siklingar, a Danish royal race
Sigarsvellir (HH 8): "Sigarr's Field"
Sigfǫðr (Grm 48; Vsp 55): "Victory-Father"; Óðinn
Siggeirr (Gðr. II 16): One of the Siklingar, a Danish royal race
Siggeirr (HH 41): Slayer of Elyimi, father of Sigmundr and Signý
Sigmundr (Gðr. II 28): Sigurðr's son (?)
Sigmundr (Gðr. II 16; Hdl 2; HH 6; Sd 1): Vǫlsungr's son

Sigrún (HH 30; HH. II prose): Daughter of Hǫgni, wife of Helgi; a valkyrie

Sigtúnir (Hi 3): Major trade center on the northern shore of Lake Mälar in Sweden; modern Sigtuna

Sigtýr (Akv 30): "Victory-God"; Óðinn

Sigurðr (Gðr. I 1; Gðr. II 1; Ghv 4; Hlr prose; Hm 7; Hrók 11; Od 19; Sd prose): Great hero of the Vǫlsungar; husband of Guðrún and slayer of the dragon Fáfnir; see Turville-Petre 1964

Sigyn (Vsp 35): Loki's wife

Sindri (Vsp 37): A dwarf; famous goldsmith

Sinfiǫtli (HH 8): Sigmundr's eldest son

Sinthgunt (MeC 2): A goddess

Sísarr (Vk 12): King of Kiev

Síðhǫttr (Grm 48): "Broad-Hat"; Óðinn

Síðskeggr (Grm 48): "Broad-Beard"; Óðinn

Skatalundr (Hlr 9): "Grove of Heroes" (?); same as Hindarfiall

Skaði (Grm 11): The giant Þiazi's daughter, wife of Niǫrðr

Skeggiǫld (Grm 36): "Axe-Age"; a valkyrie

Skilfingr (Grm 54): "Shaker" or "Reed" (?); Óðinn

Skinfaxi (Vm 12): "Shining-Mane"; Dagr's horse

Skíðblaðnir (Grm 43): "Wooden-Bladed"; Freyr's ship; one of the three treasures made by the dwarves for the gods

Skǫgul (Grm 36; Hák 1; Vsp 30): "Raging" (?); a valkyrie

Skǫll (Grm 39): The wolf who will devour the sun

Skuld (Vsp 20): "Future"; one of the Norns

Skuld (Vsp 30): A valkyrie

Skúma (Vk 2): One of Víkarr's warriors

Slagfiðr (Vkv prose): "Finn-Smith" (?); Vǫlundr's brother

Slane (FíH 15): Area near the River Boyne, north of Dublin; site of early monastery

Sleipnir (Gest 72; Grm 44; Sd 15): Óðinn's magic, eight-legged horse

Slíðr (Vsp 36): "Fearful"

Snæfiǫll (HH 8): "Snow-Fell"

Snorri goði (Sk. II 11): Chief figure in the *Eyrbyggja saga*; d. 1031

Sodom (Gen III; TrT):

Sǫkkmímir (Grm 50): A giant

Sǫkkvabekkr (Grm 7): "Sinking Hall" (?); Sága's hall in Ásgarðr

Sǫrkvir (Vk 7): One of Víkarr's warriors

Sǫrli (Hm 9): Son of Iónakr and Guðrún; Hamðir's brother

Sogn (HH 50): A fjord and district in western Norway

Sól (Vm 23): The sun

Sólfiǫll (HH 8): "Sun-Fell"

Sólheimar (HH 47): "Sun-Home"; dwelling of Hǫðbroddr

Solomon (TL):

Sóti (Hi 1): Hiálmarr's companion

Sparinsheiðr (HH 51): "Sparin's Heath"

Sporvitnir (HH 51): "Spur-Wolf" (?); a horse

Stafnsnes (HH 23): "Stave Ness"

Stari (Hrók 14): One of Hálfr's warriors
Starkaðr (Vk): Legendary hero; he descended from giants and was noted for his wisdom; see Turville-Petre 1964
Staðr (Vk 8): Place in western Norway
Steinar (Hrók 13): The two sons—Innsteinn the older and Útsteinn the younger—of Gunnlǫð
Steingrimr (Hrók 14): One of Hálfr's warriors
Steinþórr (Vk 8): One of Víkarr's warriors
Stephen, Saint (TL): Protomartyr; stoned to death ca. 36
Stiklarstaðir (Sk. II 5): Site in Prándheimr of the battlefield where King Óláfr died
Storð (Hák 7): Island off Norway
Strindir (Sk 6): Inhabitants of Strindafylki in Prándheimr, Norway
Stúfr (Hrók 14): One of Hálfr's warriors
Styrr (Vk 8): One of Víkarr's warriors
Sucat (FíH 2): St. Patrick's original name
Sumar (Vm 27): Summer
Sunna (MeC 2): A goddess (?)
Surtr (Vm 50; Vsp 52): Giant who guards Muspell; he will set the fire beginning Ragnarǫk
Suttungr (Háv 104; Skm 34): A giant; son of the giant Gilling and protector of the mead of poetry
Sváfnir (Grm 34; Haf 46): "Sleep-Bringer"; Óðinn
Svanhildr (Ghv 15; Hm 2): Daughter of Sigurðr and Guðrún; married to Iǫrmunrekkr
Svarinshaugr (HH 31): "Svarin's Hill"; Granmarr's dwelling-place
Svásuðr (Vm 27): "Gentle One"; father of Sumar
Sveggiuðr (HH 47): "Lithe" (?); a horse
Sveinn (Hrók 23): Called "the Victorious"; king rejected by Brynhildr
Svipall (Grm 47): "Changing One"; Óðinn
Svipuðr (HH 47): "Swift" (?); a horse
Sviðrir (Grm 50): "Wise One"; Óðinn
Sviðurr (Grm 50): "Wise One"; Óðinn
Svǫl (Grm 38): "Cooling"; the shield before the sun
Sweden (Hild 1; Vk 21):

Tacianus (LaG): Datianus, a Persian king; see Haubrichs, pp. 209 ff.
Taliesin (Gdd XLVIII; TrT): According to Nennius, *Historia Brittonum*, a renowned late sixth-century British poet
Tara (FíH 10; FT): Irish "Temair"; the inaugural site of the southern O'Neill kings during the Middle Ages; located near the River Boyne
Tassach (FíH 27): Also spelled Asacus or Assicus; identified as St. Patrick's "artificer" in the "Book of Armagh"
Tenby (PrT 6): Place name in Pembrokeshire; in Welsh *Dinbych* and thus identical with *Denbigh* in North Wales
Tethra, House of (Ams): Western ocean; Tethra is a pagan deity
Tetragrammaton (TrT): The four consonants of the Hebrew word for God, Yahweh: Y H W H

Theodoric (Hdbr): See Þióðrekr
Thing (LaG): See Þing
Tigris (AE 1585):
Tiw (AbN 9): Early Germanic war god
Tobias (TL): Both the blind, dying father uttering the charm and the son being protected by it; see the apocryphal *Book of Tobit*
Trebwll (Cyn 14): Place name in Powys
Tren (Cyn 3; EaP 43): Place or river name; perhaps the Tern in Shropshire
Trǫnoeyrr (HH 24): "Tronu Strand"
Troy (TrT): Traditionally, Britain was founded by Brutus, descendant of Aeneas, who fled after the Trojan War
Tudfwlch the Tall (Gdd XIII): Warrior who fought at Catraeth
Tveggi (Los 25): "Two-Faced' (?); Óðinn
Týr (R 12; Sd 6): Son of Óðinn; a god of war
Tyrfingr (Gest 73): A sword
Tyrhennian sea (FíH 6): The Mediterranean between Italy and Corsica, Sardinia, Sicily

Þakráðr (Vkv 39): "He Who Gives Pleasant Counsel"; a thrall of King Níðuðr
Þekkr (Grm 46): "The Welcome One"; Óðinn
Þiazi (Grm 11): The giant who stole the goddess Iðunn and the golden apples
Þing (Gðr. II 4; Háv 25; LaG): Germanic judicial and legislative assembly
Þióðmarr (Gðr. III 3): Þióðrekr's father; a warrior under Attila
Þióðrekr or Þióðrikr (Gðr. III 2; RöS): Theodoric or "Dietrich"; Þióðmarr's son and king of the Ostrogoths (d. 526)
Þióðrǫrir (Háv 160): A dwarf
Þióðvitnir (Grm 21): "The Great Wolf"; Fenrisúlfr
Þóra (Gðr. I end; Gðr. II 14): Hákon's daughter
Þorfiðr (Es chap. 53): Egill's standard-bearer
Þórólfr (Es chap. 52; Sk 3): Egill Skallagrímsson's brother; fought on the English side at the battle of Vínheiðr
Þórr (Grm 4; Vk 18; Vm 51; Vsp 26): Son of Óðinn and Fiǫrgyn; second to Óðinn in power; the guardian of gods and of earth; the god of thunder
Þórsnes (HH 40): "Þórr's Ness"
Þrándheimr (Sk. II 6): A district in Norway; modern Trøndelag
Þríði (Grm 46): "The Third"; Óðinn
Þrór (Grm 49): "Inciter to Strife" (?); Óðinn
Þróttr (Sk. II 3): "Strength"; Óðinn
Þruma (Vk 1): Norwegian island
Þrúðgelmir (Vm 29): A giant
Þrúðheimr (Grm 4): "Land of Strength"; Þórr's realm
Þrúðr (Grm 36): A valkyrie
Þrymheimr (Grm 11): "Noise-Home"; Þiazi's mountain realm
Þund (Grm 21): "Noisy" (?); the river flowing around Valhǫll (?)
Þundr (Grm 46; Háv 145; Sk. II 6): "The Roaring One" (?); Óðinn

Úlfdalir (Vkv prose): "Wolf Dales"

Úlfr (Vk 7): One of Víkarr's warriors

Úlfr (Vm 53): Fenrisúlfr

Úlfsiár (Vkv prose): "Wolf Lake"

Ullr (Akv 30; Grm 5; Sk 7): "Glory" or "Brilliance"; god associated with archery; son of Þórr's wife Sif, from a former marriage

Ulrich, Saint (JC): Bishop of Augsburg; (ca. 890–973; the first recorded person to be solemnly canonized by a Pope

Unavágar (HH 31): "Una Bay"

Unnr (HH. II 31): "The Wave"; a daughter of Ægir

Unnr (Vk 1): Mother of Starkaðr

Uppsalir (Hi 11; Vk 21): The religious and political center of ancient Scandinavia; modern Uppsala

Urien (Arg; ApU; Des 159; Gwy; PrU): Late sixth-century British ruler of Rheged; fought against the Anglo-Saxons

Urðr (Vsp 19): "Fate" or "The Past"; a Norn

Uðr (Grm 46): Óðinn

Útsteinn (Haf 44): Town in Norway just north of Hafrsfjǫrðr

Vænir (Vk 12): (Modern) Lake Vänern in Sweden

Vafðrúðnir (Vm): "Strong in Riddles"; a giant

Váfuðr (Grm 54; Hák 5): "The Wanderer"; Óðinn

Vakr (Grm 54): "Wakeful"; Óðinn

Válaskiálf (Grm 6): "Shelf of the Slain"; Óðinn's first hall in Ásgarðr

Valbiǫrg (Gðr II 33): Fictitious place name (?)

Valdarr (Gðr II 19): A Danish king

Valfǫðr (Grm 48; Vsp 1): "Father of the Slain"; Óðinn

Valgrind (Grm 22): "Gate of the Slain"; outer gate of Valhǫll

Valhǫll (Grm 8; Hák 1; Hdl 1; Los 18; Vsp 33): "Hall of the Slain"; Óðinn's hall where the Einheriar live

Váli (Vsp 34): Son of Loki

Váli (Vm 51): Son of Óðinn

Valland (Es chap. 53; Vkv prose): Explained either as "Land of the Battlefields" or as "Land of the Welsh," i.e., "Foreigners"; usually refers to France

Valr (Hrók 15): One of Hálfr's warriors

Vanaheimr (Vm 39): "Realm of the Vanir"

Vanir (Sd 18; Vm 39; Vsp 24): Fertility gods who fought the Æsir and later settled down with them

Varinsey (HH 37): "Varin's Isle"

Varinsfiǫrðr (HH 26): "Varin's Fjord"

Véi: "Holiness" (?); brother of Óðinn and Víli; see Bestla

Vémundr (Hrók 17): King Hálfr's standard-bearer

Veratýr (Grm 3): "God of Men"; Óðinn

Verdalr (Sk. II 6): Valley on the Norwegian coast

Verðandi (Vsp 20): "The Present"; a Norn

Vetr (Vm 27): "Winter"

Victor (FíH 4): In his "Confessio," St. Patrick reports that a "Victoricus" came to him in a dream with the message to return to Ireland; usually considered an angel

Vifill (Hrók 2): Son of Haki's Jarl Heðinn

Vígríðr (Vm 18): "Field of Battle"

Víkarr (Vk): King of Agðir in Norway

Vikings (Es chap. 52):

Vílir or Víli (Los 23): "Will" (?); brother of Óðinn and Véi

Vilmundr (Od prose): Borgný's lover

Vínbiǫrg (Gðr II 33): Fictitious place name (?)

Vindsvalr (Vm 27): "Wind-Cold"; Vetr's father

Vínheiðr (Es chap. 52): Site of the Battle of Brunanburh (?)

Vinuskogar (Es chap. 52): Name of a Russian forest given to an English wood

Virgil (Bat): Roman poet who enjoyed a reputation as a magician in the Middle Ages

Víðarr (Grm 17; Vm 51; Vsp 55): "Far-Ruler" (?); son of Óðinn and Grið (a giantess); avenged Óðinn by slaying Fenrisúlfr at Ragnarǫk

Viðrir (HH 13): Óðinn

Viðurr (Grm 49): Óðinn

Volla (MeC 2): A goddess (?)

Vǫlsungar (HH 52): Race descended from Vǫlsungr, Sigmundr's father

Vǫlundr (Vkv): Weyland the smith

Welsh (Es chap. 53):

Wodan (MeC 2): God of battle worshipped by the Germanic peoples; Óðinn is his successor; see Davidson

Ýdalir (Grm 5): "Yew Dales"

Yggdrasill (Grm 29; Vsp 19): "Yggr's Horse"; the World (Ash) Tree; its three roots sank into Ásgarðr, Iǫtunheimar, and Niflheimr

Yggiungr (Vsp 28): "The Terrifier" (?); Óðinn

Yggr (Grm 53; Vm 5): "The Terrible One"; Óðinn

Ylfingar (HH 5): The royal race to which Helgi Hundingsbani belongs

Ymir (Grm 40; Vm 21; Vsp 3): Giant from whom the world was formed; see Aurgelmir

Ynglingar (Vk 21): A Swedish royal race

Yngvi (HH 52): Son of Hringr

Yngvi (Hák 1; HH 55): Traditional ancestor of the earliest Swedish kings; title of Freyr

Ysgyrran (Gdd IV): His son fought at Catraeth

Zion, Mount (GT 15): Hill in Jerusalem where Solomon's temple stood

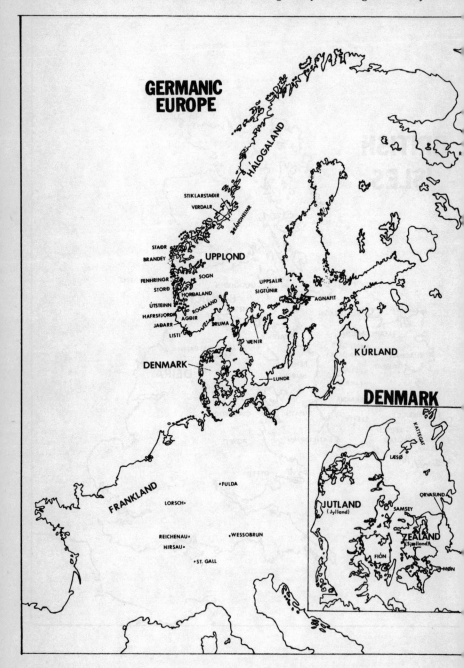